This is the first full-length study of Byron's influence on Victorian writers, concentrating on Carlyle, Emily Brontë, Tennyson, Bulwer Lytton, Disraeli, and Wilde. Rather than treating influence in terms of source study or of intersubjective struggle, it demonstrates how institutions of cultural production mediate the access that later writers have to earlier ones. These institutions produced a ritual of the Victorian authorial career in which writers repeatedly defined themselves against what they understood Byron to represent. In many cases, they did not reject him outright. Instead, they created fictions of personal development away from values associated with Byron towards those associated with themselves as mature Victorian writers.

CAMBRIDGE STUDIES IN NINETEENTH-CENTURY
LITERATURE AND CULTURE 4

BYRON AND THE VICTORIANS

Nineteenth-century British literature and culture have been rich fields for interdisciplinary studies. Since the turn of the twentieth century, scholars and critics have tracked the intersections between Victorian literature and the visual arts, politics, social organizations, economic life, technical innovations, scientific thought – in short, culture in its broadest sense. In recent years, theoretical challenges and historiographical shifts have unsettled the assumptions of previous scholarly syntheses and called into question the terms of older debates. Whereas the tendency in much past literary critical interpretation was to use the metaphor of culture as "background", feminist, Foucauldian, and other analyses have employed more dynamic models that raise questions of power and of circulation. Such developments have re-animated the field.

This new series aims to accommodate and promote the most interesting work being undertaken on the frontiers of the field of nineteenth-century literary studies: work which intersects fruitfully with other fields of study such as history, or literary theory, or the history of science. Comparative as well as interdisciplinary approaches are welcomed.

Titles published

BYRON AND THE VICTORIANS

ANDREW ELFENBEIN

Assistant Professor of English, University of Minnesota

CAMBRIDGE
UNIVERSITY PRESS

Published by the Press Syndicate of the University of Cambridge
The Pitt Building, Trumpington Street, Cambridge CB2 1RP
40 West 20th Street, New York, NY 10011-4211, USA
10 Stamford Road, Oakleigh, Melbourne 3166, Australia

© Cambridge University Press 1995

First published 1995
Reprinted 1996

Transferred to digital printing 1998

Printed in the United Kingdom by Biddles Short Run Books

A catalogue record for this book is available from the British Library

Library of Congress cataloguing in publication data

Elfenbein, Andrew.
    Byron and the Victorians/Andrew Elfenbein.
        p.   cm. – (Cambridge studies in nineteenth-century literature
    and culture, 4)
        Includes bibliographical references and index.
        ISBN 0 521 45452 2 (hardback)
            1. English literature – 19th century – History and criticism.
        2. Byron, George Gordon Byron, Baron, 1788–1824 – Influence.
        3. Influence (Literary, artistic, etc.) 4. Romanticism – Great
        Britain, 1. Title. 11. Series.
        PR468.R65E44   1995
        820.9′ – dc20   94-20629   CIP

ISBN 0 521 45452 2 hardback

Contents

Acknowledgments

In his dedicatory epistle to canto IV of *Childe Harold's Pilgrimage*, Byron thanked Hobhouse for "the social advantages of an enlightened friendship." I, too, have had the pleasure of many enlightened friendships during the composition of this book. Leslie Brisman was a model of tact and encouragement as the director of this project when it was a dissertation. Numerous teachers and colleagues have read drafts of all or some of this book and have helped me refine large concepts and small details: Marie Borroff, David Bromwich, Marshall Brown, Jill Campbell, Paul Fry, Kevis Goodman, Sara Suleri Goodyear, Elizabeth Helsinger, Jerome McGann, Ellen Messer-Davidow, Herbert Tucker, and Alexander Welsh. Michael Cooke was fertile with suggestions during the project's early stages. My series editors, Gillian Beer and Catherine Gallagher, and the readers for the Press, J. Hillis Miller and Peter Manning, all contributed to improve the manuscript; to the latter I, like so many students of romanticism, owe a special debt for his extraordinary insights. At Cambridge University Press, Kevin Taylor, Josie Dixon, and Christine Lyall Grant have been unfailingly helpful.

Curators of the Beinecke Rare Book and Manuscript Library at Yale University, the Bodleian Library at Oxford University, and the Tennyson Research Centre in Lincoln, England, gave permission to use manuscript materials in their care; Eva Reichmann allowed me to reproduce the Beerbohm drawing as a cover illustration. Earlier versions of parts of chapter 3 have appeared in the *Carlyle Annual* and in *Victorian Literature and Culture*; a portion of chapter 6 has appeared in *Modern Language Quarterly*. I am grateful to the editors of those journals for permission to reprint.

In its various stages, my work has been supported by a fellowship from the Mrs. Giles D. Whiting Foundation and by various grants from the University of Minnesota. I am particularly grateful for the McKnight–Land Grant Fellowship, which allowed me to complete the book. It also gave me three exceptional research assistants: William Young, Daniel Birkholz, and Lauren Marsh. My colleagues at Minnesota, including Rita Copeland, David Wallace, Michael Hancher, George T. Wright, and many others, have been constant sources of encouragement.

To say that every sentence in the book has been debated, formulated, reformulated, and revised with the help of John Watkins indicates only the smallest fraction of what I owe to him. My last and greatest words of thanks go to those whose help has extended far beyond enlightened friendship, my parents Myra and Lowell Elfenbein.

Abbreviations

CL   Thomas and Jane Welsh Carlyle, *The Collected Letters of Thomas and Jane Welsh Carlyle*, ed. Charles Richard Sanders *et al.*, 21 vols. to present (Durham: Duke University Press, 1969–).

CW   Carlyle, *Works of Thomas Carlyle*, ed. H. D. Traill, 30 vols. (London: Chapman and Hall, 1896–99).

LJ   George Gordon, Lord Byron, *Byron's Letters and Journals*, ed. Leslie A. Marchand, 12 vols. (London: John Murray, 1973–82).

M   Thomas Moore, *Letters and Journals of Lord Byron with Notices of His Life*, 2 vols. (London: John Murray, 1830).

NB   Carlyle, *Two Note Books of Thomas Carlyle*, ed. Charles Eliot Norton (New York: Grolier Club, 1898).

SR   Carlyle, *Sartor Resartus: The Life and Opinions of Herr Teufelsdröckh*, ed. Charles Frederick Harrold (New York: Doubleday, 1937).

WW   Oscar Wilde, *The First Collected Edition of the Works of Oscar Wilde*, ed. Robert Ross, 15 vols. (1908–22; rpt. London: Dawsons, 1969).

Note on the text

All quotations of Byron's poetry are from the *Complete Poetical Works*, eds. Jerome McGann and Barry Weller, 7 vols. (Oxford: Clarendon, 1980–1993). *Childe Harold's Pilgrimage* and *Don Juan* are cited by canto and stanza number; the verse dramas by act, scene, and line number; and other poems by canto and line number or by line number alone as appropriate.

Introduction: on influence

"Influence" has been a controversial term in critical studies because of its different definitions. For some, it conjures up an outmoded model of source study. For others, source study remains useful in practical criticism despite challenges posed to it by poststructuralism. Yet for the most part, Harold Bloom's theory of the anxiety of influence has superseded the association of influence with source study. Bloom's work has had its own influence, particularly on feminist critics who have revised his paradigms to describe how female writers relate to a patriarchal tradition.[1] More recent critics have preferred "intertextuality" to "influence." "Intertextuality" has been particularly associated with Julia Kristeva's work, such as *Le Texte du Roman*. She argues that the illusion presented by a work as a coherent expression of its author's mind should be disrupted so that "the notion of a 'person-subject of writing' becomes blurred, yielding to that of 'ambivalence of writing.' "[2] This ambivalence leads to treating texts as mosaics of other texts, which include for Kristeva any form in which meaning is inscribed, not just other books. Kristeva insists on the irreducible plurality of what Anglo-American critics had traditionally understood to be unified: the individual author and the literary tradition.[3]

Jay Clayton and Eric Rothstein have analyzed the popularity of Kristevan intertextuality, as opposed to Bloomian influence, as a theoretical model.[4] They isolate several factors behind influence's decline, all of which point to the perceived necessity of discarding the concept of the author whose isolated genius provides the source of literature. Intertextuality avoids the problematics of agency and canonicity associated with traditional source study and with Bloom's oedipalization of influence. Instead, it replaces them with a more open notion of the relations that may

I

exist between texts. In particular, if culture itself is read as a
web of signs, then possible candidates for intertextual relationships increase dramatically. Even more than influence, intertextuality is an umbrella term that can be used to describe widely
differing hermeneutics, from Roland Barthes's stress on the infinity of codes that a text might engage to Michael Riffaterre's
exploration of textual matrices that point to a unitary reading.

Jonathan Culler has suggested that intertextuality's weakness
is the enormous range of texts that it opens to interpretation,
since when the concept is used as the basis for practical criticism
it either regresses to source study or narrows itself to particular
texts for convenience.[5] John Mowitt, in contrast, suggests that
intertextuality undermines disciplinary assumptions governing the
interpretation of texts, including the assumption that theoretical
insights should be evaluated by their helpfulness in producing
close readings.[6] Nevertheless, insofar as critics have appropriated
Kristeva's theory in Anglo-American literary study, they have
severely neutralized it. Rather than fundamentally challenging
the literary work's status, intertextuality has merely provided an
attitude toward textual origins, a reminder that they are never
self-generating. Much criticism of the 1980s embraced such an
attitude even when it did not necessarily highlight intertextuality
as a theoretical starting-point. For example, new historicist critics
who developed Foucault's insights about power assumed that
particular texts must be understood as intersections between or
competitions among larger cultural discourses.

The neutralization of Kristevan intertextuality suggests that
influence may not be so easy to dismiss, limited though its
assumptions may be, because it fits into the academic construction of literary criticism as a discipline. Clayton and Rothstein
point out but do not pursue the irony whereby theorists of
intertextuality, who attempt to go beyond the concept of the
author, have had tremendous influence as authors.[7] Although
Barthes proclaimed the death of the author, his effect on literary
criticism has been as a highly ingenious writer; interest in the
relation between sexuality and his criticism has heightened his
life's importance.[8] Even if one rejects the ideology of canonicity
or wishes to move beyond the problematics of individual agency,
it is difficult to think oneself out of the degree to which individual
authors have influence that involves their lives as well as their

works. The cultural fiction of the author is not "just" a fiction because the practices and institutions of literary study underwrite it in innumerable ways.

Influence, understood as the way that the work of one author shapes that of a later one, now has the peculiar status of being everywhere and nowhere. As an approach to literary analysis, it has become intellectually suspect and professionally unfashionable. Yet a glance at footnotes of books or articles in the field reveals that the discipline of literary study is obsessed with documenting influences. The older interest in tracing literary-historical lines of influence has not so much disappeared as been transformed into tracing the effects of major theorists. This book reexamines the historicity of influence partly because influence has become so central to how literary study constitutes itself as a discipline. Doing so demands exploring the construction of the author as a figure who can have influence.

The title and outline of this book have an allusive relation to George Ford's *Keats and the Victorians*, a classic source study.[9] Although, like this book, it examines a major Romantic poet and his influence on later, canonical Victorian writers, assumptions have changed. Ford relies on a self-contained understanding of literary history as a process determined by changes in taste. Influence depends on parallel passages, and sometimes less on verbal echoes than on general similarities in diction and language. More generally, his work conceives of historical action in terms of intending subjects who impose their will on their environment with little structural constraint. Yet treating Ford as a theoretical strawman is less interesting than responding to the genuine challenge that his work offers to reconceptualize the cultural practices producing literary influence as a historical phenomenon.

As W. J. T. Mitchell has noted, influence itself has a history and is "influenced" by its materials.[10] By arguing eloquently for influence's historicity, Mitchell suggests that the diachronic aspect of influence has not been sufficiently investigated. In particular, new historicists have privileged synchronic explanations over diachronic ones: they are more likely to analyze the political pressures of a particular moment than the constraints exercised by literary conventions or classic authorities. Yet Raymond Williams's statement about tradition applies more narrowly to certain forms of literary influence: "[T]radition is in practice the most evident expression of the dominant and hegemonic pressures and limits."[11] Even if influence does not express the dominant tradition, it still has political significance.

Several writers suggest promising directions for developing Mitchell's concern with influence's historicity. Foucault, especially in "What Is an Author?," has drawn attention to the author not as an individual but as a discursive category giving a privileged status to certain texts.[12] Nancy Armstrong and Leonard Tennenhouse's *The Imaginary Puritan* continues and partly challenges his work by investigating the appearance of "the author" in seventeenth- and eighteenth-century Britain. Their book describes the agency of writing in locating subjectivity inside the body and history outside of it, so that writing seems to come from inside the author's physical person. Like Armstrong and Tennenhouse, I am interested in the power of writing to create the inner self, especially because I understand Byron's career as a critical turning-point in the relations between author, text, and audience, when the text became not merely an author's product but an eroticized expression of the most authentic depths of his or her personality.

Yet a welcome stress on the agency of writing leads Armstrong and Tennenhouse to downplay, although not to ignore, the role of institutions and reception as catalysts for this agency. While this role is hardly outside of or prior to writing, it cannot be traced solely within the frame of the text itself. Likewise, their paradigm-shattering account of the relation between American captivity narratives and Richardson's *Pamela* relies on imaginary readers to support arguments about relations between texts: "[M]ost readers appear to have accepted Pamela's view that it was better to die than have sex with anyone but one's husband. Could it be that they heard in her protests the sentiments of colonial heroines responding to the Indian menace? What else would have made the loss of her virtue equivalent to losing one's English identity?"[13] The rhetorical questions about audience suggest a simultaneous appeal to and discomfort with modes of source study that might establish the path from captivity narratives to *Pamela*. Armstrong and Tennenhouse rigorously avoid empiricism, by which I mean the writing of history as if facts simply could speak for themselves. Yet if writing is to be granted historical agency, and Armstrong and Tennenhouse demonstrate that it must, the question arises of how anything else can be described as having agency if one is to avoid empiricism.

Two critics who suggest possible answers are Hans Robert Jauss and Pierre Bourdieu. Jauss's *Rezeptionsästhetik* proposes to analyze a work by considering the contemporary "horizon of expectations" in which it was written and by investigating whether it meets or disrupts these expectations:

The analysis of the literary experience of the reader avoids the threatening pitfalls of psychology if it describes the reception and the influence of a work within the objectifiable system of expectations that arises for each work in the historical moment of its appearance, from a pre-understanding of the genre, from the form and themes of already familiar works, and from the opposition between poetic and practical language.[14]

Jauss foregrounds the importance of acknowledging diachronic and synchronic perspectives on literature simultaneously. His insistence on "the historical moment" of a work's appearance demands that the "system of expectations" involve more than just literature, because "the social function of literature manifests itself . . . only where the literary experience of the reader enters into the horizon of expectations of his lived praxis, preforms his understanding of the world, and thereby also has an effect on his social behavior."[15] In such an emphasis, he shares with Barthes a concern for the "already read," the unwritten assumptions of readers that are an inevitable and often ignored element in the production of meaning.

Yet Jauss's ideas are exciting in theory but disappointing as realized in practice.[16] The problem lies in his desire to elevate reception to an aesthetic, an emphasis that leads him to avoid the specifics of a historical study of audience, despite his claim for the existence of an "objectifiable system of expectations." Authors such as Janice Radway have demonstrated the effectiveness of doing what Jauss does not by analyzing the responses of actual readers to challenge generalizations about how literature functions in society.[17] Nevertheless, Jauss raises a crucial issue by suggesting that writers can situate their reactions to other authors only in relation to a larger cultural reception. He takes Foucault's question "What is an author?" one step further by asking, "What is an author to his or her audience?" A work's historical significance involves not only how it responds to contemporary ideological problems but also how contemporary readers responded to it.

If, following Jauss, we acknowledge that an influential writer is available to later writers not as a unified entity but as a network of cultural responses, it is also possible to conceive of writers who are influenced not as self-determining monads but agents within a system of production. The theorist most useful in picturing how such a system affects influence is Pierre Bourdieu. Bourdieu is best known for his sociological studies of how education and culture reproduce symbolic capital, which he defines as a kind of power that takes the form not of money but of prestige, status, or recognition. The concept of symbolic capital helps Bourdieu to avoid simply recording "reality" in his sociological histories: he is arranging information so as to highlight how symbolic capital works. He has not, to my knowledge, been discussed as a theorist of literary influence. Yet his sociology of art analyzes how a literary system conditions the attitudes of later writers toward earlier ones.

Bourdieu takes nineteenth-century France as his model for the cultural field. This field, which consists of the totality of relations between writers, publishers, reviewers, and readers, arranges itself around a basic principle: the inverse relation between economic and symbolic capital. Writers aiming for the greatest amount of symbolic capital adopt an ethos of art for art's sake: they are interested in success or failure solely in aesthetic terms, which an elite coterie of other artistic producers define. At the other end of the spectrum are writers who sell their art, such as journalists or hack dramatists. In between are a range of different positions arising from tensions between these two poles.

Bourdieu's model treats influence in terms of the struggle for symbolic capital. Younger writers positioned to achieve symbolic capital oppose established ones:

The ageing of authors, schools and works is far from being the product of a mechanical, chronological slide into the past; it results from the struggle between those who have made their mark . . . and who are fighting to persist, and those who cannot make their own mark without pushing into the past those who have an interest in stopping the clock, eternalizing the present state of things.[18]

Where Bloom sees the agonistic position of younger writers towards precursors as an internal psychological struggle, Bourdieu demystifies it as the structural result of a competition for symbolic capital. Originality, for Bourdieu, does not arise from the strong poet's psychological need but from a cultural market-place's demand that for writers to accumulate symbolic capital, they must "push into the past" more established writers. For Bourdieu, authors who simply imitate the current trends are not "weak," as they are for Bloom. Instead, their positions in the cultural field (typically as writers needing to earn money) lead them to capitalize on whatever constitutes popular taste.

As a sociologist, Bourdieu is not concerned with producing interpretations of the kind associated with Anglo-American literary criticism. He demonstrates how symbolic capital functions in a sociological field, not how to interpret literature. As a result, his models raise the problem of distinguishing between a work's social determinants and the work itself. Although "the work itself" may be a mystified concept, Bourdieu produces a purely formal description of the cultural field that rarely refers to the content of different works. Given his terms, it would be difficult to distinguish texts that occupy similar positions in the field of cultural production. Moreover, he tends to simplify the variety of possible positions that later writers can take toward earlier ones. While he maintains that younger writers refuse everything their artistic "elders" are and do, refusal can mask ambivalence or indebtedness. Here, Bloom provides a considerably subtler guide to influence's intricacies.

Moreover, Bourdieu describes the cultural field at one stage in its history. He assumes the existence of full-blown capitalism and offers few suggestions for how the cultural field came to assume a particular form or how it has changed. As a result, neither his model nor his terminology can be transposed to a different period without considerable modification. Nevertheless, his work offers some of the most promising areas for historicizing influence because it insists on the structural determinants of cultural production.[19]

A pre-text or a precursor is always already interpreted, so that influence is never a purely intersubjective activity, as Bloom represents it. A writer's influence involves far more than texts that she or he writes. It depends on the apparatus whereby that work is produced, disseminated, reviewed, consecrated, or forgotten. Equally important, it depends on how this apparatus constructs the writer's life in relation to the work. Later writers encounter differing versions of an earlier one, so that their authorial positions in the cultural field are conditioned not only by their role in the literary system but also by the access that they have had to models of authorship. This book will demonstrate the importance of expanding and complicating the notion of pretext or precursor by insisting on the range of discourses through which earlier writers become accessible to later ones. A historical investigation of influence needs to account less for all the possible associations that any given writer may have had for later ones than the ways in which the career of a writer intersected with practices determining the reception of earlier writers. I take as axiomatic that the pull between treating texts as the products of individual authors and as products of larger systems of discourses, practices, and institutions is not simply a problem that can be solved by thinking about it hard enough. My choice has been to steer my analysis away from the psychological vocabulary that has dominated the study of influence. The histories that the following chapters construct underscore how circumstances of literary production condition the texts that later writers produce in relation to earlier ones.

While "influence" is one area of concern in this book, the other is "Byron," whom I introduce in the words of a nineteenth-century admirer:

Why, if the fairest test of genius were to be tried by the influence it exerts on cotemporary [*sic*] literature, I hardly know how high we are to rank the name of BYRON. What a change he has created, not only in our poetry, but in our dramas, novels, and almost national character! ... He quite sublimated the quiet English out of their natures, and open shirt-collars, and melancholy features; and a certain *dash* of remorse, were as indispensable to young men, and are so still, as tenderness, and endurance, and intense feeling of passion among the fair sex.[20]

The passage begins by describing Byron's effect on literature yet soon recognizes that Byron is not just an author, but an unprecedented cultural phenomenon. His work affects not only the novel, poetry, and drama, but fashion, social manners, erotic experience, and gender roles. This description suggests that any account of BYRON's influence will have to consider far more than the poetry written by George Gordon, Lord Byron.

The movement from "George Gordon" to "BYRON" can represent an array of new developments in the production of literature. Although other writers have used "Byronism" to refer to a set of traits supposedly characterizing Byron's texts, I use it to refer to developments that allowed Byron to become a celebrity in Britain. Byronism involves roughly three interpenetrating levels: Byron's poems, biographies of Byron, and adaptations of and responses to both. The first level involves the apparatus that associated Byron's name with a set of mostly poetic texts through publications, reviews, collections, annotations, illustrations, forgeries, and imitations. Yet the cult of Byron resulted from what was perceived to be his personality as much as from his poems. Byronism includes the biographies, legends, reminiscences, rumors, and gossip that surrounded every aspect of Byron's life. Byron's contemporaries felt that the importance of Byron's life and character to his work made him distinctively new as an author. The stereotypes of the Byronic character, a passionate hero with a darkly mysterious erotic past, acquired so much prominence that they could soon stand for clichéd and outmoded forms of literature, behavior, or characterization. Finally, Byronism refers to the variety of responses to the poems and biographies by Victorian men and women, from professional writers to casual diarists. Not all responses were written ones: British entrepreneurs tried to capitalize on Byron's appeal with an assortment of Byroniana. The products of Byronism have no essential or defining characteristics other than their perceived relation to the life and work of Lord Byron.

This study attempts to avoid essentializing either "Byron" or "influence" even while recognizing that their historical power has come from their role as perceived essences. Surprisingly, no book has been written about Byron's influence. The closest is Samuel C. Chew's *Byron in England*, which is about Byron's reputation, not his influence. Shorter studies have focused chiefly on transformations of the "Byronic hero," a type that later writers imitated with varying degrees of ambivalence. The problem with such an approach to Byron's influence is that it overlooks the enormous complexity of possible institutions, discourses, and practices that made both Byron and influence available to Victorian writers.[21] While it is true that the clichéd Byronic hero represents an important element in Byronism, the type is less interesting in itself than for what it suggests about Victorian representations of subjectivity. The Byronic hero's fascination lay less in his intrinsic qualities than in the fact that he was supposed to represent Byron, the man. The ramifications of the easily stated equation between Byron and his heroes were immensely complicated. Rather than arguing that Byron's life was as important as his poetry for later writers, I want to stress the extent to which "Byron's life," "Byron's work," and the relations between them all resulted from how the Victorians produced what counted as literature and culture.

The writers on whom I concentrate could hardly have been more different from Byron and from one another. Yet all wrote texts that engaged Byron and the market in Byron so as to be among the most daring and unexpected productions of Victorian literature. Four in particular, Carlyle, Emily Brontë, Tennyson, and Wilde, ruptured, often with considerable violence, contemporary aesthetic decorums, as the shocked initial receptions that greeted their Byronic works attest. In different ways, they departed radically from the author's established role, even though the content of their work was not necessarily what contemporary politicians would have called radical. Looking at them allows me to demonstrate the complexity of Byronism in Victorian literature by exploring how their work challenged possibilities for what literature was supposed to do.

The sheer diversity of forms through which "Byron" and "influence" were available to nineteenth-century writers prevents a single neat account of Byron and the Victorians. My goal is to suggest how historicizing the workings of influence, with particular reference to Byron, enables a rethinking of the significance of Victorian texts. Although the representation of subjectivity is a common theme throughout this book, each chapter is necessarily self-contained to the extent that each author engages with literary production and the representation of Byron differently. Nevertheless, certain core issues cluster for each writer around his or her relation to Byron. For Carlyle, these center on class; for Brontë, gender; for Tennyson, popularity; and for Bulwer Lytton, Disraeli, and Wilde, sexuality. These are not mutually exclusive areas of emphasis, but general areas of concern in which "Byron" and "influence" played a formative role.

I began this book hoping that examining Byron and his

influence would allow me to break down what seemed to me the artificial barriers between Romanticism and Victorianism as fields of study. As I have worked on it, this desire has realized itself through questions about the history of the author as celebrity, the materiality of influence, and the representation of subjectivity in the nineteenth century. Few authors other than Byron provide so rich a starting-point for narrating the development of the Victorian authorial self. Byron's representation of subjectivity and its reception in Victorian culture challenged writers who defined themselves as literary subjects in relation to what they understood Byron's subjectivity to be.

CHAPTER I

Byron and the secret self

Byron's descriptions revealed such insight into what early nine-teenth-century readers had learned to consider the most intimate aspects of human emotion that they seemed to be transcripts of experience, not portrayals of imaginary beings. Walter Scott noted about Byron, "We must recal [*sic*] to the reader's recollection that since the time of Cowper he has been the first poet who, either in his own person, or covered by no very thick disguise, has directly appeared before the public, an actual living man expressing his own sentiments, thoughts, hopes and fears."[1] Scott's passage describes Byron's career as a spectacle. The adverb "directly" suggests that Byron's writing and Byron, the "actual living man," are all but indistinguishable. In Scott's account, the public hardly seems to respond to Byron's poetry at all, only to the "sentiments, thoughts, hopes and fears" for which the poetry is "no very thick disguise."

For Byron's contemporaries, the sense that Byron was his heroes struck them with an oddly irresistible force. Scott, for example, wrote about *Childe Harold's Pilgrimage*, "You cannot for your soul avoid concluding that the author as he gives an account of his own travels is also doing so in his own character."[2] Although only a few readers actually knew Byron personally, many supposed that his poems provided an almost unmediated knowledge of his mind. The most secret, intimate aspects of his personality were widely felt to be public property.

This perceived equation between Byron and his heroes still dominates modern criticism of his work. Although his self-dramatizations are no longer taken to be as direct as they once were, the topic of Byron's self-representations is ubiquitous in Byron criticism.[3] Jerome J. McGann, the most influential recent critic of Byron, has repeatedly emphasized that "[a]ll of his heroes, we know, are surrogates of himself, more or less displaced."[4] Jerome Christensen has most vigorously challenged the view whereby Byron's poems "are imagined as an elaborate code that, by way of a handily metamorphic secret . . . can be brought into some determinate relation with a singular circumstance of Byron's life."[5] Yet even Christensen avoids asking why this coding came to be associated with Byron in the first place. He emphasizes the importance of Byron's publisher, John Murray, in developing "the copyrighted domain named Byron, which was institutionalized . . . as a self-reflexive machine for producing poems and profit."[6] Yet while the Murray circle manufactured several successful authors at the beginning of the century, only Byron was supposed to have created a revolutionary relation between author, text, and audience. The question still remains of why Byron's first readers were so eager to believe that his heroes were indeed self-portraits.

I wish to suggest how strange this phenomenon was. The issue of whether Byron did or did not really portray himself in his heroes does not help to answer the question of why, after reading *Childe Harold's Pilgrimage* or *The Corsair*, hundreds of readers who knew nothing about Byron aside from what they had read believed that they had seen the authentic depths of a "real" human psyche belonging to George Gordon, Lord Byron. The issue is not simply that writing, especially fiction, played a critical role in producing models of subjectivity, because by the early nineteenth century, the writing of subjectivity was nothing new.[7] Nevertheless, while few readers equated Robert Southey with Madoc or George Crabbe with Peter Grimes, much of literate Britain assumed that Conrad or Lara was Byron. The challenge is to explain why Byron's representation of subjectivity in particular gave rise to such a response.

It is tempting to explain Byron's success in terms of the notoriety of his life: his scandalous reputation made his readers eager to read him into his rebellious heroes. Yet the equation between Byron and his heroes was established *before* the details of his personal life became public property. His scandalous aura arose almost as if to justify the qualities of the poetry. Biography was not read back into poetry; from the start, his poetry was understood to be confessional. When readers reacted as if the connection between Byron and his heroes was a revolutionary novelty, their reaction was neither obvious nor inevitable. Rather than starting from the premise that Byron's poems involve some element of self-dramatization, as most Byron criticism does, I wish to examine how and why this premise was established in Byron's lifetime.

This chapter will concentrate on Byron's poetry, especially the representations of subjectivity in four texts, *The Corsair*, *Childe Harold's Pilgrimage*, *Manfred*, and *Don Juan*. My discussion is not meant to provide an exhaustive overview of Byron's career, but to examine the changing status of Byronic subjectivity in some of the texts most important to Byron's nineteenth-century readers. My overall concern is not with how Byron revealed himself in his heroes but with what in his writing made his first readers certain that he did.

Although Byron's first readers occasionally commented on his radical politics or his exotic treatment of the East, he became famous for his portrayal of passion. Supposedly he had felt such intense passions that his experience allowed him to describe them with exceptional vividness. Sincerity was the key to the logic behind the equation between Byron and his heroes: Byron could not have portrayed passion as he did unless he had experienced it first. Yet the sole proof of his sincerity was the vividness of the descriptions themselves; as Annabella Millbanke wrote of his heroes in 1814, "It is difficult to believe that he could have known these beings so thoroughly but from *introspection*."[8] Because his descriptions seemed to exceed the powers of mere invention, they supposedly had to be records of the truth of his experience.

As McGann has emphasized, Romantic sincerity is a rhetorical effect that is achieved by seeming not to strive for effect.[9] Although the first place to look in Romantic poetry for such sincerity might be the Romantic crisis lyric, Byron's career challenges expectations about genres in which authors are supposed to reveal themselves. The Byron who seemed to reveal to his public the inner depths of his soul was primarily not a lyricist, but the poet of *Childe Harold's Pilgrimage* and the Turkish Tales, even though he did write a few confessional lyrics that became quite famous, especially "Fare Thee Well!." Most Romantic lyrics did not electrify contemporary readers into believing that they had become acquainted with the most secret thoughts of "an

actual living man." Yet Byron, supposedly the most confessional
of the Romantic poets, wrote in modes that seem at first glance
much less obviously confessional than the lyric.

For Byron's readers, the most popular poetic mode was the
verse narrative. The equation between Byron and his heroes has
its background in narratives such as Scott's *Marmion* (1808). I
take as a representative moment from the latter a scene in which
the hero, after hearing a song about an unfaithful lover, is stricken
with guilt for his misdeeds:

> High minds, of native pride and force,
> Most deeply feel thy pangs, Remorse!
> Fear, for their scourge, mean villains have,
> Thou art the torturer of the brave!
> Yet fatal strength they boast to steel
> Their minds to bear the wounds they feel,
> Even while they writhe beneath the smart
> Of civil conflict in the heart.[10]

When the narrator discusses Marmion's remorse, his language
becomes highly generalized: he gives no details about Marmion's
mind in particular, but refers to "[h]igh minds" and to "the
brave." Marmion's situation is attractive to Scott's narrator
because it lets him describe not merely Marmion, but the suffering of noble minds. Abstraction gives significance to the individual situation, so that this narrative does not appear interested
in details about Marmion's past, but in how his mental state,
at this moment, acquires the force of a type.

Yet the abstracting movement of the passage also invites curiosity about the circumstances provoking these feelings. Marmion
is wrapped in an aura of mystery that the abstract descriptions
heighten. The interest of the language pulls in two directions at
once: toward abstractions about high minds and toward absent
particulars about Marmion as an individual. Scott's narrative
eventually explains the origins of Marmion's remorse in terms
of his guilt about his past criminal deeds. Not until he has been
fatally wounded in battle does he admit, in the presence of a
monk, that he has betrayed his mistress and pursued the woman
to whom he is engaged only for her wealth. The narrative suggests
that finding out the details about him is the symbolic cause of
his death: he lives only while his psyche retains its mystery.
Once the causes for his remorse are known, the abstractions for

which his mind provided the type are less applicable. He gains his individual history at the cost of his suggestiveness as a representative of the human mind itself.

Byron's famous descriptions of the "human heart" derive directly from Scott, as the following passage from *The Corsair* demonstrates. It describes the introspection of the hero Conrad after he has been imprisoned:

> Even in that lonely hour when most it feels
> And to itself, all—all that self reveals,
> No single passion, and no ruling thought
> That leaves the rest as once unseen, unsought;
> But the wild prospect when the soul reviews—
> All rushing through their thousand avenues.
> Ambition's dreams expiring, love's regret,
> Endangered glory, life itself beset;
> The joy untasted, the contempt or hate
> 'Gainst those who fain would triumph in our fate;
> The hopeless past, the hasting future driven
> Too quickly on to guess if hell or heaven;
> Deeds, thoughts, and words, perhaps remembered not
> So keenly till that hour, but ne'er forgot;
> Things light or lovely in their acted time,
> But now to stern reflection each a crime;
> The withering sense of evil unrevealed,
> Not cankering less because the more concealed—
> All, in a word, from which all eyes must start,
> That opening sepulchre—the naked heart
> Bares with its buried woes, till Pride awake,
> To snatch the mirror from the soul—and break. (II.336–57)

Byron's critics often singled out this moment or ones like it for special praise. For example, John Hodgson in the *Monthly Review* praised the passage for demonstrating the "author's acquaintance with the workings of the heart," which had "seldom been depicted with so much force."[11] Byron owed the equation between himself and his heroes to the rhetoric of such passages. These, rather than lyrics like "Fare Thee Well!," led readers like Scott to assume that he was "expressing his own sentiments, thoughts, hopes and fears."

At first glance, this reaction seems peculiar. This passage does not look confessional at all because it is so abstract, even more so than Scott's. Conrad's significance, like Marmion's, would seem to be that his experience allows generalizations about passion. Conrad the individual character disappears from the passage that is supposed to reveal his innermost torment. It presents no specific details about his past. "Deeds, thoughts, and words" are mentioned, but they remain without content. Not only does Byron give no specific reason for Conrad's remorse, the passage does not even make it clear that the remorse described is Conrad's. Byron's references to "self" (II.337), "our fate" (II.345), and "the naked heart" (II.355) carefully avoid any language that would individualize the emotion.

The description's abstractness invites the reader to make connections with particular experiences because Conrad's remorse is presented as if it were the interior of any psyche submitted to intense self-scrutiny. As in Scott, the passage projects a fantasy that under the heat of self-interrogation, a common depth of human feeling appears that subsumes specifics of identity. These are made to seem unimportant, mere artificial categories of civilization that vanish before the universal abstractions of the naked heart. Conrad embodies the Enlightenment fantasy of a universal self, one divorced from the externals of history and subject solely to its own control. At the core of this universal self is desire. Although in a list like "Ambition's dreams expiring, love's regret, / Endangered glory, life itself beset" (II.342–43), love is only one abstraction among others, the pile-up of items suggests the restlessness of a desire that is larger and more deeply eroticized than what Byron calls "love." The key to the naked heart in Byron is the eroticization of all inner emotions in terms of desires so profound that they can never be fulfilled.[12]

The works of Michel Foucault underscore the broader significance of Byron's confessional rhetoric. In volume 1 of *The History of Sexuality*, Foucault argues that since the sacrament of confession, the discourse of sexuality has become a privileged site for discovering the truth of the inner self. After the Reformation, confession gradually lost its ritualistic character and spread into a variety of social forms; Foucault concentrates on its nineteenth-century medicalization. Almost in an aside, he notes that the Western obsession with confession produced a new kind of literature, one "ordered according to the infinite task of extracting from the depths of oneself, in between the words, a truth which the very form of the confession holds out like a shimmering mirage."[13] Foucault's description is striking because it applies more aptly to Byron's work than to any previous writings in British literary history, even those designating themselves as autobiographies. In Byron, for the first time, the description of a "genuine" inner self is linked with a discourse placing desire at that self's center.

The "shimmering mirage" that Byron's poetry held out was "Byron himself," an image of the "real" man who supposedly was the original of the poetic representations. Influential as the work of Richardson, Cowper, Rousseau, and others had been in shaping the portrayal of subjectivity, none had meshed subjectivity and eroticism in a secularized confessional mode quite as Byron had. The only competition that Byron's representation might have had during the early nineteenth century was Wordsworth's *Prelude*, which remained out of the public eye until the middle of the century. By that time, Byron's model dominated British literature.

With his mesh between subjectivity and eroticism came a new picture of the mind as a site of infinite depth. This mental topography parallels the collapse, which Foucault traces in an earlier work, *The Order of Things*, at the end of the eighteenth century in the power of representations to hold together elements of knowledge. Whereas earlier knowledge had depended upon systems of classification that organized knowledge in charts and tables, Foucault demonstrates the emergence of transcendental terms that designated a reality prior to and outside of representation. These terms, such as "organic structure" in biology, "labor" in economics, and "inflectional system" in grammar, were generative origins whose effects alone could be traced.[14] The confessional soul in Byron works along a principle similar to that of these transcendental terms; it is a "deep" source generating visible effects but not itself representable. It is held out as an endless source of ever greater mysteries, an inexhaustible well of desire and pain. This invisibility authenticates the representation itself. Sources that are announced as unimaginable are supposed to seem more real than representable ones.[15]

Unfathomable as the Byronic hero's soul may be, the abstractness with which it is described promotes, as in Scott, curiosity about the origins of the hero's situation. The critical difference between Byron and Scott is that Scott satisfies this curiosity, while Byron does not. Byron never reveals the origins of the hero's feelings within the context of the fiction. The reader does not learn what particular relevance "stern reflection" (II.351) or "evil unrevealed" (II.352) may have for Conrad. Byron gives a powerful description of a mind in torment, but no clues about that torment's sources except a rhetoric that gestures memorably but vaguely to unfulfilled desire.[16] Where Scott relates a narrative, Byron presents a sensibility surrounded by mystery. Where Scott suggests a visible motive for tormented consciousness, Byron shrouds motives in mystery. This invisibility of origins is the critical turn that Byron's rhetoric performs on the tradition of sensibility and its representation of the inner self. While, as David Marshall has argued, the sense that characters have no real access to the inner selves of other characters haunts much eighteenth-century writing, Byron foregrounds this lack of access as the dominant characteristic of the Byronic hero.[17] All that remains visible is a superstructure built upon baffled desire.

The central paradox of Byron's rhetoric was that he was taken to be at his most confessional when he was at his most abstract. His language of the human heart carried its greatest power when individuating details vanished. Since the fiction provided no origin for the hero's torment, readers looked outside the frame to "Byron" himself, the fiction that could not be acknowledged as such. As John Wilson noted of Byron and Rousseau,

They have gone down into those depths which every man may sound for himself, though not for another; and they have made disclosures to the world of what they beheld and knew there—disclosures that have commanded and enforced a profound and universal sympathy, by proving that all mankind . . . are linked together by the bonds of a common but inscrutable nature.[18]

Byron was equated with his heroes more because of what he did not tell than because of what he did. Byron's life appeared as a reality for his readers once he had stretched representation to the point where an absence of origins made it impossible for his characters to be read as fiction. The real Byron had to be invented as the absent cause of what was inexplicable within the poems themselves. The equation between Byron and his heroes offered the author's soul, rather than his skill, imagination, or genius, as the genuine source of his representations. The next step for Byron's readers was biography, which might provide the answers that fiction did not. Eventually, Byron's poems took a second place to the cult of Byron himself, since the poems were interesting only for what they revealed about the "real" man.

In the rest of this chapter, I want to explore how the universality of Byron's rhetoric of subjectivity posed challenges for creating plots supposedly about particular individuals. In Turkish Tales such as *The Corsair*, he faced these challenges by putting the Byronic hero in relation to a Byronic heroine. Simple as this solution sounds, the Byronic heroine created considerable difficulties. Gender offered a fundamental challenge to the Byronic hero as a universal Enlightenment subject. If the inner recesses of the mind that Byron portrayed really belonged to a common but inscrutable human nature, then gender should not affect the ability of both men and women to share the essence of the naked heart. The fantasy of a passage like the one I quoted from *The Corsair* is that subjectivity is the same in everyone. Yet if a woman could possess a subjectivity that was no different from a man's, then she could be a Byronic hero just as well as he. Any differences between men and women would become the superficial effects of culture, not the basic ones of nature. But having a woman and a man in the same poem who both possessed the essentials of the "naked heart" would rob the male Byronic hero of his supposedly unique soul. Byron's fame depended on creating heroes who represented one man only, Byron. For a woman as well as a man to take on such subjectivity in the same poem would weaken the power of the Byronic hero to represent the "real" Byron. Such transgendering would dismantle the assumption that a male author's self-expression must occur through a male character.

Some critics have assumed that Byron responded to this problem by representing women with no subjectivity at all, so that his poems show the supposedly universal "naked heart" as belonging only to male heroes. Yet Byron's images of women are considerably more complicated, as Caroline Franklin has demonstrated.[19] It is true that in his letters and journals, Byron could not have been more patriarchal in his attitudes: he often treats women as wholly other, and sometimes as wholly contemptible. In his poetry, however, he inherited a language that purported to represent a subjectivity purified of gendered traits. These two attitudes can be understood as versions of two competing ideologies of gender. The first assumed that men and women had fundamentally different natures and therefore fundamentally different social roles; these differences made women naturally subordinate to men. The second stemmed from the category of what David Hume called the "natural and inherent principles and passions of human nature," which were "inalterable"; the category of "human nature" claimed to address an essential humanity that transcended codes like gender.[20] The two positions, both of which appear in Byron's poetry, had differing implications for the structure of desire between the sexes. The first implied that heterosexual desire must derive from difference, as in Milton's Eden. The second suggested that it must stem from likeness, or what eighteenth-century writers called "sympathy," since there was no essential difference between male and female souls.

This double inheritance of ideologies of gender meant that Byron's portrayals of erotic relations were torn between the positions that desire depended on an absolute difference between men and women, and that it depended on an absolute identification between fundamentally similar subjectivities, which happened to be lodged in opposite sexes.[21] In Byron's poetry, the second position appears in his obsessive explorations of literal or symbolic sibling incest.[22] Incest represents the possibility that desire arises from an identification between male and female versions of the same psyche. If subjectivity is truly universal, then genuine otherness does not exist. Desire can be based only on identification.

Yet incest is hardly a comfortable possibility for Byron. His poetry is haunted by the fear that a universalized conception of the inner self might not make men and women different enough. When women in his poetry really possess the naked heart as much as men, they are usually punished for it. Rather than suggesting that both men and women are equally entitled to subjectivity, Byron tends to represent passion as a zero-sum struggle over its possession: the more a female character asserts her right to it, the more passive and conventionally feminine a male character becomes. In the end, an emphasis on difference always cancels out one on similarity, usually at the cost of the woman's disappearance or death. The preservation of difference rescues the equation between Byron and his hero by reinforcing the paradoxical uniqueness of the hero's universality.

In *The Corsair*, two heroines embody the conflict between desire based on difference and on identification: Medora is entirely different from Conrad, while Gulnare is his double. Even Byron's early readers saw the oddity of Conrad and Medora's match. His first biographer, John Watkins, noted that "we cannot help wondering at the sort of love that could unite two hearts apparently so ill fitted to each other."[23] Medora is sociable, domestic, civilized, and beautiful, while Conrad is alienated, wandering, aggressive, and sublime. Their mutual incomprehension is absolute. From her first appearance, she seems more dead to him than alive, as her opening song reveals: "Remember me—Oh! pass not thou my grave / Without one thought whose relics there recline" (1.355–56). The fears she expresses of being forgotten by Conrad point to more pervasive absences in her relation to him. These appear in her futile attempts to make him stay with her through promises of domestic bliss, dancing, singing, and reading Ariosto, while he is planning a raid on Seyd, a Turkish Sultan. Although Conrad briefly pities her, it is impossible to imagine him being attracted for long by activities so alien to him.

For Conrad, the private domestic space that Medora offers is unnecessary. He is preoccupied enough with his own inner spaces, which he has parceled out with scrupulous precision into love for Medora and hatred for all others; as he tells her, "My very love to thee is hate to them" (1.403). She exists for him chiefly as an ideal anchoring this polarization. Insofar as she is not purely an ideal but a character who expresses her own needs and desires, she appears to him as a trap, and he wastes no time in abandoning her. During the raid, he disguises himself as an escaped prisoner to distract Seyd's attention while his men overwhelm the palace. The disguise itself metaphorically suggests that Conrad's life with Medora has been an incarceration. Once he knows that his men are in the palace, he throws off the disguise to become the figure of pure aggression that Medora wished to hold in check. In public action, away from the stifling domesticity of Medora's bower, he achieves what the poem represents as the freedom of masculine violence.

Yet this violence disappears almost immediately when he encounters Seyd's favorite, Gulnare. Once she enters the plot,

the gender difference that was so absolute between Conrad and
Medora begins to waver. His psyche is structured as if Medora
were the only woman in a world of men; his mental polarization
between absolute love and hate depends on her uniqueness. But
the plot introduces a new possibility when Conrad meets Gulnare.
Because she is a possible object of erotic attraction for him, her
presence unsettles Medora's exclusive claims. Hearing the cries
of Seyd's women in the burning harem, Conrad decides to halt
the attack and rescue the women. He suddenly forgets that he
is supposed to hate all except Medora because he had not
reckoned with the possibility of his "all" including women as
well as men. This psychic balance, which depended on treating
the world as exclusively male except for Medora, topples:

> Man is our foe, and such 'tis ours to slay:
> But still we spared—must spare the weaker prey.
> Oh! I forgot—but Heaven will not forgive
> If at my word the helpless cease to live.   (ii.205–08)

In the slip between "spared" and "must spare," Byron represents
Conrad's lingering uneasiness about showing mercy to "the
weaker prey" and thus belying his claim to hate all except
Medora. Beginning in the past tense, as if narrating a deed of
mercy, he suddenly remembers that he has not yet accomplished
the deed. The narrative justifies his uneasiness: in pausing to
save Gulnare from the blaze, he permits Seyd's men to rally and
defeat his forces. It is as if he were being punished for having
deviated from the polarization that demanded the worship of
Medora and hatred for all else; he loses everything by upsetting
this balance.

Gulnare, as a result, assumes control of the action. She visits
Conrad, who has been thrown in prison after his defeat, first to
offer thanks and sympathy, later to suggest how he can escape
by murdering Seyd. Her literal penetration of his prison cell
prefigures her more central act of identification with him: she
takes on his character until she becomes his double. As Byron
emphasizes, her status as Seyd's slave parallels that of Conrad
as Seyd's captive: "She was a slave—from such may captives
claim / A fellow-feeling, differing but in name" (iii.202–03). She
rescues Conrad just as he rescued her; in the most scandalous
turn of the plot, she murders Seyd, as Conrad had planned to

do. In the end, Conrad and Gulnare cause, directly or indirectly, the deaths of their original partners. Both are "extreme in love or hate, in good or ill" (III.521); if Conrad has one virtue and a thousand crimes, Gulnare has one crime and a thousand virtues.

This interpenetration of selves differing in nationality, gender, race, and social status embodies the fantasy projected by a passage such as Conrad's self-examination, which bypasses cultural differences for the abstractions of the naked heart. Gulnare increasingly lays claim to an inner self that before was only Conrad's. Her enforced relations with Seyd have developed in her a version of Conrad's "secret spirit free" (I.248), as she suggests when she says of Seyd:

> But still—he goes unmourned—returns unsought—
> And oft when present—absent from my thought.
> Or when reflection comes, and come it must—
> I fear that henceforth 'twill but bring disgust.   (II.519–22)

As Conrad grows more passive, Gulnare grows more active in asserting her own deep emotions. When he asks why she seeks Seyd's death, she justifies herself in terms of a Conrad-like bitterness about her past disappointments: "My youth disgraced—the long, long wasted years, / One blow shall cancel with our future fears" (III.378–79). By a kind of unconscious sympathy between Conrad and Gulnare, she takes on his sensibility.

The poem never lets the doubling between the two erase gender distinctions entirely. Gulnare's passions never have the vagueness about origins that encouraged contemporary readers to equate Conrad with Byron. Gulnare has specific reasons for her feelings, her love for Conrad and her hatred for Seyd, so that Byron's descriptions of her subjectivity never attain the generality of Conrad's. Nevertheless, her experiences seem to be a better realization of the passions attributed to Conrad than those of Conrad himself. While he dwindles into a hero of sensibility, she grows into a Byronic hero.

When Gulnare offers Conrad a knife with which to murder the sleeping Seyd, he disdains the subterfuge and argues that he had come to attack Seyd in battle, not with "the secret knife," because he "who spares a woman's seeks not slumber's life" (III.364–65). This Conrad bears little relation to the earlier one who plotted to ambush Seyd's camp; as critics since Jeffrey have noted, Conrad's aggression strangely vanishes when Gulnare suggests that he kill Seyd. As a result, Gulnare takes the murder upon herself and returns to Conrad's cell with a small spot of blood on her forehead that reveals her deed. When Conrad sees it, he is as shocked as Milton's Adam upon Eve's return from the Tree of Knowledge: "But ne'er from strife—captivity—remorse . . . / So thrilled—so shuddered every creeping vein, / As now they froze before that purple stain" (III.422, 424–25). He reacts as if he, rather than Seyd, had been stabbed; his thoughts "bleed within that silent cell—his breast" (III.479). Her orchestration of the details of their escape reduces him to apathy: "Nor cared he now if rescued or betrayed" (III.449). Following her passively, he is led from Seyd's prison back to his camp, where his followers greet him and Gulnare.

The Corsair's most peculiar moment then follows because the poem does not know what to do with Gulnare. Conrad embraces her in gratitude for having saved his life, and she is never mentioned again. Although most critics have simply ignored Gulnare's disappearance, the reviewer who in 1814 said that the narrative left him "full of anxiety for what may be the lot of the self-devoted Gulnare" was more sensitive to its strangeness.[24] In Byron's first draft, she vanished from the narrative even more abruptly than she did in the final version. The entire section describing the embrace between Gulnare and Conrad was an afterthought; as Byron explained to John Murray, "I have added a section for *Gulnare* to fill up the parting—& dismiss her more ceremoniously" (*LJ*, IV: 24). Byron's comment is strange because Gulnare is not dismissed ceremoniously: she simply disappears from the text. Immediately after describing the embrace of Conrad and Gulnare, the narrative shifts to Conrad's reaction to Medora's sudden death and his grief at her loss.

The awkwardness of this ending arises from a collision between two possibilities for love in Byron's narrative: likeness and difference. Although Franklin maintains that Gulnare is "willing to accept the authority of Conrad, her superior in rank, race, and sex,"[25] the climactic embrace between the two suggests that they are more alike than Franklin allows: "He clasp'd that hand—it trembled—and his own / Had lost its firmness, and his voice its tone" (III.539–40). Their mutual trembling figures their closeness. Both experience a passion too deep for words, which only the body's language can express. The elaborate sentimentality with which the narrative describes their embrace reads like a defensive gloss for a highly unconventional situation in early nineteenth-century narrative: the equality of male and female souls.

Yet, after having played with the possibility that Conrad might recognize one who is his second self, the poem reasserts the gender relations with which it began when an emphasis on difference cancels one on likeness. The cost of this reassertion is the elimination of all female characters: Medora dies and Gulnare disappears. Although Daniel P. Watkins notes that Medora "must die because her validity as an ideal and the hope she represents have been destroyed," it would be more accurate to say that she dies to fulfill her validity as an ideal of a woman who poses no threat to masculine autonomy.[26] Only through her death and Gulnare's disappearance can Conrad regain his "secret soul":

> By those, who deepest feel, is ill exprest
> The indistinctness of the suffering breast;
> Where thousand thoughts begin to end in one,
> Which seeks from all the refuge found in none;
> No words suffice the secret soul to show,
> And Truth denies all eloquence to Woe.   (III.640–45)

Conrad is once again a Byronic hero; the poem returns to the abstractions of the universal subject and to the earlier polarization of Conrad between love for Medora and hate for all others. When Conrad is with Gulnare, he seemed to lose his deep inner self, but after her disappearance, it returns. Byron's narrative restores the uniqueness of the hero's naked heart. It demonstrates, however awkwardly, that the inner self is a less universal possession than it might seem to be. Even at the desperate cost of obliterating all female characters, Byronic heroes remain Byronic heroes, not heroines. Conrad's exhaustion is the only sign of the strain to which Gulnare subjects the uniqueness of the male hero. His ego at the end is only a shadow of his former self, a "stricken soul" on which "exhaustion prest" and which "stupor almost lull'd . . . into rest" (III.646–47). Conrad's experience with another self like his own depletes rather than enriches him.

While Scott's *Marmion* closes after the secrets of Marmion's torments are discovered and he is punished, Byron gives no such ultimate revelation about Conrad; we are not even told of his death. Instead, the poem emphasizes that Conrad has little self left to hide. Since it refuses to reach closure through a dramatic revelation of the hero's past sins, it substitutes a sense of psychological exhaustion, a spiritual death that matters more than a literal one.[27] Part of the seductiveness of the naked heart described in Byron's poetry is the sense that it is not as strong or as lasting as it is supposed to be. Having deep but invisible passions turns quickly into having no passions at all. Byron's work displays for its readers the pleasures of a subjectivity that is perpetually at risk, whose depths are so precious that they need to be protected from depletion. As Christensen suggests, one strategy to shore up this potentially exhausted interiority is to repeat the portrayal of the naked heart in poem after poem, even though the need for repetition is itself a sign of fragility.[28]

Byron's heroes provided a pattern whereby individuals could imagine themselves to be unique by following a carefully constructed model. The key to this uniqueness was passion. By eroticizing subjectivity, sexuality came to be Byron's master trope for the workings of an inner self that could be read only as Byron's. His first readers were right to concentrate on his portrayal of passion, because its implications for the representation of subjectivity, far more than his radicalism or his representation of the Orient, exercised a decisive effect on later writing. It made concerns like politics seem less essential than the fundamental display of the author's naked heart.

The scandalous events of 1816, climaxing with Byron's separation from Lady Byron, altered his relation to his language of the naked heart. The separation scandal marked him because it gave the public an extrapoetic event on which to center a shocking history. Numerous such histories surfaced, from Byron's supposed affair with the actress Mrs. Mardyn to the rumor that Lady Byron left him when he demanded anal sex. The newspapers hotly debated the separation and discussed endlessly the merits and demerits of Byron and his wife. Not even Byron's dramatic death at Missolonghi stimulated a comparable outpouring of commentary.[29]

The sign of Byron's altered relation to his audience is that in much of the poetry written in 1816 and afterwards, "I" replaces "we" or "he." The universalizing language of the earlier poetry gives way to more overtly personal and lyric meditations. The changes in *Childe Harold's Pilgrimage* between cantos I and II, published in 1812, and cantos III and IV, published in 1816 and 1818 respectively, most vividly register how Byron rewrote his relation to his audience. To demonstrate this rewriting, I will concentrate on the poem's changing relation to the conventions of topographical poetry. As John Guillory has argued, in the eighteenth century such poetry oscillated between descriptions of scenery and abstract moralizing reflections upon it; both scenery and reflections presented to a new class of readers examples of what counted as a commonplace.[30] Guillory's argument valuably suggests why poems like Thomson's *The Seasons* and Gray's *Elegy* were so popular in the eighteenth century. They represented forms of "cultural property . . . urgently sought by an upwardly mobile professional class."[31] To be able to recognize as commonplace the scenes and sentiments expressed in these poems marked the reader as having achieved "a pleased identification with a social group, an identification through the medium of what the reader and writer possess in common, a language."[32]

By the time of the 1812 *Childe Harold*, the rules of the topographical genre had altered. The poem still oscillated between scenic descriptions and general reflections on them, but the nature of the scenery and reflections changed in response to changes in what counted as markers of class emulation. Like earlier topographical poems, the 1812 *Childe Harold* offered its version of upper-class tastes commodified for the consumption of a wider reading public. But this commodification involved not descriptions of English scenery, which no longer seemed distinctively aristocratic, but scenes in Portugal, Albania, Greece, and Spain, where only an aristocrat with Byron's money and connections could travel. Moreover, Byron's reflections on these scenes were not secularized versions of classical topoi, as in Thomson's *The Seasons*, but clichés of early nineteenth-century sentimentality, the same style that Byron skewered in *English Bards and Scotch Reviewers* after having imitated it slavishly in *Hours of Idleness*.[33] This language represented a communal ideal of refined English that was no longer tied to a classical education, as Thomson's reflections were, but could still mark the language of respectable society. In particular, it responded to the growth of a female reading audience and the consequent need for a new standard of polite speech.

One example of the topographical poem's characteristic reflections on a scene occurs in canto II after Byron describes the
straits of Calpe:

> 'Tis night, when Meditation bids us feel
> We once have lov'd though love is at an end:
> The heart, lone mourner of its baffled zeal,
> Though friendless now, will dream it had a friend.   (II.23)

William St. Clair has discovered that the stanza containing these
lines was the passage from *Childe Harold* most frequently copied
into ladies' albums in the early nineteenth century.[34] Although,
as he also notes, it would not be likely to appear in modern
anthologies, his discovery situates *Childe Harold* as a poem whose
value lay in disseminating what counted as cultivated sentiment,
in this case, the melancholy pleasures of "Meditation." Byron's
scenic descriptions and his thoughts on them became the commonplaces of those wanting to demonstrate their participation in
polite culture by copying refined expressions. The picturesquely
ordered English scenes and classical commonplaces of eighteenth-
century topographical poetry give way in Byron to exotic scenes
and aesthetic sentimentality; these serve as the communal standards of language and sentiment to which all desiring respectability ought to aspire.

Even the poem's political outrage arises in the context of
sensibility. As Peter Manning demonstrates, the poem pointedly
sets itself against the jingoism previously associated with the
genre of the chivalric verse romance.[35] It does so by placing
values of sensibility above those of British nationalism. For
example, Byron targets Lord Elgin's appropriation of Greek art
because it spoils the aesthetic beauty of Greece itself. Speaking
of Seville, he notes, "Soon, soon shall Conquest's fiery foot
intrude, / Blackening her lovely domes with traces rude" (I.45).
Characteristically, language mingling aesthetics and eroticism
expresses his scorn for political aggression. Invading forces of
"Conquest" ruin the pure, feminized beauty of the lands to
which he travels. Political outrage in these cantos arises from a
sentimental conception of foreign countries as beautiful women
who must be protected.

The most striking innovation in *Childe Harold*'s dissemination
of cultivated sensibility is Harold himself. Harold has little sub-

stance as a character in the 1812 poem; he is a fiction that allows Byron to enclose abstract feeling in a particular character. Yet shadowy as Harold is, he allowed the class-specific language of the poem to be read as uniquely personal in a way that earlier topographical poetry was not. The key to his personality was his highly conventional erotic melancholia. When readers of the 1812 *Childe Harold* equated Byron with Harold, "Byron" was a personification of the commonplaces of polite literature, who had been given the shadow of a self through Harold. Reading Byron through Harold's sensibility grounded the poem's commodification of polite language in the body of a "real" aristocrat who functioned as a type.

By 1816, the situation had changed. Byron was no longer a type because the notoriety of his marital separation had given him concreteness, whether he wanted it or not. When he resumed *Childe Harold*, he was writing as a man with a past that gave him a specificity that none of his heroes had. As a result, Harold is more than ever a mere fiction, as Byron eventually admits in the preface to canto IV. The interest of the second half of *Childe Harold* lies in Byron's reinvention of himself as an individual. He does so partly through specific references to his family situation, as when he mentions Ada at the opening and closing of canto III. But his more powerful device is a myth of self-development. While Harold and the narrator in cantos I and II are entirely static, the Byron of cantos III and IV insists on what McGann terms "the necessity of constant development and painful growth."[36] Self-development is Byron's strategy for inventing individuality. His poem shifts from presenting himself as a type to presenting himself as a man whose capacity for self-development defines his uniqueness.

The presence of "Byron the individual" alters the oscillation between scene and reflection developed in the 1812 poem by offering new norms for class emulation. The paradox of the poem's second half is that the norm is one of individual experience so private that it cannot be communicated. The scenes that Byron views are no longer exotic. He travels to places that had been closed off because of the Napoleonic wars, but which would soon be open to British tourists. In cantos III and IV of *Childe Harold*, Europe becomes a catalogue of important sights. The poem presents a sequence of fetishized greatness: great men,

events, scenes, authors, and art, most of which look strikingly
alike. The canon of European civilization becomes the equivalent
of the commonplaces of earlier topographical poetry. It is all
available to nourish the refinement of the inquiring mind.

The critical difference occurs in the way that Byron reflects
on these sights. Rather than appearing as an embodiment of
sensibility, like Harold, he invents himself as "Byron" the individual. Reflecting on these sights provides the evidence of his individuality because it becomes the spur to his self-development.
He says famously at the beginning of canto III that the purpose
of writing poetry is "to create, and in creating live / A being
more intense" (III.6). Yet the verb "to create" is out of place in
Childe Harold. A more appropriate one would have been "to
tour." *Childe Harold* teaches nineteenth-century readers that the
European tour is a mode of individual soul-making.

One sign of this individualism is that language emphasizing
inexpressibility increasingly replaces older language of aesthetic
sentimentality, although this never disappears entirely. In a
famous passage, after viewing a spectacular storm over the Rhône,
Byron is speechless:

> Could I embody and unbosom now
> That which is most within me,—could I wreak
> My thoughts upon expression, and thus throw
> Soul, heart, mind, passions, feelings, strong or weak,
> All that I would have sought, and all I seek,
> Bear, know, feel, and yet breathe—into *one* word,
> And that one word were Lightning, I would speak;
> But as it is, I live and die unheard,
> With a most voiceless thought, sheathing it as a sword.   (III.97)

The communal language of sentimentality gives way to a language that insists on the priority of private experience. While
the topos of inexpressibility was itself a cliché of sentimentality,
it is revitalized when Byron incorporates it into his myth of
self-development. Byron's feelings upon seeing the storm are so
special, so intensely his own, that they cannot be described.
Before the Venus de Medici, he is similarly "[d]azzled and drunk
with beauty, till the heart / Reels with its fulness" (IV.50) and
scorns those who with "paltry jargon" would attempt to describe
the sculpture's ineffability. His poem is the culmination of the
tradition in which topographical poetry served as a privileged

genre for transmitting knowledge of cultivated sentiment to those seeking to assume respectability. The poetical, historical, political, and artistic monuments of Europe become a form of cultural private property because Byron can experience them so as to reinforce his individuality. As James Buzard has documented, Byron's invention of his experience of European greatness as unique, privileged, and profoundly individual proved to a be a boon to the Victorian tourist industry. Early Victorian guidebooks included substantial quotations from Byron's poems, especially *Childe Harold*, to guide tourists to develop themselves by copying Byron.[37] He revealed how all could become unique by doing precisely what he had done.

Byron's success in imagining individual self-development in cantos III and IV of *Childe Harold* depended partly on avoiding the problems with erotic relations that rendered the plot of *The Corsair* so peculiar. Given the fact that his history featured sexual scandal, he faced a considerable challenge after 1816 in developing any plot involving a Byronic hero and heroine. His solution in *Manfred* was to turn to drama and put the Byronic hero in the novel position of speaking for himself. *Manfred* is simultaneously more and less personal than the Turkish Tales. Insofar as it addresses sibling incest, it acknowledges the scandalous rumors circulating about Byron's separation from his wife. Yet the generalized vocabulary of the naked heart that encouraged readers to equate a hero such as Conrad with Byron no longer pertains to Manfred. As a dramatic character, he does not have the privilege of evaporating into abstractions as Conrad did.

Sexual transgression haunts Manfred far more explicitly than any previous Byronic hero. In the relation between Conrad and Gulnare, *The Corsair* toyed with the possibility that the inner self might belong to a woman as much as to a man, only to reassert gender difference in the end. In *Manfred*, the incestuous love between Manfred and Astarte returns to the moment when the narrative of *The Corsair* collapsed. *The Corsair*'s hint of symbolic incest between Gulnare and Conrad becomes the full-fledged incestuous love of Manfred for Astarte. The drama confronts sibling incest far more directly than *The Corsair* did as an image for the possible identity of male and female subjectivities.

Manfred spends the first two acts reacting against this possibility by insisting vehemently on his uniqueness. Although he is often seen as the epitome of the Byronic hero, Byron's change of genre from verse narrative to closet drama significantly altered the representation of the hero's inner self. *The Corsair* often alluded to the inner depths of Conrad's heart but elaborated them only in a few generalized passages. Moving to drama blocked the universalizing of Byron's earlier confessional rhetoric; the narrator of *The Corsair* speaks of "we" and "our," but Manfred speaks of "I" and "mine."

As a result, Manfred seems far more embattled than Conrad partly because he lacks the luxury of a narrator to describe his privileged interiority. He tells the Chamois Hunter, "Preach [patience] to mortals of a dust like thine,—/ I am not of thine order" (ii.i.37–38). When he describes himself to the Witch of the Alps, he maintains that his "spirit walk'd not with the souls of men, / Nor look'd upon the earth with human eyes" (ii.ii.51–52). He is happy only when alone; to meet others is for him to feel "degraded back to them" (ii.ii.78). Manfred loudly rejects the idea that his interiority is like that of anyone else and acknowledges no kinship with the universal naked heart exemplified by Conrad. Instead, he insists that he is so unique as to be incomprehensible.

He cannot be taken at his word. Far from finding him incomprehensible, many of the other characters know him well. In the play's first scene, the Spirits reduce him to a senseless heap because they read him better than he wants to admit. After he boasts that "there is no form on earth / Hideous or beautiful" to him, the Seventh Spirit undercuts him by appearing as "*a beautiful female figure*" (i.i.184–85, 188); Manfred takes her to be Astarte, whether or not she is, and promptly faints. This scene clues the reader that Manfred is not as incomprehensible as he wishes to appear, for the Spirits easily puncture his mask of indifference. Throughout the play, his reputation seems to precede him. The Witch of the Alps, for example, tells him, "I know thee, and the powers which give thee power; / I know thee for a man of many thoughts, / And deeds of good and ill, extreme in both" (ii.ii.33–35). The First Destiny, proclaiming "Avaunt!— he's mine," describes Manfred in terms much like those Manfred uses to describe himself to the Witch: "[H]is aspirations / Have

been beyond the dwellers of the earth" (II.iv.50, 58–59). Even
the Abbot, whose orthodoxy limits his sympathies, epitomizes
Manfred's character:

>   He
> Hath all the energy which would have made
> A goodly frame of glorious elements,
> Had they been wisely mingled; as it is,
> It is an awful chaos.   (III.i.160–64)

While his description may seem inadequate, it closely resembles
Manfred's own self-description: "[W]e, / Half dust, half deity,
alike unfit / To sink or soar, with our mix'd essence make / A
conflict of [the world's] elements" (I.ii.39–42). With the exception
of the Chamois Hunter, the other characters quickly seize upon
the central tensions of Manfred's psyche. Even if they do not
understand the specific circumstances behind his self-division,
they nonetheless reveal that he is not as incomprehensible as he
claims.

In *The Corsair*, no one in the fiction was privileged to see into
Conrad's mind, not even Gulnare; only the narrator could expose
the universal abstractions of Conrad's inner self. In *Manfred*, the
nature of the hero's psyche and the relation of other characters
to it are reversed. Unlike Conrad, Manfred never dissolves into
a universal subject; he is unique, as he repeatedly insists. Yet
because he speaks so frequently about himself, the characters
have access to his inner self in a way that was available only to
the narrator in *The Corsair*. Not only does Manfred speak about
himself incessantly, the other characters seem at times to have
heard what he will say before he says it.

Astarte alone destabilizes Manfred's sense of his uniqueness,
because in his eyes, she threatened not only to know him, but
to be him. Manfred describes her as having been almost exactly
his double; she had "the same lone thoughts and wanderings"
as he, but also had "pity, and smiles, and tears," which he had
not (II.ii.109, 113). While the differences between them are the
accidental effects of gender stereotypes, the similarities between
them are essential. She embodies the possibility that "a mind / To
comprehend the universe" (II.ii.110–11) might not be Manfred's
exclusive possession. Even after her death, she haunts him
because her memory still subverts his faith in the uniqueness of

his interiority. Yet she is also absolutely "other" because his internalization of her arose from her death, under mysterious circumstances. If she is like Gulnare in being the hero's second self, she is like Medora in being always absent. Astarte represents the collapse into a single character of the competing possibilities of desire based on likeness and difference, which *The Corsair* had embodied in two different characters.

The relation between Astarte and Manfred centers on the fatal moment when Astarte had an unmediated view of Manfred's heart:

MANFRED: Her faults were mine—her virtues were her own—
    I loved her, and destroyed her!
WITCH: With thy hand?
MANFRED: Not with my hand, but heart—which broke her heart—
    It gazed on mine, and withered.   (ii.ii.116–19)

Manfred's nearly incoherent language describes the core of the tragedy. While readers from the drama's first appearance have been tempted to invent histories for Astarte to explain what really happened, this passage is not about Astarte but about Manfred. The issue is not what happened, but what he thinks happened. According to him, the cause of her death was not incest but her gazing upon his heart. While he initially takes the guilt upon himself, claiming that he "destroyed her" and "broke her heart," when he describes the fatal moment, agency passes from him to her as his heart becomes the object of her gaze. Although we could interpret this passage to mean that she learned of his sinful love for her and could not bear the knowledge, this reading gives Manfred's language more specificity than it invites.

Instead, for Astarte to gaze upon Manfred's heart is to experience her own superfluity.[38] If Manfred and Astarte indeed "had one heart" (ii.i.26), as he tells the Chamois Hunter, then for her to penetrate to the depths of his heart would be to discover not mutuality, but repetition. Her heart withers because it is not distinctive enough to survive alone. In their relations, the zero-sum logic that pertained in *The Corsair* between Conrad and Gulnare returns. The more interiority there is for him, the less there is for her. His account even suggests a bit of *Schadenfreude* because her death proves that he was the stronger. Alan Richardson notes, "Manfred's love necessarily destroys its object, because his end is not union with Astarte but the assimilation of her."³⁹ But assimilation is less Manfred's goal than a situation from which he wishes to escape; it results from the impossibility of sharing the identity of his inner self. Assimilation is inadequate for Manfred because Astarte, even as a memory, challenges the supremacy of his narcissism. His greatest wish is not to assimilate her but to restore her existence so as once again to externalize what he has made internal.

Acting upon his wish, Manfred conjures up her Phantom in the last scene of Act II. Although we would expect their encounter to be the play's most private moment, it is actually the most public, witnessed by Arimanes, Nemesis, Spirits, and Destinies, all of whom comment on the action. The inclusion of onlookers emphasizes how, in summoning the Phantom, Manfred is already compromising his interiority by confronting an image of Astarte that is not purely a product of his own mind. The assembled audience magnifies awareness of the extent to which he must break out of himself to meet the Phantom.

His bizarre conversation with her is a desperate attempt to regain some of what he has lost. Manfred addresses the Phantom as if speaking to his ideal Astarte; he wishes to hear from a woman who exists entirely for him, unlike the Astarte who competed with him to her cost. It is one of Byron's masterstrokes that Manfred does not get the Astarte he expects. Instead, Byron presents an image of Astarte with no subjectivity at all; it is not even clear if this is the real Astarte or merely a phantom with her image. Whether or not the Phantom is understood to be Astarte, it is enough that Manfred takes her to be so, because their conversation effectively breaks her hold on him. Manfred at last confronts an Astarte who is entirely outside himself: if in life, they held such close communion that they had one heart, in her phantasmic appearance, they are entirely different. The Phantom speaks not as an identical version of him but as an impersonal voice of necessity. Her announcement, "Manfred! To-morrow ends thine earthly ills" (II.iv.152), is so entirely different from what he asks for that it shatters his internalization of her.

The sign of this shattering is that after this scene, Manfred never mentions Astarte again, not even to anticipate a reunion with her after death. Until the close of Act II, his subjectivity

revolves around his tormented eroticism. Once that torment stops,
the source of his inner conflict vanishes, and he has to become
a new character. Byron had trouble continuing the drama because
the third act of *Manfred* is one of the few times in his career that
he had to imagine a plot with a Byronic hero, but no Byronic
heroine.

He develops two possibilities for what masculine subjectivity
might look like without its characteristic depths of erotic torment.
The first appears in Manfred's lyrical speech recalling the Coliseum. In it, sexual relations are recast as relations between
masculine history and feminine nature. Manfred's imagery transforms Astarte's gaze into the more benign power of beautiful
landscape. He recalls how the moon "cast a wide and tender
light,"

> Leaving that beautiful which still was so,
> And making that which was not, till the place
> Became religion, and the heart ran o'er
> With silent worship of the great of old!—
> The dead, but sceptred sovereigns, who still rule
> Our spirits from their urns.   (III.iv.36–41)

The moon has Astarte's "gentler powers" of tenderness, but none
of her subjectivity's potential invasiveness. Instead, its influence
creates a luminous continuity that raises all it touches to beauty.
Manfred's erotic past gives way to his fantasy of male associations
extending through history. Though this vision is his alone, the
sovereigns belong to a community larger than himself, as he
emphasizes when he asserts that they rule "[o]ur spirits"
(III.iv.41). For the first time he admits that he might worship
something outside of himself and even be led by "the great of
old" (III.iv.39). His speech suggests the possibility of a self that
no longer needs to be defined in terms of rigidly exclusive
interiority, but that gathers strength from seeing itself as part of
a historical, masculine continuum. The cost of this strength is
the projection of the feminine entirely into nature.

The vision of the Coliseum is Manfred's most tranquil scene
of self-discovery, but Byron does not permit him to sustain it.
The second possibility for Manfred's subjectivity in Act III is an
insistence on absolute autonomy. Just as the end of *The Corsair*

replaces an emphasis on similarity with one on difference, so in *Manfred* the vision of masculine continuity gives way to a ferocious insistence on isolation. In the final scene, as a demon rises from the earth to possess his soul, Manfred insists loudly on the power of his individual mind:

> The mind which is immortal makes itself
> Requital for its good or evil thoughts —
> Is its own origin of ill and end —
> And its own place and time. (III.iv.129–32)

The speech belies everything else in the drama: Manfred can make it only after Astarte has vanished from his consciousness. As Cooke notes, "It is worth stressing that Manfred becomes a hero less for what he can do than for what he can do without."[40] In this fantasy of masculine independence, Manfred puts aside all except his own absolute narcissism.

In doing so, he insists loudly on his own uniqueness in language transparently stolen from Milton's Satan. It is as if, without Astarte, Manfred has nothing left to confess, so Byron imports his mind from Milton. Manfred's subjectivity is running on empty because eroticism is so central to Byronic representation that once Manfred has abandoned Astarte, he has nothing left to say when he wishes to bare his soul. The hollowness of his death scene derives from a rhetoric that has lost its underpinnings.[41] The point is not that Manfred has reached an endpoint of narcissism, but that without Astarte he has nothing left to be narcissistic about. The dying Manfred is a hero with no secrets.

After *Manfred*, Byron's relation to his heroes and to his audience became more exploratory; in the works of his Italian period he tried out modes from satire to philosophical drama. As much modern criticism has emphasized, Byron never entirely abandoned a "romantic" mode for a "satirical" one. Yet nineteenth-century discussions of Byron usually split his career between the early *Childe Harold* side and the later *Don Juan* one, thus preserving the familiar eighteenth-century division between sentiment and satire. As a result, I am going to bypass Byron's closet dramas, fascinating as they are, because they took a second place to *Don Juan* in nineteenth-century treatments of his later career.

Don Juan relentlessly pokes fun at the Byronic style that exhausted itself in *Manfred*: "And the sad truth which hovers o'er my
desk / Turns what was once romantic to burlesque" (iv.3).
Throughout, as McGann has argued in *"Don Juan" in Context*,
Byron mocks his audience's desire to see his poetry as an embodiment of his life:

> Here I might enter on a chaste description,
>   Having withstood temptation in my youth,
> But hear that several people take exception
>   At the first two books having too much truth;
> Therefore I'll make Don Juan leave the ship soon,
>   Because the publisher declares, in sooth,
> Through needles' eyes it easier for the camel is
> To pass, than those two cantos into families.   (iv.97)

Byron's teasing insistence on the chastity of his imagination
resembles Sterne's, but the specifically Byronic twist in the passage is his claim that he could describe Juan's seduction because
he himself "withstood temptation" in his youth. He implies
that his unwritten passage would have exemplified the equation
between author and hero on which the success of his earlier
poetry depended. Yet if he really portrayed himself in his hero,
the results would be unacceptable to the public. What respectable
families want from him is the clap-trap of the naked heart, not
the truth of George Gordon, Lord Byron. Having made this
elaborate bow to propriety in not describing Juan's seduction,
he goes on to narrate Juan's misadventures in a harem, an
episode not calculated to make the poem more acceptable to
families who rejected the earlier cantos. Byron produces a scandalous poem by repossessing the category of truth. If this poetry
is not acceptable to the hypocritical British public, then it demonstrates that he has a privileged relationship to the representation
of reality.[42]
I have argued that the rhetorical source of the equation
between Byron and his heroes lay in the manipulation of a
universalizing language that eroticized a psyche undetermined
by social constraints. With engaging aplomb, *Don Juan* largely
jettisons this language. Although little in the poem is not open
to retraction, Byron foregrounds his impatience with the mysteriousness of his earlier representations: "I hate all mystery, and
that air / Of clap-trap, which your recent poets prize" (ii.124).

Characteristically, he professes his hatred of "clap-trap" in connection with events that are utterly unmysterious: his zeal for exposing mystery is more a comment on his previous career than on *Don Juan*. Except in the final Gothic episodes, he creates an air of mystery only about the obvious, as when he describes the name of Miss Protasoff's "mystic office" at Catherine's court, " 'l'Eprouveuse,' " as "[a] term inexplicable to the Muse" (IX.84). Even the Gothic clap-trap is not sustained for long; the Black Friar is soon unveiled as "her frolic Grace—Fitz-Fulke!" (XVI.123). The poem's real mystery lies not in the hidden, eroticized depths of the characters but in the narrator's unpredictable digressions, which are far more seductive than anything in the plot.

When Juan imitates the dying Manfred by protesting his independence to Gulbeyaz, "Heads bow, knees bend, eyes watch around a throne, / And hands obey—our hearts are still our own" (V.127), the narrator comments tartly, "This was a truth to us extremely trite" (V.128). A fundamental assumption of Byron's previous poetry was that the heart remained independent of all constraints of society, but *Don Juan* casually treats this assumption as a threadbare commonplace. Even though *Don Juan* does not dismiss the language of the naked heart entirely, it no longer privileges such language as the vehicle of absolute truth about the psyche. Instead, the poem questions whether any language can assert such truth, since the variability of human behavior suggests that a universal inner self is either illusory or permanently invisible.

Questioning the depth of the universalized inner self involves not only the narrator's remarks but also Juan's character. Whereas the Byron of cantos III and IV of *Childe Harold* invented himself as an intensely realized consciousness undergoing painful self-development, Juan is "a little superficial" (XI.51). Although some critics persist in seeing Juan as a complex character who undergoes continuous moral development, Juan matters little except as an occasion to generate a kaleidoscopic variety of incidents. Like its hero, the whole of *Don Juan* is "a little superficial," by which I do not mean that it is trivial or inconsequential, but that it deliberately discards the obsession with universalized inner depths that made Byron's previous poetry famous.[43]

As a result, erotic relations also change because men and women become as different as society makes them. Recognizing that gender roles are products of civilization, *Don Juan* asserts the gender differential as an absolute of human experience. As Wolfson has demonstrated, differences between men and women in the poem are never more pronounced than when they seem to be transgressed.[44] Byron employs literal and figurative cross-dressing in *Don Juan* not to suggest the androgyny of human nature but to puncture the ridiculousness of men and women who attempt to take on the traits characteristic of the opposite sex. As socially imposed abstractions, "Man" and "Woman" remain in a stable polarity, although individual characters may refuse to recognize it. If *Don Juan* repeatedly exploits and draws attention to the constructedness of gender roles, it does not challenge their validity. It recognizes that certain stereotypes are arbitrarily enforced, especially at the expense of women, but does not argue that they therefore should be removed.

For example, Catherine the Great in *Don Juan*, like Gulnare in *The Corsair*, possesses stereotypically masculine characteristics, but the significance of the gender-crossing is entirely different in the two poems. The doubling of Conrad and Gulnare suggested a fundamental identity in the constitution of their inner selves; differences between them seemed to be merely the effects of culture rather than of nature. In *Don Juan*, female characters like Catherine take on a parodically overwhelming erotic aggressiveness, as if to compensate for Juan's superficiality. The fraught struggles of Byron's earlier heroes and heroines give way to situations in which women easily dominate, although their domination is usually seen as comic. While a few characters, such as Leila and Aurora Raby, are exceptions to the general rule, Byron's women in *Don Juan* generally conform to Pope's maxim, "Every woman is at heart a rake." The poem's often noted eighteenth-century quality arises in part because Byron treats gender more according to Augustan norms of Pope and Fielding than according to bourgeois ones of domestic fiction that competed with and eventually replaced those of the Augustans.[45]

Insofar as "the secret self" exists in *Don Juan*, it belongs to heroines:

> But Adeline was not indifferent: for
> (*Now* for a common place!) beneath the snow,

As a Volcano holds the lava more
   Within—*et caetera*. Shall I go on?—No!
I hate to hunt down a tired metaphor:
   So let the often used volcano go.
Poor thing! How frequently, by me and others,
It hath been stirred up till its smoke quite smothers.

I'll have another figure in a trice:—
   What say you to bottle of champaigne?
Frozen into a very vinous ice,
   Which leaves few drops of that immortal rain,
Yet in the very centre, past all price,
   About a liquid glassful will remain;
And this is stronger than the strongest grape
Could e'er express in its expanded shape.   (XIII.36–37)

Byron does not scorn the volcano image merely because it is a
commonplace but because in his earlier work it had been associated specifically with his male heroes. He also used it in his
famous definition of poetry as the lava of the imagination; critics
such as Francis Jeffrey had applied Byron's metaphor to himself
by calling him "a volcano in the heart of our land."[46] The
volcano metaphor was a privileged figure to express the intense
passions of Byron's masculine inner self.

Byron rejects it in *Don Juan* because it would be inappropriate
to use the same figure that described a masculine subjectivity
to describe a feminine one: the poem abandons the (almost)
gender-blind language of the naked heart in the Turkish Tales.
Since society makes men and women fundamentally different,
the same figure cannot be used to describe them both. The
champagne metaphor that Byron substitutes for the volcano femi-
nizes suppressed passion by making it a force of culture rather
than nature. A precious glassful of concentrated champagne is
as different from spouting lava as female subjectivity is from
male.

Nothing was more shocking to the poem's first readers than
its treatment of gender roles, which flew in the face of what such
writers as Hannah More and Maria Edgeworth promulgated as
the ideal of a proper domestic woman. Despite the oddity of
Byron's previous treatments of erotic relations, he had created
heroines such as Medora in *The Corsair* who conformed to their
ideal. *Don Juan*, however, disregarded it almost entirely. In seeing

Don Juan as a poem that was designed to shock, I disagree with
the still influential argument of E. D. H. Johnson that Byron's
satire in *Don Juan* arose because he misunderstood the British
public. He argues that Byron, living in exile in Italy, would not
have known that the Regency had ended and that a more severe
Evangelical morality was dominating society.[47] Johnson underestimates the extent to which Byron's poem positions itself as a
radical rejection of contemporary mores, which may have helped
to define what those mores were by demonstrating what they
were not. If in *Childe Harold* Byron had used the topographical
genre to reinvent the commonplace, *Don Juan* presented scenes
and reflections that could never be so appropriated, as the poem's
epigraph suggests. While the outcry greeting the 1819 *Don Juan*
dismayed Byron, it also gratified him because it signaled that
he was not merely an audience-pleasing hack. As he suggested
throughout the poem, he had become too good for his audience.

It is easy to overstate the differences between *Don Juan* and
Byron's earlier poetry partly because the division between the
two became so common in the nineteenth century. There is only
a slender distinction between Manfred's final posturing and the
ease with which Byron mocks Juan's speech to Gulbeyaz.
Likewise, *Don Juan* occasionally indulges in melancholy generalizations about human experience that recall the earlier poems,
although these generalizations never carry a similar authority as
ultimate revelations because they are not attached to particular
characters. But the most challenging figure to analyze regarding
the continuities and discontinuities in Byron's work is the narrator. If the characters in *Don Juan*'s plot have impoverished
subjectivities next to the loudly proclaimed depths of Byron's
earlier heroes, the narrator becomes a different kind of character
who can be read as "Byron himself." The chief characteristic of
his subjectivity is what he calls "mobility," a general skepticism
about following any established system of belief.[48] Mobility subverts the confessional language of the previous poems by suggesting that it exists only as one pose among many rather than as
language holding the key to ultimate truths. Analyzing how
gender affects the narrator's stance is tricky. For Wolfson, Byron's
treatment of mobility suggests that gender divisions in the poem
are less secure than they seem to be; mobility succeeds in being
"loyal to no sex, itself showing mobility across gender lines."[49]

For her, mobility is not gender-specific because it belongs both to the masculine character of the narrator and to the feminine one of Adeline. She suggests that mobility is *Don Juan*'s revision of the language of the naked heart, a characterization of subjectivity that does not make exclusive claims on the basis of gender.

Yet Adeline's mobility and the narrator's differ. Hers is the role-playing of a skilled hostess, and we are assured that underneath it lies a soul that she betrays "only now and then" (xvi.96). The narrator, in contrast, repeatedly punctures the illusion that he has any essential core to his personality. He exemplifies a purely rhetorical self and mocks those sentimental enough to want to read his mobility as a flight from supposedly more sincere, deeper feeling. Furthermore, while Adeline's mobility is imposed on her by her social situation, the narrator's demonstrates his freedom from such constraints. He manifests his absolute control of his plot and his mastery over changes in epic tone. His mobility is a constant reminder of his masculine position of dominance.

Although the maleness of Byronic mobility does not resemble the normative masculinity emerging at the century's beginning, it reinvents the Augustans' lordliness. Refusing to conform to any particular code of gendered behavior becomes his sign of a behavior based on class, an aristocratic refusal of bourgeois categories. From the vantage of *Don Juan*, the monolithic inner self of the earlier poems looks too much like a concession to the littleness of those who want a private self to accompany their private property. Resisting it in *Don Juan* is the narrator's most masculine trait because it is his most lordly one. He may challenge early nineteenth-century gender stereotypes, but he does so by upholding his version of Augustan ones. Byron's politics in *Don Juan* do not mesh quite so comfortably with those of the Augustans, but gender is another matter.[50] The most vivid testimony to the gender exclusiveness of Byronic mobility is the fact that almost no later female writers imitated it, although they imitated obsessively the sentimental discourse of the naked heart, with its universalizing language of erotic subjectivity, for the rest of the century.

Don Juan was successful enough as an attack on Byronism that it closed off satire as a genre through which Victorian writers could define themselves against Byronism: Byron had done it first. The few Victorian writers who imitated *Don Juan* used its radical aristocratic ethos to license their rebellion against bourgeois norms. For Bulwer Lytton, Disraeli, and Wilde, *Don Juan* was a valuable model for homosexual performativity, especially because it challenged the existence of an essential, private self. Yet for the most part, *Don Juan* loomed as a road not to be taken. Representative work by Carlyle, Emily Brontë, and Tennyson pretended that it did not exist.

If the poem lampooned Byronism, it also generated enough scandal to allow it to be incorporated rapidly into the image of Byron's general outrageousness. Rather than being read as Byron's dismissal of Byronism, it seemed the final proof that Byron could never be a respectable author. Nevertheless, certain readers soon recuperated the poem by interpreting it as Byron's most sincere self-representation precisely because it avoided his earlier rhetoric of sincerity. This trend is evident as early as Lockhart's comment in 1821, "Stick to Don Juan: it is the only sincere thing you have ever written."[51] Carlyle's essay on Burns followed this opinion: "Perhaps Don Juan, especially the latter parts of it, is the only thing approaching to a sincere work, he ever wrote" (*CW*, XXVI: 269). Such portrayals provided the background for Eliot's famous opinion that in *Don Juan*, "we get something much nearer to genuine self-revelation" than in Byron's previous work.[52] For these readers and for many later critics, *Don Juan*'s style of confession provided a far more convincing portrait of Byron than the confessions of the Turkish Tales or *Childe Harold*.

Understanding the significance of the reception of *Don Juan* involves a larger investigation of the cult of Byron in British culture. In the next chapter, I will turn from a discussion of the rhetoric of subjectivity in Byron's poetry itself to the reception of Byron. The division between Byron's poetry and its reception is not an absolute one; as I have argued, each successive poem was itself part of the reception of Byron's earlier poetry. Yet Byron's reception had as much to do with the making of his image as with his actual poetry. While Byron's poetry helped to create the fictitious "real" Byron who portrayed himself in his heroes, it alone was not enough to create BYRON, the figure whose fame spread across the globe. BYRON was a creation of the literary institutions of nineteenth-century Britain.

CHAPTER 2

The creation of Byronism

This chapter will examine Byron's reception. Although this subject deserves a book-length treatment, I will concentrate only on
the aspects of Byronism that had the most significance for Victorian writers. In particular, I will examine the marketing of
Byron's subjectivity, because his fame depended on making it
accessible to a wide audience, including many who never read
him. Byron the celebrity was for Victorian writers a vivid and,
to some, distasteful image of what fame meant in a capitalist
literary system.

George Gordon, Lord Byron, the individual whose life and
writings are familiar from the work of scholars such as Marchand
and McGann, now largely disappears from my analysis. "Byron"
henceforward refers to Byron the celebrity, my interpretation of
a multifaceted cultural phenomenon. No necessary connection
exists between these two Byrons except that both depend partly
upon twentieth-century academic readings of nineteenth-century
materials. "George Gordon, Lord Byron" is an author responsible
for certain texts. As Foucault suggests in "What Is an Author?,"
such a construction imposes a cultural authority on these texts
and perpetuates the assumptions whereby individuals are
assumed to be responsible for texts whose origins may be far
more multiple.[1] "Byron the celebrity," in contrast, has no such
specificity. He was a name without a stable identity, available
to be damned, consecrated, or ignored, but in all cases accessible
only through the marketing of cultural goods.

Although the word "celebrity" may suggest a twentieth-century
Hollywood star system, the celebrity was an invention of Victorian capitalism. I distinguish the celebrity from merely famous
people as a figure whose personality is created, bought, sold,
and advertised through capitalist relations of production. Pope,

47

Sterne, and Radcliffe were famous authors, but Byron was the first to belong to a fully commercial society.[2] He was a literary celebrity not simply because his poems were widely read but because they were marketed as more than poems. They supposedly offered not merely instruction and delight, but a "real" man's subjectivity. Throughout the century, Byron was the model for a new authorial role as a "personality."

For Byron the celebrity to circulate, his subjectivity became an invisible commodity lying behind more tangible ones, such as books, reviews, illustrations, sheet music, and dinner sets. In a famous passage, Marx discusses commodity fetishization as a process that mystifies social relations as relations between things; in the capitalist economy,

the existence of the things *qua* commodities, and the value-relation between the products of labour which stamps them as commodities, have absolutely no connexion with their physical properties and with the material relations arising therefrom. There it is a definite social relation between men, that assumes, in their eyes, the fantastic form of a relation between things.[3]

Relations between things (money and commodities) effectively mask the people and institutions making them possible. Byron the celebrity was a peculiar commodity because the "thing" that gave value to his products was his subjectivity. Poems, biographies, recollections, editions, refutations, plays, sheet music, paintings, dinner services, and illustrations about Byron were the actual items, but their attraction depended on their ability to reflect a prior reality: Byron's soul.

Byron was attractive as a celebrity because his presence compensated for the alienation that Marx describes as typical of capital. His legend transformed commodities that existed in "the fantastic form of a relation between things" back into "social relations between men" (and more especially women) because buying an item by or about Byron supposedly established a personal relation between author and reader. The allure of the Byron market was that items like books or engravings acquired the distinctively fascinating mark of his personality. Marketing Byron as a celebrity masked the fetishization of commodities by personalizing them.

If commodity fetishization turned relations between people into relations between things, Byron the celebrity seemed to rehumanize economic exchange. Byron the celebrity replaced person-to-person contact between producer and consumer with a person-to-"personality" contact between consumer and fetishized subjectivity. As scores of contemporary accounts reveal, the relations of nineteenth-century readers to Byron were intensely personal, sometimes more so than any relations existing in mere ordinary life. Nothing about the reception of Byron is more striking than how he was present with no mediation to generations of British consumers. For them, he was no commodity: he was the thing itself.

Men and women whose labor went into the actual products of Byronism retreated into invisibility behind the glamor that the products received from Byron the celebrity. References to Byronism as an economic phenomenon depending upon labor are rare except from those who stood to gain by it, such as John Murray. Far more typical of the mystifications produced by Byron the celebrity are comments like Thomas Carlyle's: "A gifted Byron rises in his wrath; and feeling too surely that he for his part is not 'happy,' declares the same in very violent language . . . Byron speaks the *truth* in this matter. Byron's large audience indicates how true it is felt to be."[4] For Carlyle, Byron's popularity depends on his ability to speak truth. It has nothing to do with buyers, printers, reviewers, and others. Indeed, from Carlyle's description, it is not even apparent that Byron was a writer. This passage reveals how effectively Byron was marketed because Carlyle writes as if it were possible to ignore this marketing altogether. For him, Byron's voice is simply present for all to hear. The rest of this chapter will explore how Byron became so available.

In thinking about Byron's celebrity, it is useful to avoid traditional notions of "the middle class" or "the bourgeoisie," which historians have increasingly rendered problematic.[5] Byron's audience was less a monolithic middle class than a loose accumulation of lower gentry, wealthy farmers, tradesmen, ambitious artisans, professionals, and members of a variety of other groups. Byronism is interesting because it was a force to unify these people by giving them a common representation of subjectivity. Rather than seeing Byronism as a tool of a particular class, it is more useful to see it as offering norms to members of groups who were aspiring to a common identity as respectable consumers.

These norms have less to do with class than with the desire to achieve a social standing. According to Jean Baudrillard, social standing is a universal code produced by consumer society: "Within 'consumer society,' the notion of status, as the criterion which defines social being, tends increasingly to simplify and to coincide with the notion of 'social standing.' "[6] For Baudrillard, possessions confer a particular status upon the owner. The incentive to buy is often not need, but the desire to be recognized as having achieved such status. Advertising invites consumers from differing backgrounds to attain an identical social standing through their purchases. The implicit lure held out is that status conferred by commodities erases any other social categorization.

When Baudrillard maintains that social standing replaces older systems of social organization, including class, he underestimates the historical strength of consumerism. Given the evidence of historians about the rise of a consumer culture in eighteenth-century England, it would be possible to argue that "social standing" does not follow class as a system of social organization, but precedes and helps to create it, especially for what has traditionally been designated as the "middle class."[7] The attractions of Byronism can be best understood in terms of incentives toward improved social standing that it offered to consumers. Byronism held out hope of giving the consumer the privileged sense of being above the merely commonplace. Having an opinion about Byron marked one as belonging to the privileged social group consisting of the respectable members of society, a category that could unite men and women separated by older categories like rank.

The equation between Byron and his heroes did not depend solely on the rhetorical effects analyzed in the first chapter. It also involved not merely Byron's words but also their relation to his perceived social position. Byron's readers did not divorce his words from the circumstances of the man who was supposed to have produced them. Most obviously, he was an aristocrat, and his readers were always aware of him as *Lord* Byron. While Christensen in *Lord Byron's Strength* has characterized the "Lord" in "Lord Byron" as Byron's principle of resistance to pressures of commercialization surrounding his career, I want to emphasize instead what Byron's rank meant to his audience, since his commercialization profited from it. When Walter Scott described "the novelty and pride which the public felt, upon being called as it were into familiarity with a mind so powerful, and invited to witness and partake of its deep emotion," he captured not only the public's interest in Byron's poetic intelligence, but also Byron's allure as a man of power, an aristocrat.[8] He attracted notice simply because print focused public attention on aristocrats' private lives: newspapers and journals routinely reported their births, marriages, and deaths. Notices of his parliamentary speeches appeared in the newspapers even before he became famous as the author of *Childe Harold*.

Byron's rank guaranteed for consumers that his subjectivity was special. Although novels represented fictional aristocrats or gentry to entertain readers of lower rank, Byron was a genuine baron with an ancient name. His social position was far above that of the average British writer. When aristocrats published imaginative literature, they typically produced respectable but mediocre verse, as Byron had in *Hours of Idleness*. For an aristocrat to demonstrate real literary genius, as reviews announced that Byron had done in the 1812 *Childe Harold*, was a striking novelty. Byron's combination of rank and poetic power allowed him to be presented as an almost magically privileged being. Reading his work offered the opportunity to identify with one of society's most elite members. Perhaps even more importantly, reading him let consumers demonstrate that they knew how to achieve such an identification. Byron's poems brought a new twist to the market in vicarious experience because his subjectivity created a new arena in which class emulation might occur.[9]

Byron's rank did more than make him a "natural" object of attention: it also increased the credibility of the equation between him and his heroes. Whatever Byron's rank may have meant to him, for those reading him it meant for the most part that they belonged to a social group different from his, a group that read about certain experiences rather than having them for themselves. His poetry's veiled hints at unspeakable crimes were more plausible because they came from an aristocrat. His travels to the Near East, which provided the stimulus for the 1812 *Childe Harold* and the Turkish Tales, reminded Byron's audience of the power of his money and connections. He had access to a world closed off to most of his readers.[10] His poetry appeared as a special realm of experience available to most only through his represen-

tations. Byron the aristocrat lived so that lower orders could
imagine. His rank was thus both a sign of his inherited blood
and a product of the literary market. His poems were successful
because they supposedly reflected an aristocrat's mind, but that
mind was available only through modes of production that the
aristocracy did not control.

Byron the aristocrat had a wider range of internal, as well as
external, experience than his readers. Tourism in the eighteenth
century had already marketed the aristocracy as having more
interior space than the rest of society. Carole Fabricant has
described the explosion in domestic tourism at the end of the
eighteenth century during which British travelers flocked to view
the grounds and interiors of aristocratic mansions. She argues
that this tourism encouraged the viewers to identify vicariously
with the possessors of landed wealth.[11] Her discussion could
apply, with a few changes of wording, to Byron's cult. Buying
a poem that was supposed to reveal an aristocrat's mind transferred to a psychological arena the attractiveness of paying to
see the inside of an aristocrat's mansion. In both cases, the reader
was privileged to view and identify with a secret aristocratic space
not ordinarily open to public view. Learning about Byron's inner
self could be sold as a voyeuristic delight even more powerful
than viewing estates.

The commodification of Byron developed not only from practices like domestic tourism but also from the circumstances of
literary production. Scott's comment that the public felt privileged
to be invited to read about Byron's mind raises the question of
how the book trade encouraged readers to experience certain
emotions. The selling of Byron established an unprecedented
closeness between the author's image and his or her audience at
a time when writers in general were becoming increasingly distant
from their readers. In the eighteenth century, institutions and
practices like patronage, the salon, and publication by subscrip-
tion had been predicated upon intimacy between author and
reader: Richardson and his coterie or Johnson and his club are
familiar examples of authors with a particular audience. But as
the century progressed, technological developments, a growing
leisure class consisting largely of women, and the success of the
novel allowed for a mass market for literature to develop, at
least in nascent form.[12] By the century's beginning, even poetry

could be an item for large-scale consumption. Scott's *Marmion* in 1808 sold 2,000 copies in the first month; Byron's *Corsair* set a record by selling 10,000 copies on the day it was published in 1814.[13]

With this growing market went an increasing anonymity in authors' relations to their readers. Marketing Byron's subjectivity placed the older closeness between author and audience on a new footing. The periodical reviews, themselves a product of the vastly expanded book trade, were a prominent vehicle through which Byron's readers could learn that they were supposed to feel closer to him than to any previous author:

[Byron] has awakened, by literary exertion, a more intense interest in his person than ever before resulted from literature. He is thought of a hundred times, in the breasts of young and old, men and women, for once that any other author is,—popular as are many of his living rivals.[14]

Previously, readers could know authors personally, but Byron's audience read in the reviews that they knew him more than personally: they knew his soul, or so they were encouraged to think. Paradoxically, it was precisely because these readers were not acquainted with Byron as a man in "real" life that the reviews could tell them that they knew him through his poems. Those who met Byron after having known him only through his poetry were usually surprised to find him quite different from what they had expected. Byron's career generated a model of success whereby the book trade responded to the mass market's anonymity by offering readers a simulacrum of intimacy. Byron's mind compensated for publishing's increased bureaucratization; poetry grew more nakedly personal as relations of production became less so.

Periodicals commodified responses to Byron. They gave the British reader a model for thinking about his specialness, and few Victorian evaluations of him departed substantially from those first developed in the reviews. While they were not solely responsible for his success, they developed the language in which he was discussed and understood. Although they are often remembered only for their obtuse reactions to much of the greatest Romantic poetry, it is impossible to overestimate the significance of periodicals in shaping public opinion not only about Byron

but about the role of the educated reader. For many, the periodicals decided what did and did not count as culture. Maria
Edgeworth attested to their influence when she noted of Ireland
in 1820, "The Edinburgh and Quarterly Review are now to be
found in the houses of most of our principal farmers: and all
therein contained, and the positive, comparative, and superlative
merits and demerits of Scott, Campbell, and Lord Byron, are
now as common table and tea-table talk here, as in any part of
the United Empire."[15] As beacons of culture to those unable to
reach artistic inner circles, they broke down the sense that culture
was only for an elite in major cities. When Irish farmers read
the periodicals, they could believe that they had as much access
as anyone to a total vision of culture.

Periodicals defined readers like Edgeworth's Irish farmers not
as members of an economic class but as participants in an
intellectual community defined by certain common interests.[16]
They performed in intellectual discourse what Byron's poetry
performed in subjectivity: they developed a universalizing language through which to interpret the truths of human experience.
Simultaneously, however, the sheer proliferation of periodicals
registered the existence of different audiences with different ranks
and interests. In the face of these differences, a few periodicals
established preeminence with a wide circulation, while many
faded after a few issues. For later readers, the preeminence of a
small group of periodicals continued because the work of leading
reviewers, such as John Wilson or Francis Jeffrey, was collected
and reprinted. Their comments were also appended to some
editions of Byron's poetry, so that they were available even to
those who did not read the original review. As a result, only a
few of the many reviews at the beginning of the century had a
substantial effect on Byron's reception during the rest of the
century. The generalizations that I will make about Byron's
critical reception reflect not the opinions of all reviewers, but of
reviewers who achieved the greatest prominence.

Regardless of a critic's opinions, a typical review was interest-
ing because it included extensive quotations and detailed plot
summaries; such excerpts widened Byron's potential audience.
When excerpting, critics avoided the controversial parts of
Byron's texts in favor of selected "beauties." For example, Francis
Jeffrey's review of *The Corsair* introduced excerpts with such

phrases as "one of the powerful passages of this searcher of dark bosoms," "the following beautiful strain of pure and enchanting tenderness," "the following beautiful and truly feminine exclamation," "the following beautiful and characteristic passage."[17] He disintegrated the poem into prose plot summary and beautiful poetic passages, separable from the plot, to be admired on their own. Purchasers of *The Corsair* might own the poem, but those who knew it from the periodicals were guided to the most beautiful passages. The 11-year-old Elizabeth Barrett's comments are revealing:

I have been reading Lord Byron's Corsair &c how foolish I have been not to read them before they did not entertain me much as I have perused the extracts and the reviews on them—Malgré this however I think many of the passages exquisitely beautiful the parting of Conrad and Medora & the intercesory between the hero and Gulnare are in my humble opinion two of the MOST beautiful.[18]

She has so internalized the mode of the reviews that *The Corsair* itself is disappointing. Instead, she appreciates the same beautiful passages that critics like Jeffrey singled out to be excerpted. The content of the poem faded before the privileging of particular segments as "beauties."

Excerpting did not merely reflect the need to acquaint the public with plots. It continued the process that I described in the previous chapter whereby Byron's poems became repositories of cultural commonplaces, especially the commonplace known as the mind of Lord Byron. The reviews extracted these commonplaces from the poems and reproduced them as "beautiful" moments, to be admired by those aspiring to taste and discrimination. Indeed, Byron may have written the purple passages in *Childe Harold* and the Turkish Tales with the knowledge that they would be excerpted. Eventually, publishers gathered such excerpts into books, which were known as collected "beauties" from Byron.[19] A further twist in beautification occurred once Byron had become so closely associated with respectable culture that his characters could stand for his poetry. In the 1830s, the Finden brothers' *Byron Beauties* appeared as one of a series of collections that projected standards for female beauty through pictures of literary heroines.[20] Byron's work did not merely define the language and nature of subjectivity; it even provided a basis through which to disseminate norms of physical appearance.[21]

The reviews' incessant discussions of Byron legitimized him and his poetry as a leading cultural event. They guaranteed that individual readers such as Edgeworth's farmers would find in Byron's poetry a subject for intellectual, aesthetic, and moral debate. Ian Jack has summarized well the developing attitudes toward Byron.[22] Although his poetry was always controversial, a set of typical reactions can be traced: initial enthusiasm for *Childe Harold* and the Turkish Tales, puzzlement at *Manfred*, disappointment with most of the verse dramas, and scandalized anger at *Cain* and *Don Juan*.

Although each periodical had its own audience, biases, and idiosyncrasies, the amount of common ground among the major reviewers is surprising. When discussing Byron, reviewers, both positive and negative, Whig and Tory, sharply distinguished the task of the artist from that of the critic. In them, the ease with which eighteenth-century writers like Johnson or Goldsmith had moved between critical and creative activity gave way to a more marked boundary between the poet as genius and the critic as interpreter. This division had a direct effect on the tone in which they approached their subject. While Byron's interest derived from the fascination of his particular subjectivity, the reviewers' authority came, in contrast, from their more universal point of view. They played as great a role as Byron did in fashioning the romantic poet as a privileged being set apart from ordinary humanity. Byron could "look with a steady eye upon those terrible wonders of our common nature, of which other minds have only had some faint and occasional perceptions"; he held up to view "those high and dread passions of men, which our ordinary life scarcely shows."[23] These critics, in contrast, did not evidence such passions in their work but evaluated the efforts of those who did.

Although M. H. Abrams did not consider Byron's reception when he traced the movement from mimetic to expressive theories, it would be possible to narrate this development as a response to Byron's career.[24] Abrams's influence has partly blinded later readers from seeing how the theory of the romantic artist first gained widespread currency through Byron's reviewers. As early as the first cantos of *Childe Harold*, Francis Jeffrey noted that "the sentiments and reflections which he delivers in his own name, have all received a shade of the same gloomy and misanthropic colouring which invests those of his imaginary hero."[25] By the time of canto III of *Childe Harold* Jeffrey announced that "it is really impracticable to distinguish" Byron from Harold. A reviewer in the *British Critic* grumbled, "The hero of the poem is, as usual, himself: for he has now so unequivocally identified himself with his fictitious hero, that even in his most querulous moods, he cannot complain of our impertinence in tracing the resemblance."[26] Few readers of the reviews could have avoided learning that Byron was supposed to be his heroes.

Critics sometimes intensified the sense of familiarity with Byron by giving him psychological counseling. For example, William Roberts wished that he "would wake for ever from the feverish dreams of a morbid temperament, and consign his faculties to subjects more agreeable to the lofty vocation of his genius," while Walter Scott hoped for a time when Byron would "bring his powerful understanding to combat with his irritated feelings."[27] Byron's poetry alone was the grounds for their judgments, as if after reading him, they knew enough to evaluate his psyche. They provided readers with a model for reacting to poetry not in terms of the author's technical skill but in terms of a personal response elicited by the author's supposed character.

Even critics who disliked Byron reinforced the practice of reading Byron the man through the poetry. No critic was more hostile than William Hazlitt, who attacked Byron because his "love of singularity" resulted from his "conscious sense that this is among the ways and means of procuring admiration."[28] Hazlitt did not attack Byron because his poetry was unskillful or followed a flawed aesthetic program. Instead, he attacked Byron's character, which he had gauged by reading the poetry. In it, he recognized insincerity that he assumed arose from the "conscious sense" with which Byron manipulated his readers. While Hazlitt may not have believed that Byron's heroes were direct reflections of his mind, he believed that Byron's writing was. His accusations and others like them further promoted the assumption that Byron could be read through his poems. Accusations of hypocrisy had force only if Byron was assumed to be trying to convince his audience of his sincerity. Although I argued in my previous chapter that the equation between Byron and his heroes arose in response to the veiled origins of the heroes' torment, this equation could not have become so widespread from Byron's poetry alone. The periodical reviews gave to British readers a model for understanding why Byron was unlike previous poets. They encouraged them to construct a relation with Byron more intimate than any that had previously existed between a poet and his audience.

While the reviewers were only a few men, Byron's readers numbered in the tens of thousands. It cannot be assumed that every British reader read Byron exactly as the reviewers did, despite their undoubted influence. Tracing the "common reader's" reaction to Byron is more difficult than might be supposed, partly because the common reader, like the middle class, had no clear definition in the early nineteenth century. Nevertheless, many early observers took one aspect of Byron's audience for granted: his most passionate admirers were supposed to be women. Almost all later critics writing about Byron's reception have believed this assumption, and the evidence of surviving letters, diaries, biographies, and autobiographies suggests that many women did indeed feel passionately about Byron. Nevertheless, like most clichés, the association between Byron and female readers did not simply reflect a prior reality. It was also useful for those who believed it because it performed certain kinds of cultural work.

Byron enjoyed boasting ambivalently about his popularity with female readers. According to Trelawney, he told Shelley, "John Murray, my patron and paymaster, says my plays won't act . . . He urges me to resume my old 'Corsair style, to please the ladies.' "[29] In one of his squibs to Murray, he described the works that Murray valued most: "Along thy sprucest bookshelves shine / The works thou deemest most divine— / The 'Art of Cookery' and Mine / My Murray" ("[To Mr. Murray (1818)]," 13–16). By noting that Murray's most profitable publications were his poems and a cookbook, Byron implied that the works attracted a similar audience. Women wishing to buy the "Art of Cookery" were the ones buying, or asking their husbands to buy, Byron's poetry.[30] He later told Medwin, "I am sure I was more pleased with the fame my 'Corsair' had, than with that of any other of my books. Why? for the very reason because it did shine, and in *boudoirs*. Who does not write to please the women?"[31] Murray and Byron were not alone in assuming that Byron's most enthusiastic readers were women. William Gifford growled in a review, "Certain we are, that the most dangerous writer of the present day finds his most numerous and most enthusiastic admirers among the fair sex."[32] The *Christian Observer* complained, "How long, indeed, an abused British public, and our fair countrywomen in particular, will suffer themselves to be held in the silken chains of a poetic enchantment . . . is more than we can tell."[33] Mary Russell Mitford believed that Medwin's *Conversations* would "have one good effect," because it would "disenchant the whole sex."[34]

Although later in this chapter I will examine reactions from women who actually read Byron, I first want to treat the clichés about his female readers as symptomatic of changes in the book trade at the beginning of the century. Behind Byron's comments about the literature of the boudoirs was an explosion of reading designed for women, especially novels.[35] In 1809, Hannah Rathbone wrote to a friend, "I think if I had nothing else to do I could sit and read from ten o'clock in the morning till ten at night."[36] According to Thomas Peacock, "the stream of new books . . . float[ing] over the parlour window, the boudoir sofa, and the drawing-room table . . . furnish[es] a ready answer to the question of Mr. Donothing as to what Mrs. Dolittle and her daughters are reading."[37] Fashionable novels centered on fictional representations of private life, so that the new female reading public was closely associated with the desire for learning intimate details about the lives of other people.[38] David Hume had maintained that women did not read history unless "it be *secret* history, and contain some memorable transaction proper to excite their curiosity."[39] Rousseau argued that "the world was the book of women" because women had a special ability to interpret the minds of men as if they were books.[40] The discussions of such eighteenth-century writers had gendered the desire to penetrate into the minds of others through reading as distinctively feminine.

Byron's verse romances assimilated the feminized genre of the novel and carried it in new directions by introducing the personality of the author.[41] Byron's representation of subjectivity meshed perfectly with a stereotypically feminine fascination with "*secret* history." In Caroline Lamb's *Glenarvon*, the heroine reads the Byronic hero just as women described by Hume and Rousseau were supposed to read novels: "She seemed to dive into the feelings of a heart utterly different from what she had ever yet observed: a sort of instinct gave her power at once to penetrate into its most secret recesses."[42] Reviewers claiming that Byron's readers were chiefly female connected the stereotypically feminine interest in the inner self with Byron's poetry, which they praised for the intensity with which it explored his subjectivity. Insofar as they constructed the chief attraction of Byron's poetry as the man behind the poetry, they placed any reader in a feminized position, as Sonia Hofkosh has argued.[43] The widespread association in writing by men between Byron's poetry and a female audience arose less from the magnetism of Byron's personality than from the gendered codes through which male and female writers responded to the gendering of the reader's role.

Yet the question remains of how women actually reacted to Byron's work. My evidence comes largely from writings by women who either were authors or were members of the upper classes because, with few exceptions, only they had their personal writings collected and published, usually after their deaths. What is striking in their reactions is the intensity with which they describe either liking or detesting Byron. Susan Ferrier in 1816 was typical when she wrote to a friend, "Did you ever read anything so exquisite as the new canto of 'Childe Harold'? It is enough to make a woman fly into the arms of a tiger; nothing but a kick could have hardened her [Lady Byron's] heart against such genius."[44] Ferrier values Byron not because he conforms to established rules but because the personality projected by his poetry is so attractive that she cannot understand how Lady Byron could have left him. Women who may not ordinarily have read poetry because they were unfamiliar with the laws of poetical criticism could find in Byron a writer who encouraged a more personal response. If judging Byron did not depend on knowing an established body of poetic rules, then they might find his work more accessible because it could be judged with reference to their own feelings. As I have suggested, these "feelings" were themselves a product of imaginative writing. Literature taught its readers to experience the emotions with which they would judge later literature.

Reactions like Ferrier's are part of the larger trend whereby personal judgment became an increasingly important standard of evaluation during the end of the eighteenth century and beginning of the nineteenth.[45] When Johnson and Boswell quarreled about literature, they appealed to standards of nature and decorum.[46] Similarly, in 1800 when Thomas Green read John Moore's *Zeluco*, whose hero is often cited as a predecessor of Byron's, he admired not the hero but the author's moral purpose and technical skill: "This character is well contrived to purge the selfish and malignant passions, by exhibiting the hideous effect of their unrestricted indulgence; and the crush of the sparrow at the outset, and of the child at the close is felicitiously conceived for this purpose."[47] But by 1822, Harriet, Countess Granville, wrote after listening to her husband read *Cain*, "Tell dear George that I think 'Cain' most wicked, but not without feeling or passion. Parts of it are magnificent, and the effect of Granville reading it out loud to me was that I roared till I could neither hear nor see."[48] For Countess Granville, *Cain*'s power has little to do with Byron's ability to mirror nature or to conform to neoclassic decorum. Even though she finds it "most wicked," presumably because of its blasphemy, what stands out in her description is her emotional reaction. Her reactions were not unique. For Lady Morgan, the 1812 *Childe Harold* had "more *force, fire,* and *thought* than anything [she had] read for an age."[49] Samuel Rogers claimed that he knew "two old maids in Buckinghamshire who used to cry over the passage about Harold's 'laughing dames' that 'long had fed his youthful appetite.' "[50] Elizabeth Barrett felt that the final canto of *Childe Harold's Pilgrimage* contained "all the energy, all the sublimity of modern verse," and Jane Welsh believed that the sun and the moon had gone out of the sky when she heard that Byron was dead (*CL*, IV: 69–70).[51] In all cases, what mattered was the personal intensity of their reactions rather than their appeals to standards of judgment or general nature.

Although Byron's poems were first available only to the wealthy, they gradually filtered to the rest of the population through a variety of means: Murray and his successors made them available in cheaper editions, circulating libraries purchased them, and illegal piracies appeared. By the 1830s the reactions that women of lower social ranks had to Byron echoed the reactions that more economically privileged women had had earlier. He was quite popular even with those who might have been expected to disapprove of him because of their religious beliefs:

The Castle Book Club in Colchester carried his works, and even the Thaxted Book Society read his *Life* in the 1830s. His publications were received with emotional enthusiasm not only by those with radical sentiments, such as the daughter of a Birmingham manufacturer . . . but by others for whom his appeal is somewhat more unexpected . . . Jane Ransome Biddell . . . was such an admirer of Byron that she and her farmer husband named one of their sons "Manfred" . . . An Essex Quaker tanner's wife compared her adored husband to Byron in looks and temperament, despite their sober domesticated lifestyle with nine children, while Mary Wright Sewell, daughter of a strict Quaker farmer, read Scott, Southey and Byron with delight.[52]

By the 1830s, Byron's poetry was not merely for the London elite. Knowing him was a touchstone of respectability for women in varying religious, geographic, educational, social, and economic positions.

The most telling evidence that I have found regarding the reaction of working-class women to Byron appears in a letter of 1841 by John Clare, in which he asks for the return of his Byron editions: "One of your labourers Pratts Wife borrowed—'Childe Harold'—& Mrs Fishs Daughter has two or three or perhaps more all Lord Byrons Poems & Mrs King late of the Owl Public house Leppits Hill & now of Endfield Highway has two or three all Lord Byrons & one is The 'Hours of Idleness.' "[53] The responses of Pratt's wife, Mrs. Fish's daughter, and Mrs. King have not survived, and it is difficult to speculate about what they might have been. Perhaps borrowing Byron indicated their desire to get what seemed to them to be "high culture." By 1841, Britain's literary elite had moved far beyond Byron, in part because women like Mrs. Fisher's daughter and Mrs. King had gained access to him. Once Byron became available at such a broad social level, he lost his attractiveness for those who wanted to believe that they were on the cutting edge of artistic trends.

While the appeal of Byron to women may have varied across class lines, one of its strongest components was undoubtedly erotic, as the comments of Susan Ferrier and Countess Granville suggest. Quotations from Byron added a touch of romance to many encounters during the century. The fashionable Jane Digby acquired the nickname "Aurora" (after Aurora Raby) from one of her admirers soon after her debut; she herself preferred "Ianthe" from *Childe Harold's Pilgrimage*.[54] The Quaker manufacturer

Barclay Fox in 1842 wrote in his journal: "Chenda [the daughter of Sir Thomas Fowell Buxton] was talking to me of some sea view from the Alban Hill & Lord Byron's lines on it, & as the fresh breeze blew back her curls & gave a deeper rose to her cheek, I thought she never looked so beautiful."[55] While neither Barclay nor Chenda was imitating Byron, Chenda's quotation from Byron heightened the scene's romantic atmosphere. After reading William Fletcher's account of Byron's death, the Quaker schoolgirl Mary Jane Taylor wrote in 1850,

I can well understand how he who gazed on the pale, silent, but beautiful face of the illustrious dead must treasure up the remembrance of that moment ... Oh, how can Lady Byron endure to think that she did not soothe her husband in his dying hour, and that she did not guard him with that affection which she ought to have felt![56]

Like Ferrier, Taylor reproaches Lady Byron for being a bad wife, and implicitly suggests that she would have handled him better. She, unlike Lady Byron, would have felt the appropriate degree of affection. For Jane Digby, Chenda Buxton, and Mary Jane Taylor, Byron became part of daily life because reacting to him influenced their sexual roles.

While conduct-book writers such as Sarah Ellis were codifying respectable female sexuality more rigorously than ever before, Byron's subjectivity as expressed in his poems and then in the biographies about him provided an alternative model for sexual expression. His work offered itself as an escape into a realm of transgressive sexuality, love with a glamorous aristocrat who seemed to cry out for female companionship. As such, it was a prototype of the twentieth-century mass-produced fantasies for women that Janice Radway has analyzed. Her words about contemporary romances might be applied directly to the case of Byron's female readers: "Romance reading supplements the avenues traditionally open to women for emotional gratification by supplying them vicariously with the attention and nurturance they do not get enough of in the round of day-to-day existence."[57] Whether or not one wants to invoke Althusser's category of "interpellation," the Byron market molded female attitudes toward sexuality by providing women with a fantasy image of desire. Byron's heroes suggested the possibility of a secret inner life of passion, which could never be expressed, but which pro-

vided a vivid alternative to what then became the dullness of
the external world.

Yet statements such as Radway's reify female sexuality by
assuming that women have an innate need for "emotional gratification." To conceive of Byron as supplying nineteenth-century
women with a fantasy realm of sexual fulfillment that they were
denied in actuality overlooks the extent to which Victorian sexual
mores were not simply inflicted by men upon a passive female
population. The women who reacted passionately to Byron were
the same ones eagerly embracing the doctrines of such writers
as Hannah More and Sarah Ellis. In both cases, reading provided
a path toward respectability. The writing of More and Ellis
shaped an understanding of "real life," the particular ideals that
women were supposed to actualize in the domestic realm. Reading
Byron, in contrast, belonged to the appreciation of "high culture"
as a special realm set off from the everyday. The fact that such
prominent writers as Gifford and Ellis herself disapproved of
Byron's popularity among women only heightened the attraction
of Byron as a commodity.

Perceived transgressiveness was part of Byron's commodification because it increased his desirability. Byron's negative pub-
licity sharpened the distinction between the supposed dullness of
everyday life and the excitements of the cultural marketplace.
Although consuming works by and about Byron may have
appeared to some critics as an example of female waywardness,
it only followed the process by which entrepreneurs marketed
the desire for distinction. Rather than treating the reading of
Byron as a means through which women rebelled against oppress-
ive sexual norms, reading Byron was a way to maintain those
norms by containing sexual passion entirely within fiction, and
therefore within the realm of cultural production.

Part of the transgressive charge that Byron carried was that
his sexual attractiveness may not have have been based entirely
on difference. As I suggested in my first chapter, Byron's poems
before *Don Juan* developed the possibility that the "naked heart"
belonged to women as much as to men, although they eventually
reasserted masculine priority over the possession of subjectivity.
Female readers may have found it possible to bypass the narrative
and concentrate instead on Byron's heroes, who were supposed
to represent a universal inner self. The identification of women

with the Byronic hero is most obvious in the second half of the nineteenth century, beginning with the vogue for female characters who revivified Byronic romanticism by appropriating its clichés, such as Mary Elizabeth Braddon's Aurora Floyd or Thomas Hardy's Eustacia Vye. It is difficult to find evidence of women's identification with Byron's characters in surviving personal writings earlier in the century. Such female writers as Felicia Hemans, Caroline Lamb, Mary Shelley, and Charlotte Brontë, however, reproduced the Byronic hero in their writing not merely as an object of desire but as a figure for themselves as authors. Rather than trying to reinvent the Byronic hero as a heroine, they used the hero himself as the center of their plots. The tendency for so many female writers to recreate the Byronic hero suggests that the figure was available not solely for desire and admiration, but also for imitation and identification. As I will argue in chapter 4, *Wuthering Heights* both continues and critiques this tendency in the writing of early Victorian women.

For women who were not writers, Byron's marketing may have encouraged identification across genders. As I discuss in chapter 6, biographical writing on Byron drew attention to his femininity. In addition, while reviewers commented on Byron's skill in portraying the "naked heart," a category that transcended gender difference, portraits of Byron, which were tremendously popular, captured this transcendence by making Byron androgynous. Especially as he was represented in the popular Harlowe engraving, Byron's appearance conformed to stereotypes of feminine beauty as much as to masculine ones.[58] A fictional representation of Byron's androgyny occurs in Charles Dickens's *The Old Curiosity Shop* (1840). When Miss Monflathers, head of a local school for young ladies, takes her pupils to visit Mrs. Jarley's wax museum, Mrs. Jarley modifies her sordid exhibits by such deft changes as "turning a murderess of great renown into Mrs. Hannah More." One transformation involves Byron:

Mary Queen of Scots in a dark wig, white shirt-collar, and male attire, was such a complete image of Lord Byron that the young ladies quite screamed when they saw it. Miss Monflathers, however, rebuked this enthusiasm, and took occasion to reprove Mrs. Jarley for not keeping her collection more select: observing that His Lordship had held certain opinions quite incompatible with wax-work honours.[59]

Dickens does not explicitly connect the scream of Miss Monflathers's young ladies to the androgyny of Mrs. Jarley's image.
Nevertheless, the gender-crossing is suggestive. Dickens hints that
the young ladies may scream louder at a Byron derived from
Mary Queen of Scots than they would have at one derived from
a different male figure. While Miss Monflathers presumably refers
to Byron's religious opinions when she reproves Mrs. Jarley,
Dickens juxtaposes her disapproval with the transvestite image
of Byron so as to suggest that his androgyny is part of his allure.
Underneath the Byron who provokes screams is a figure closer
to the young ladies than they know.

The whether Byron's attractiveness stemmed from identification,
difference, or a piquant combination of the two, representations
such as Dickens's suggest how Byron was marketed in terms of
his supposed attractiveness to a female audience. The erotic
charge that reading Byron produced became a signal for how
women might participate in respectable culture. His celebrity
helped to draw nineteenth-century women into consumerism by
offering to satisfy desires that they may not have known they
were supposed to have. The attractiveness of Byron was not that
he tapped into innate desires that existed outside of social norms.
Rather, his work's reception defined female eroticism as a
phenomenon stimulated by books. Since books were available as
commodities, the system of production used female desire to drive
consumption.

The stereotype of Byron's popularity with women suggests as
much about male readers as it does about female ones. For some
reviewers, Byron's female readers were a source of considerable
amusement. John Gibson Lockhart, for example, satirized them
by imagining a conversation about Byron among characters from
Jane Austen's novels:

Now, tell me, Mrs. Goddard, now tell me, Miss Price, now tell me, dear
Harriet Smith, and dear, dear Mrs. Elton, do tell me, is not this just the
very look, that one would have fancied for Childe Harold? Oh! what eyes
and eyebrows!—Oh! what a chin!—well, after all, who knows what may
have happened. One can never know the truth of such stories.[60]

Lockhart's ladies are well acquainted with Byron's unhappy
marriage, but they have little to say about his poetry. His comic
picture of women falling over themselves to admire Byron as a

man, not as a poet, became a cliché of Victorian literature: Arthur Clough's *Amours de Voyage* (1855), George Eliot's *Felix Holt the Radical* (1866), Anthony Trollope's *The Last Chronicle of Barset* (1867), and Samuel Butler's *The Way of All Flesh* (1903) are only a few of the many works in which women are criticized or made to seem ridiculous for admiring Byron.

Although Lockhart satirizes Byron's female readers partly because they respond to Byron's looks and personality, not his poetry, women would have learned this response from such male reviewers as Lockhart in the first place. Moreover, this response to Byron would have been encouraged by the way that imaginative writing created and then sustained the supposedly feminine interest in what Hume called "*secret* history." Nevertheless, Lockhart reasserts male sophistication by treating female reactions to Byron as naive. His reactions and those of other reviewers who described Byron's female admirers could therefore appear more refined in contrast. The passionate female admirer of Byron became a convenient image onto which male reviewers could project a degraded aesthetic response. They could demonstrate their superior morality and judgment by scorning the female reader's supposed naïveté.

The image of Byron's female admirers also had its uses for men who were not reviewers. If Byron was what respectable women wanted, the cultured heterosexual Englishman could take his cue accordingly. Although women were supposed to keep their admiration for Byron purely ideal, men might dare them to cross the line by imitating Byron. Byron's success at least influenced the way they had to perform erotic roles. As John Edmund Reade, whom I quoted in the Introduction, claimed in 1829, "open shirt-collars, and melancholy features; and a certain *dash* of remorse, were . . . indispensable to young men." They were indispensable because Byron had turned them into the signs associated with the fascinating male hero.

Yet Reade's image of remorseful young men, like Lockhart's image of passionate female admirers, did not simply reflect a prior reality. It helped to shape the perception, widespread in late 1820s and early 1830s, that young men, who were not necessarily of the best classes, were trying to be sophisticated by imitating Byron. While it is impossible to know how many men actually imitated Byron, contemporary letters and diaries make clear that many read and admired his poetry. To name only a few men of widely varying backgrounds, Keppel Craven, John Hamilton Reynolds, John William Ward, James Losh, Joseph Jekyll, Henry Fuseli, John Bright, and Douglas Jerrold all attested to their admiration in their letters and diaries. As one reader noted,

> My bosom has often thrilled beneath the witchery of his potent spells—my soul kindled beneath the breathings of his impassioned strains; my hand shook with eagerness; my heart leaped with emotion as I have hurried with ardent eye through those scenes of tenderness, and terror, and grandeur, which his mighty mind had so naturally and strikingly pourtrayed [*sic*]: until borne away by the tide of sympathetic excitement, I have bowed my soul in idolatrous reverence to the creations of his genius, and hailed their exaltation with the most rapturous delight: but the enthusiasm of my devotion gone by,—I have turned my eyes inwardly; my heart yet heaved with the impulse communicated, but its waves were turgid with the storm, and polluted with the spoils of virtue, and the wrecks of civilization floating in rude confusion upon its troubled elements. My understanding was beclouded, my affections defiled, my passions excited.[61]

This passage is one of the most interesting descriptions of reading Byron that I have found, both because it is so vividly melo-dramatic and because it is anonymous, although the National Union Catalogue attributes it to Thomas Bailey. If the attribution is correct, Bailey ventriloquizes an extreme version of what would have been gendered as a "feminine" reaction to Byron. More typical may be Francis Boott's comment written in 1832: "Byron in many respects is above all Poets & I say so, without doing any violation to my unmixed Idolatry of Genius in any age— Read the immortal passage in Childe Harold on the Grecian Daughter, and match it for me in any page of inspiration."[62] Boott is characteristic of most records from men in that he is interested in Byron not as a personality, but as a poet. He mentions passages that he admires, rather than praising Byron's appearance or his life. For the most part, when men mention Byron, the emotional temperature is lower than it is for women. They quote from his poetry in passing or mention a casual biographical anecdote. One example among many: in 1854 on his way to the Crimea, Richard Temple Godman noted that he "fully experienced the truth of Byron's lines: 'There is no sea the Traveller e'er pukes in / Whose waves are more deceptive than the Euxine.' I am not sure my quotation is quite correct."[63] For Godman, Byron's couplet provided a witty comment to incorporate into his description of military experience. The quotation is more a sign of wide reading than a comment on his admiration for Byron's personality.

Another indication of how men read Byron is the frequency with which women mention that Byron has been read to them:

Your papa and I sat over the fire in the dining room and fancied ourselves young people, with a baby, or two perhaps, in the cradle upstairs, and read together more beautiful poetry [canto III of *Childe Harold*] than any other pen I am acquainted with has yet produced.[64]

Lord Rosslyn read to us "Lara," Lord Byron's new tale.[65]

He [Mr. Ellice] *would* read passages of Don Juan to us and to tell you the truth the best of us and Lady Elizabeth herself could not help laughing.[66]

Be sure to bring the next cantos of Don Juan, as I am immoral enough to enjoy the wit of it, when *you* read it—there is a saving clause and sanction to my conscience.[67]

The fact that men read Byron to women is not in itself distinctive; reading aloud was widespread. Yet it further reinforces the need to avoid taking the cliché of Byron's female audience as truth. Such quotations complicate any model of reception that would assume that because certain genres were feminized, its readers were always women.

Likewise, they remind us that the physical act of reading Byron's images of the solitary, alienated hero often occurred not in solitude, but in heterosocial settings. A new poem from Byron might become the occasion not for a lonely reader's meditation on his or her alienation but for husbands and wives to enjoy domestic felicity or for friends to entertain one another. Although the examples that I have cited come from the middle and upper classes, reading aloud was even more prevalent among the working classes because many would have depended for knowledge of Byron on having his work read to them. Byron's representations of the intensely private "naked heart" must have been accessible to many in the form of a group activity, reading aloud, that reinforced existing social bonds.

Given the evidence of the male admiration for Byron and of

the extent to which reading aloud ensured that men as well as women read his work, the scarcity of representations or discussions of male admirers of Byron's poetry in fiction or journalism is striking. Almost the only fictional representation of a male admirer of Byron written during his life was by a woman: Jane Austen in *Persuasion* (1818).[68] I can only speculate about the reasons for this cultural reticence, but I suspect that it may have stemmed from a desire to keep the homoerotic element of Byron's appeal hidden from view. For reviewers, the image of Byron's female admirers effectively mediated the fact that many men might have felt just as strongly about him. Although their language could become quite enraptured, as John Wilson's work in *Blackwood's Magazine* and the *Edinburgh Review* demonstrates, the image of the female admirer protected reviewers from the awkwardness of seeming to admire Byron too much. For other men, reading aloud may have allowed them to indulge in a version of what Diana Fuss calls the "homospectatorial look," the possibility of appropriating heterosexual representations for same-sex desire.[69] Perhaps under the guise of "slumming" by reading literature for women, they could experiment with erotic possibilities that for the most part were strictly off limits. In chapter 6, I discuss three writers who were attracted to the homoerotic aspects of Byron's personality, as they understood it. Yet I suspect that male attraction to Byron was more widespread than surviving evidence indicates, just as I suspect that the success of male celebrities in the twentieth century depends as much on the market's ability to make them appeal to men as on the ability to make them appeal to women. When a figure is successfully commodified as an icon of desirability, as Byron was, the representation cannot be assumed to reach one gender alone.

I suggest in my previous chapter that Byron's poetry let his readers sustain the paradox of imagining themselves to be special while they were behaving like everyone else. Yet, from the first, not all readers swallowed this paradox. Instead, many registered their superior discrimination by pointedly not succumbing to the supposed fascination of Byron's celebrity. Instead, such readers established an association between Byron and the commonplace. While Byron's admirers saw in him a startling, unprecedented originality, others found him clichéd. This second reaction is sometimes blamed on Byron's many imitators, but it was an inevitable product of Byron's success. Once enough people admired him for his originality, the possibility of seeing this admiration itself as merely commonplace soon followed. Particularly for presumptive members of Britain's social or artistic elite, Byron was significant less because of his supposed sexual attractiveness than because his career allowed them to distinguish themselves from the reactions of "ordinary" readers. Such elite readers were attracted to Byron as a means through which to demonstrate the fineness of their cultural judgments by criticizing him in a uniquely "personal" way. Byron's subjectivity was less attractive than the opportunity it offered to demonstrate the refinement of their own.

Evidence of such critical distance appears in letters or diaries expressing some reservation about the prevailing view of Byron:

I suppose anyone would be torn to pieces who ventured to criticize this little poem ['Ode to Napoleon Bonaparte'] and not give unqualified admiration . . . but I want to know what Lord B. means by upbraiding him [Napoleon] with "hoarding his own blood." Does he blame him for not committing suicide?[70]

I have read . . . Lord Byron's "Corsair," which *I* think does not deserve the commendations it has received.[71]

Since I last wrote I have read the Siege of Corinth, which in some parts is so horrid as to be absolutely ludicrous.[72]

I have heard many express the wish that he had lived to retrieve his character and change his opinions for his own sake, and for the example to society; but I had no hope that this would be the case.[73]

Are there any more new books to talk of, or can we close this talk of literature without remembering one who has pleased us more than we ought to be pleased, and shocked us less than we ought to have been shocked? . . . I think I felt his powers as deeply as those who talked loudest in their praise; but then my conscience never slept; indeed, my moral taste would have revolted at the guilty gloom that hung over his heroes, though I had no higher principle to direct me.[74]

Critical distance from Byronomania is familiar to students of Romanticism since the canonical male Romantics either loathed Byron, like Wordsworth, or had strongly ambivalent reactions to him, like Shelley; many of the writers quoted above were also professional authors. Yet their reactions indicate more than professional jealousy. For them, it was important not merely to have read Byron, but to have thought about him enough to be able to commit to paper an opinion that seemed to be truly personal.

Given that the stereotypical admirer of Byron was female, the reactions of educated women are particularly interesting with regard to distancing. Since women were supposed to be in love with Byron's subjectivity rather than with his poetry, a comment like Lady Stanley's about the meaning of an image in the "Ode to Napoleon Bonaparte" resists the assumption that all women were so infatuated with Byron as not even to notice his poetry. In making critical remarks about Byron, a woman separated herself from the stereotypical image of the female reader and assumed a role closer to that of the male reviewer as a judge of artistic production.

The question of the female reaction to Byron becomes trickiest with *Don Juan*. Male reviewers often maintained that the poem was unsuited for women; one thought that they should read it only to cure them of their admiration for Byron: "The many fine eyes that have wept dangerous tears over his descriptions of the Gulnares and Medoras cannot be the worse for seeing the true side of *his* picture."[75] Personal writings from the period suggest that some women followed the advice of the reviews and avoided *Don Juan* altogether, such as Anne Grant, who wrote "I am in great measure a stranger to the works that disgraced his last years."[76] Nevertheless, the personal writings of many educated women, such as Amelia Opie, Lady Morgan, Countess Granville, Hester Piozzi, Maria Edgeworth, and Lady Spencer-Stanhope, suggest that the reviewers do not provide an accurate image. These women read *Don Juan* precisely because it was supposed to be unsuitable. Opie, for example, thought that its scandalousness was overrated: "And when I heard some highly virtuous and modest women tell me they had read it, and were 'not ashamed,' and when I recollected that I had read Prior, Pope, Dryden and Grimm, I thought I would e'en add to my list of offences that of reading 'Don Juan.' I must say that the account of its wickedness is most exaggerated."[77] Her remarks suggest that *Don Juan* was a test case through which women could divorce themselves from cultural stereotypes about proper reading. Enjoying *Don Juan*, or at least finding merits in it, allowed them to prove their sophistication by avoiding the crudity of vulgar outrage. As late as 1869, a Victorian debutante quoted *Don Juan* in her diary to illustrate that she was "not romantic" and did not "believe in people dying of misplaced affection and broken hearts."[78] Quoting *Don Juan* was a rhetorical strategy whereby she could demonstrate a practicality greater than that of women who had succumbed to an idealized picture of marriage.

Because stereotypical views of Byron's male admirers were less pervasive than ones of his female admirers, distancing carried less weight for men than for women. Nevertheless many men, often professional writers, recorded their dim opinions of Byron. The young Anthony Trollope, when annotating his mother's sentimental poem on the death of Byron's daughter Allegra, wrote, "This is vast nonsense—his Lordship was certainly a clever man—but as selfish a bonvivant as ever lived and no more worthy of the ethereal character so often given him than I am."[79] While the fact that nineteenth-century male writers often denigrated Byron is no surprise, I emphasize the extent to which they wrote as if dissenting from a majority opinion. Whether or not an ethereal character really was given to Byron is less important than Trollope's claim that he was distinguishing himself by refusing to believe it. For readers like Opie or Trollope, Byron's attraction depended on the opportunity that he offered to analyze how their reactions to his work distinguished them from ordinary readers.

In escaping the contradiction whereby Byron's supposedly unique subjectivity was commodified so as to be appropriated by anybody, this group of elite readers ran into a different one. The desire to have an opinion that was not commonplace itself became commonplace. After a time, this group's position could be filled simply by not writing about Byron and by finding new literary heroes to replace him, such as the young Tennyson. For the artistic elite, Byron's fame quickly exhausted itself. After a point, discussing him seemed hopelessly old-fashioned. Byronism survived as long as it did only because of the effects of the gradually increasing circle of those who had easy access to his poetry and to information about him. At first, the most elite readers adopted a dismissive attitude toward Byron, but as more people read Byron, more were in a position to dismiss him as commonplace. Yet such reactions were only possible once members of a given social group had achieved enough familiarity with poetry that the choice of a preferred poet could signify social aspiration, whereas at an earlier period reading anything would have been a sufficient marker of class emulation.

I single out the reactions of this elite to emphasize that their opinions do not represent all British readers. In writing the history of Byron's reception, twentieth-century critics have concentrated solely on the views of this group, since theirs are most easily accessible. As a result, the history of Byron's reputation has been told as a simple story of decline: after Byron's enormous popularity, his reputation went into eclipse around 1830 and did not recover until the end of the century.[80] Such narratives are inadequate because no single narrative encompasses all reactions of all audiences reached by Byron's life and work. Throughout the century, every announcement of Byron's fading reputation can be matched with one attesting to its continued power. For example, although George Borrow in *The Romany Rye* (1855) described his shock at meeting a group of literary men and women who barely knew Byron, the Earl of Belfast in 1852 wrote that "*Byron* is still so much amongst us, because his direct influence is far from extinguished."[81] My goal is to avoid the tendency to speak of the rise or fall in Byron's popularity among a particular social group as if it could stand for Byron's fate in Britain as a whole. The surviving evidence does not permit a conclusive history of Byron's reputation in terms of a sequence of ups and downs. Rather, Byron the celebrity was a figure present with varying degrees of urgency and mediation for different social groups throughout the nineteenth century. These degrees were defined by such factors as the frequency with which his texts and texts about him were reprinted, the audiences at whom they were aimed, the numbers of writers explicitly or implicitly imitating Byron, and the availability of non-literary products, such as engravings of Byron. Having a position toward Byron, whether it was hatred, dismissal, or adoration, became a marker whereby men and women in unprecedented numbers demonstrated their ability to participate in and evaluate culture. For the first time, the members of a nation shared not merely a common government or monarch, but what was perceived as a cultural phenomenon available to all: Byron the celebrity.

Having discussed social aspects of Byron's reception, I want in the following sections to examine specifics of his commodification. Since legends cannot transmit themselves, a Byron industry ensured that his fascinating subjectivity stayed before the public for as long as it was profitable. For a time, any book or item related to Byron found an audience. My purpose is not to catalogue this material because such work has already been done by several scholars, most notably by Chew in his invaluable *Byron in England*. Although Chew sidesteps elements of Byron's reception, such as the many non-literary forms of Byronism, his book remains the most comprehensive survey of nineteenth-century reactions to Byron. Yet, fascinating as these are, with few exceptions they had little individual effect on Victorian writers. For most, the products of Byronism were important less because of their particular content than because they gave a vivid picture of one aspect of literary fame in a capitalist market. In particular, all events in the life of the commodified Byron were open to intense public scrutiny, especially the ones that seemed to be the most private.

Since reviewers had emphasized that the interest in Byron's poetry depended upon his personality, Byron biographies eventually competed for attention with Byron's poetry. An added interest to these biographies was that Murray and Hobhouse had arranged to burn Byron's memoirs.[82] Byron's poetic emphasis on the invisibility of the inner self seems almost to have scripted the burning. Although his poetry emphasized that the depths of the inner self could never be revealed, the burning suggested to the newspapers that Byron's life as revealed by himself was too scandalous to be published. Whether Murray intended it or not, burning the memoirs was an economic masterstroke. No gesture could have been better calculated to heighten the aura of scandal that surrounded Byron. For those who had known Byron, and for some who had not, the burning provided a welcome occasion to make quick money by converting their knowledge of him into print. Since the public had no way to know how true any particular account was, a range of accounts from strictly factual to pure fiction appeared in British booksellers' stock.

The memoir was a far less clearly defined genre than the review, and a far greater disparity of assumptions surfaced in the Byron memoirs than in reviews. They were not simply texts written by different people who knew Byron: they were self-conscious participants in a battle over how to present the life of the major figure in early nineteenth-century culture. Many loudly positioned themselves against the perceived inadequacies of earlier accounts so that, even more clearly than in the reviews, Byron's life was a starting-point for conflicts over interpretation. The overall effect of the many conflicts in the biographies was to make Byron the celebrity resist any single, definitive interpretation. He appeared as the center of a heated debate that invited readers to choose among several possible interpretations of his life and character. The interpretation that particular readers chose is less notable than the existence of many possibilities from which they could choose. The variety of conflicting accounts invited the consumer to buy as many as possible, since no single account could ever be fully adequate. Particularly until the appearance of Thomas Moore's biography, the lack of a definitive account may have been an incentive to buy several points of view. The sheer proliferation of material reinforced the status of Byron the celebrity as the cultural event of the day to which anyone with pretensions had to respond.

One of the first memoirs, John Watkins's *Memoirs of the Life and Writings of the Right Honourable Lord Byron* (1822), represented a transition from the review to the biography. It collected the most publicly available facts about Byron and added a series of observations about the poems, most of which would have been familiar to those who read the major periodicals. Watkins did little more than embody the opinions of the reviewers in a different form. Other biographies, such as R. C. Dallas's *Recollections of the Life of Lord Byron* (1824) and the notice found in the *Annual Biography for 1825*, followed Watkins's pattern, although Dallas had the added authority of having known Byron personally and published letters by him.

In contrast to such biographies, blatantly fictitious ones also appeared that took a far more idolizing tone. While truth and fiction about Byron were not stable categories either then or now, several accounts appeared in the 1820s and 1830s describing events quite unlike what any who knew Byron would have accepted as true. The spurious *Narrative of Lord Byron's Voyage to Corsica and Sardinia* (1824), which insisted that "no memoir of Lord Byron conveys so accurate a portrait of his Lordship's real character," described Byron's action-packed voyages to islands in the Mediterranean that Byron never visited. It represented him as a noble, generous aristocrat who kept the sabbath and performed acts of charity, such as giving money to a young couple to let them marry.[83] John Mitford's *The Private Life of Lord Byron: Comprising His Voluptuous Amours . . . with Various Ladies of Rank and Fame* (1836), a piece of soft pornography, offered a different fictional portrait by representing Byron as a stereotypical aristocratic seducer. For the most part, respectable reviews ignored such works. Except for Leigh Hunt, who debunked several, I have not found a single diarist or correspondent who mentions having seen these. Presumably their buyers were readers whose social standing was lower than those of those readers whose personal records were eventually published. Their appearance is interesting because it suggests how eager publishers were to sell Byron, even at the cost of manufacturing him *in toto*.

Reviewers attended more seriously to biographies and reminiscences by those who had known Byron personally, most of which gave dramatically competing accounts. Thomas Medwin's *Conversations of Lord Byron* (1824) started a controversy by tarnishing the noble image of the Byron who died fighting for Greek freedom. It presented instead a Byron who made gossipy and unflattering remarks about his friends. Controversy over Medwin spurred rejoinders. Some, like William Parry, who had been Byron's firemaster in Greece, defended him as a complex man who had been dedicated sincerely to liberty. Leigh Hunt, in contrast, offered an unflattering portrait in *Lord Byron and Some of His Contemporaries* (1828). His bitterness at Byron's treatment of him in Italy led him to criticize Byron as vacillating and inconsistent:

He did not care for argument, and, what is worse, was too easily convinced at the moment, or appeared to be so, to give any zest to disputation . . . He was moved to and fro, not because there was any ultimate purpose which he would give up, but solely because it was most troublesome to him to sit still and resist. "Mobility," he has said, in one of his notes to "Don Juan," was his weakness; and he calls it "a very painful attribute."[84]

Instead of seeing Byron as a Byronic hero, a mysterious mixture of good and bad moral qualities, he rewrote this moral mixture as the inherent instability of Byron's psyche. In Hunt's view,

Byron had no essential self, only a succession of poses. Work like Hunt's reinforced the view taken by those like Lockhart and Carlyle that *Don Juan* was Byron's most sincere effort precisely because it exposed his lack of a central self.

Hunt's negative interpretation so outraged Murray that he commissioned Byron's friend Thomas Moore to write a response. Moore's official biography, *Letters and Journals of Lord Byron with Notices of his Life*, was published in two volumes by Murray in 1830, and quickly established itself as the standard biography. No book had a greater impact on Victorian perceptions of Byron, and I shall refer to it frequently. It was an instant best-seller and was reprinted more frequently than any other version of Byron's life. Part of its authority came from the hundreds of letters by Byron that Moore published for the first time, which early readers agreed were brilliant. For some, they were an alternative canon even more interesting than Byron's poetry. Emily Eden wrote enthusiastically after reading the second volume,

Have you seen the 2nd Volume of *Lord Byron?* It is a wicked book, and having made that avowal it is unlucky that I feel myself obliged to own that it is much the most interesting book I ever read in my life—much. I never was so amused, and the more wickeder he is in his actions, the more cleverer he is in his writings. I am afraid I like him very much—that is I cannot bear him really, only I am glad he lived, else we should not have had his *Life* to read, to say nothing of his poetry.[85]

For Eden, Byron's letters and journals revealed even more directly than his poetry the wickedness and cleverness of his mind. Her reaction suggests how the commodification of Byron's subjectivity continued even without the presence of the poetry. His life as revealed in his letters could attain even more authority than the poems through which he initially became famous.

Byron's letters and journals remain the most interesting part of Moore's biography. Yet Moore also advanced an interpretation of Byron's character that circulated widely. While Moore's book was written to refute Hunt's, it in some ways supported his view. Both emphasized the instability of Byron's character, but while Hunt made him seem frivolous, Moore made him seem like a lively child:

The pride of personating every description of character, evil as well as good, influenced but too much, as we have seen, his ambition, and not a little, his conduct; and as, in poetry, his own experience of the ill effects of passion was made to minister materials to the workings of his imagination, so, in return, his imagination supplied that dark colouring under which he so often disguised his true aspect from the world. (*M*, II: 788–89)

Moore gave a coherent picture of Byron the man at the expense of Byron the myth, which he unmasked as a product of Byron's "pride of personating." Although many contemporary accounts emphasized that Byron was not like his heroes, Moore's book took this debunking a step further. In his account, Byron *was* like his gloomy heroes, but only when he chose to adopt one of the poses that made up his personality. At other times, he was a childish joker, a cynical lover, or an ardent patriot. The combination of Byron's actual letters with Moore's consistent characterization of him in terms of his mobility allowed the biography to develop an interpretation of Byron that explained the paradoxes in his career without damning him, exalting him, or vacillating.

To a degree, Moore did his job too well: while his Byron is not altogether respectable, his relentlessly conventional interpretation neutralized all the more shocking sides of Byron's character as the effects of "genius."[86] His biography extended the division made by the reviewers between the special world of artistic genius and the ordinary world of community, convention, and judgment. Moore's Byron embodies all the irregularities permitted to genius as they are judged through Moore's bland pieties. The sheer size of Moore's volume, along with his detailed research into Byron's life and reproduction of Byron's letters, gave his account of genius an authority that no other account could match, but he used this authority to enclose Byron within the bounds of respectability.

Moore's book never went unchallenged because no single interpretation of Byron could be trusted to be fully adequate. John Galt, for example, published his popular biography of Byron after reading the first volume of Moore because he thought that it was too lenient. Later, Edward John Trelawney's *Recollections of the Last Days of Shelley and Byron* (1858) and Harriet Beecher Stowe's *Lady Byron Vindicated* (1870), which revealed Byron's incest with his half-sister Augusta Leigh, offered other challenges to the dominance of Moore's interpretation. As I will discuss in chapter 6, Stowe's controversial account spurred late Victorian interest in Byron, and even more biographies appeared in the 1880s and 1890s. Like his heroes, Byron seemed to be an infinitely complex character who justified frequently renewed efforts at interpretation. Byron remained at the center of attention as long as he was controversial enough to attract an audience willing to pay more to learn about him and his life.

Competing accounts of Byron guaranteed that Victorian authors had no monolithic reading of him. Even Moore's biography, the closest to a standard account, prevented any totalizing interpretation through its emphasis on the variableness of Byron's personality. Each Victorian writer could, to some extent, create his or her own Byron. For those who wished to see Byron as a hero, there were numerous accounts of his noble deeds and actions, but those who wished to condemn him had abundant evidence as well. In any case, the biographies were an essential element in shaping a myth of romantic genius that tied an author's work intimately to a life open to interpretation.

While the Byron biographies were the most prominent example of how knowledge of his life was kept before the public, entrepreneurs found numerous other ways to market him. The proliferation of Byron items cued consumers that reading Byron or texts about him might not be enough to appreciate him fully. In a system of consumption that depended on stimulating the desire for ever-new sensations, these products provided alternative possibilities for gaining social standing by such acts as displaying a portrait of Byron or buying a handsome edition of his works. Byron seemed to be so extraordinary a phenomenon that he could not be experienced solely through the printed page, but needed to be made available in extra-literary forms.

Scholars have already treated some of these. Margaret Howell has demonstrated how Byron's plays enjoyed considerable success on the nineteenth-century stage, where, after cutting, they provided an occasion for spectacular scenic displays.[87] Stage managers also adapted his poems, as when Drury Lane staged an elaborate *Bride of Abydos* in 1818.[88] In another outstanding analysis, James Buzard has shown the usefulness of Byron to the burgeoning tourist industry. He suggests that Byron's celebrity contributed to a contest for distinction in the tourist industry much like the one that I analyzed in terms of readers' responses to Byron's texts.[89] Yet plays and tour books were not the only aspects of the larger commodification of Byron. He also quickly entered the academy when his poetry was excerpted for classroom instruction. The young Matthew Arnold won much admiration at Winchester for his declamation of the curse from *Marino Faliero*.[90] Elocution anthologies soon included snippets from Byron; in one, Byron's poetry illustrates such emotions as ambition, confidence, desire and dread of death, despair, disdainful scorn, grief, guilty conscience, reproof of servility, scorn, and sullenness.[91]

Given that Byron's most adoring readers were supposedly women, producers aimed many items of Byroniana at the domestic, female audience. Although Byron inspired Continental composers to some of the century's greatest music, in Britain, Byron provided lyrics for parlor songs. "Fare Thee Well!" was particularly popular, along with various settings of imagined replies by Lady Byron.[92] The *Hebrew Melodies* that Byron had written for Isaac Nathan's settings also sold well.[93] In addition to songs, consumers could buy numerous portraits of Byron, which also adorned the frontispieces of editions of Byron's poems or biographies. The absence of visible references to writing in these portraits focus the viewer's attention on Byron's personal appearance; he seems less important as a writer than as a figure to be admired.[94] By the 1850s, Byron's portrait had acquired such stature that one was included at the Great Exhibition; the young Louise de la Ramée, later famous as Ouida, noted that she had seen there "several splendid statues and an exquisite ceilling [*sic*] with Byron painted on it. Splendid!"[95]

Representations of subjects from Byron's poetry were almost as popular as portraits. Nineteenth-century catalogues list more than 200 paintings based on Byronic poems.[96] While only a few people would have seen these paintings, engravings of Byronic subjects had a much wider circulation. From early in Byron's career, Murray published engravings to accompany Byron's poems, so that the wealthy reader could bind together both the poems and the engravings. Later, Murray commissioned pictures of Byronic subjects from many of Britain's greatest artists, including J. M. W. Turner. The industrious Finden brothers compiled several books of such engravings, including *Finden's Illustrations of the Life and Works of Lord Byron, With Original and Selected*

Information on the Subject of the Engravings (1833–34).[97] These illustrations were so popular that Copeland and Garrett, the successors of Josiah Spode II, used them for a dinner service; a complete set could include 119 pieces.[98]

I sketch these items to indicate how the longevity of Byronism depended on the adaptability of Byron's appeal. Byron the celebrity could be used to sell not just poetry, but items as different as plates and sheet music. The continued appearance of Byronic items seemed to mandate that consumers continue to be interested in him. A complete dinner service seems rather far from the magic of Byron's subjectivity, but the possibility of incorporating Byron into everyday life presumably gave a touch of distinction even to the most commonplace activities.

The most interesting question about these commodities is the relation between them and the scandalousness of Byron's career. After the appearance of *Cain* and *Don Juan*, widely read religious journals, which had previously ignored Byron, opened fire. Some divines even issued pamphlets condemning Byron's immorality.[99] Byron's supposed lack of belief was a frequent source of concern. In 1847, John Cumming, a favorite divine of Tennyson's mother, used Byron to describe "*an infidel's brightest thoughts, in some lines written in his dying moments* by a man, gifted with great genius, capable of prodigious intellectual prowess, but of worthless principle, and yet more worthless practices—I mean the celebrated Lord Byron"; he then quoted from three different poems by Byron, none of which was written when Byron was dying.[100]

Such clerical denunciations guaranteed that Byron retained an aura of scandal, which was valuable to the market because it reinforced the slightly transgressive thrill that Byron was supposed to offer. Yet they also created the possibility that transgression could go too far and that Byron might be too dangerous. Sumner Jones, for example, who grew up in a Dissenting family, remembered, "Of Byron we had a mysterious notion, gathered from hearing our elders now and then speak of him shudderingly, as of some Satanic spirit who had been permitted visibly to stalk abroad."[101] Shudders like those of the elder Joneses provided a continued impetus for entrepreneurs to stress Byron's respectability rather than his scandalousness, since his scandalousness was valuable only insofar as it did not threaten his respectability too openly.

When looking at Victorian treatments of Byron, rather than finding exploitations of his sensationalism, it is far more common to find him censored or censured so as to become respectable reading. Although Marx commented that readers could be comforted that Byron died young "because if he had lived he would have become a reactionary bourgeois," a variety of Victorian institutions saw to it that he became one anyway.[102] Even the biographies that praised him rarely justified transgressions. Instead, the Byron market downplayed his sensational side. The paradox was that this effort to make Byron respectable kept alive his scandalousness, since his excesses had to be mentioned in order to be deplored. As a result, when Byron commodities appeared, consumers had a chance to have conventional norms reinforced by learning about Byron's departures from them. The reader was provided with the chance to judge a personality as complex and important as Byron's was supposed to be.

The sheer abundance of Byron products may have been the most effective means of making him respectable. Time and the ease with which Byron products entered British homes attenuated the rawness of the scandal surrounding his name. Yet Byron always retained the potential to be nudged back into scandalousness. In particular, Stowe's allegation of incest placed him once again at the center of attention because of the shocked response to it. Yet the Stowe affair was less an anomaly in the progress of Byron's reputation than the most vivid example of the extent to which his respectability depended on the whiff of scandal. His scandalousness survived precisely because of the constant efforts to tame it.

Byron editions demonstrate how Byron's respectability depended upon a continuous chastening of his scandalousness. Several critics have described Murray as a master at such chastening. The radical publisher William Hone succinctly characterized him as "Bookseller to the Admiralty, and a strenuous supporter of orthodoxy and the Bible Society."[103] When negative criticism made *Don Juan* too hot for Murray to handle, Byron published the remaining cantos with the radical publisher John Hunt.[104] Yet it is less well known that Hunt went bankrupt a few years after Byron's death, and Murray acquired rights to the few poems that he did not already possess, including the rest of *Don Juan*. For most of the century, his firm held a virtual monopoly on legitimate editions of Byron, and his publications indicate how Byron appeared to many nineteenth-century readers.[105]

The early Murray editions of Byron are strikingly plain, almost spartan. The fourth edition of *Childe Harold's Pilgrimage*, for example, is a 180-page quarto, with only two stanzas per page, leaving a generous amount of white space. The extensive notes in the back of the volume are printed in large type, as if they are meant to be read, not dismissed as footnotes. Such editions were quite expensive; William St. Clair estimates that a bound copy of the first two cantos of *Childe Harold* cost 50 percent of a gentleman's weekly income.[106] Peter Manning has given an excellent reading of Murray's octavo edition of *The Corsair* in terms of a production for an elite, moneyed audience, with its motto from Tasso, untranslated epigraphs from Dante, notes with quotations in French and Latin, and gentlemanly introductory epistle to Thomas Moore.[107] Most editions that Murray produced during Byron's life resembled this octavo, which was more affordable than the quarto *Childe Harold*, but still beyond the reach of most. As Manning notes, the poetry's appearance emphasizes that however radical its sentiments might be, its physical production kept it as property of the dominant classes.

After Byron's death, this severe plainness gave way to more obviously deluxe editions and less imposing cheaper ones. Murray's 1845 edition of *Childe Harold*, a handsome quarto printed on heavy paper that contained sixty engravings and a frontispiece of Phillips's painting of Byron in Albanian dress, was as much for showing as for reading. Although *Childe Harold* describes the political deterioration of the countries that Byron visits, illustrations in this edition depict picturesque landscapes and scenery with no trace of wretchedness. The physical appearance of the book muted the poem's radicalism. In the 1840s, Murray also produced cheap editions; by the 1840s, editions of Byron were inexpensive enough that they sold widely to members of the working classes.[108] By 1860, even *Childe Harold* was available in a one-shilling edition in the series "Murray's Railway Reading; Containing Works of Sound Information and Innocent Amusement Suited for all Classes of Readers." This edition offered train readers a Byron as politically neutral as the one offered to the socially ambitious buyer of the 1845 volume.

Murray's most significant effort to impose respectability on Byron was the seventeen-volume octavo collection edited by John Wright in 1832–33. The first six volumes included Moore's biography, so it was enshrined as the "official" word on Byron. The later volumes contained facsimile pages to demonstrate that Byron's manuscripts had been consulted, and Wright occasionally commented on differences between the manuscripts and the printed text. Just as important, the edition consecrated judgments of the reviews by using them as footnotes. Comments by Scott, Jeffrey, Wilson, and others guided readers to the poems' beauties, and further reinforced the equation of Byron with his heroes. His apparatus gave this edition the authority to define for the public what Byron truly wrote and implicitly to condemn any other edition as corrupt, such as the many editions put out by the Paris-based publisher Galignani. It packaged him as a respectable author by emphasizing niceties of textual and biographical observations and by downplaying his political and poetic radicalism.

Although Murray's Byron was the Byron most familiar to canonical Victorian authors, he was not the only Byron available in the nineteenth century. Byron was one of the few authors read by all ranks of society, and his popularity among the working classes reflects both a rise in working-class literacy and the spread of presses aimed at a working-class audience. As I have noted, cheap versions of Byron's texts became available for those striving to participate in respectable culture but not able to afford Murray's expensive publications. Yet working-class literacy introduced a second, more subversive possibility for reading Byron when some working-class readers, particularly the Chartists, appropriated him as an icon of rebellion.

St. Clair argues that Byron's audience fell into two groups: the elite readers of *Childe Harold* and the Turkish Tales and the far wider audience of *Don Juan*. *Don Juan*'s popularity is indisputable. It was available cheaply in a range of pirated editions, often produced by politically radical publishers; a preface in one such notes, "[W]e have had editions of all sorts of shapes and sizes; from the original superb quarto, to the shabby 'two-penny trash,' or weekly instalment of about twenty-four duodecimo, badly-printed pages."[109] Piracies were as much responsible for the poem's harsh reception among "respectable" critics as anything in the poem itself.[110] Nevertheless, it was quite popular: Mrs. Piozzi attested to the effectiveness of the piracies when she noted that the poem was "so seducing, so amusing, and so *cheap*, it will soon be in every hand that can hold one."[111] William Parry told Byron that he particularly liked the shipwreck, which horrified Byron's respectable readers, because "that is something we mechanics and the working classes understand."[112] As late as 1853, the publisher W. H. Smith received an angry letter letter from a man who had seen the poem on sale at one of Smith's bookstalls at Waterloo Station and who feared the effects of making so dangerous a poem available to the working classes.[113]

Yet St. Clair overstates his case when he suggests that the working classes were not interested in the earlier Byron. Keith Walker's discussion of the working-class reception of Byron indicates that numerous piracies of the earlier poems also appeared. William Hone, for example, brought out the twenty-third edition of the *Poems on Domestic Circumstances* in 1817; although Hone's edition numbers are not always reliable, his claim suggests the poems' popularity.[114] Manning's reading of Hone's adaptation of *The Corsair* further suggests the working-class interest in the sentimental Byron, and Dean and Munday published other prose versions of the Turkish Tales. Most tellingly, poems by many working-class poets, such as Thomas Cooper, William Hay Leith Tester, William McGonagall, Peter Gabbitass, and John Critchley Prince, manifest a debt not to *Don Juan* but to Byron's earlier poems. This debt suggests that poets on the margin of the literary system copied what seemed to them the most respectable side of Byron's work rather than the less elevated manner of *Don Juan*.

Of these poets, the most interesting is Thomas Cooper, the Chartist. Philip Collins has written a detailed study of him, in which he demonstrates how Cooper and other Chartists adopted Byron as a radical icon. An eye-witness account of a Chartist demonstration in Newcastle in 1838 noted that the crowd carried banners and that "a considerable number of these contained patriotic inscriptions from the works of Byron."[115] Both George Julius Harney and George Jacob Holyoake, leading agitators, often quoted lines from *Don Juan* as their motto: "I wish men to be free, / As much from mobs as kings—from you as me"

(IX.25).[116] The leading Chartist paper, the *Northern Star*, contained many excerpts from Byron's poetry and discussions about him; Ernest Jones in the *People's Paper* praised Byron's speech on the Nottingham frame-breakers.[117]

The association of Byron with political radicalism presented a different kind of transgressive charge for Victorian readers than that associated with his sexual or religious heterodoxy. Whereas a profitable aura of scandal contained Byron's sexual irregularities and his blasphemous opinions, his usefulness for the Chartists did not present Victorian entrepreneurs with a comparably profitable image. The Chartist Byron was part of a more genuinely oppositional discourse than the Byron of the divines because entrepreneurs like Murray could not appropriate his political radicalism. At the same time, the Chartists hardly had a "truer" version of Byron; indeed, the Byron discussed in their newspapers was even more idealized than Moore's. For the Chartists, Byron figured primarily as a champion of liberty at all costs. Nevertheless, the presence of this idealization guaranteed that Murray's version of Byron never attained complete dominance. His Byron had to compete not only with the religious attacks on him, but more notably with his radical Chartist appropriation. In chapter 5, I will return to the effects of this politicized counter-reception on the way that later writers, especially Tennyson, responded to Byron.

Victorian writers coming after Byron took essentially three stances: slavish imitation, rejection, or an ambivalent combination of the two. Many, like John Edmund Reade or William Whitehead, were willing to reproduce Byronic clichés to capitalize on his popularity. Their work made money for a time by appealing to the same qualities that the reviewers had enshrined as exciting in Byron's poetry. Many poets tried to pass their work off as Byron's; presumably they were less interested in artistic recognition than in the earning power of Byron's reputation.[118] Their trademark was the Byronic hero, who quickly became a stock character; indeed, it was a stock character even before Byron.[119] Yet even if the archetype of the Byronic hero did not originate with Byron, his career had left his stamp on it so indelibly that any mysterious, brooding hero was sure to be identified with him. Imitators were always inferior because none of them could claim the special attraction of Byron's subjectivity, the equation between hero and author. While Byron supposedly bared his soul in his heroes, those who copied the Byronic hero were merely baring a feeble version of someone else's soul. Imitating Byron was an impossible project because the quality that had brought Byron fame, "Byron's soul," was not available for imitation.

More ambitious writers like William Thackeray, Aubrey de Vere, or Henry Taylor scorned Byron outright because of his vulgar popularity and the poor quality of his imitators. Byron endured considerable abuse from his poetic contemporaries, and the pattern continued after his death. Taylor, for example, maintained that Byron had merely given "the charms of forcible expression" to commonplace thoughts because "the public required nothing more."[120] The writing of such men created the conditions for the inverse relation between artistic prestige and economic success that Bourdieu characterizes as the fundamental principle underlying artistic production in capitalism.[121] The perceived closeness between Byron and the public meant that for many Victorian writers, he became the type of an author who earned fame by abandoning artistic canons to please vulgar public taste. Instead of having been an artist, he was merely a striking personality. If the public's adoration was to be gained by baring one's soul in order to awaken interest, then it was better to preserve self-respect at the cost of large sales.

Against what were considered to be Byronism's commonplaces, Victorian authors could proclaim their own originality. Such proclamations more than anything else produced the perception that Byronism had indeed become commonplace. Rejecting Byron became an essential ritual of the career of the Victorian author. The often repeated declarations of the death of Byron's popularity were not simply the result of numerous individual dislikes: they reflected the systemic necessity for writers to create an audience for themselves by persuading their readers that Byron and all he represented needed to be abandoned. While these writers initially had to struggle against the dominant taste, they soon helped to define alternative cultural norms to replace those of Byronism.

The rejection of Byronism was most productive for Victorian authors when it took the form of narratives of transition. The

development away from a youthful, immature Byronic phrase to
a sober, adult "Victorian" phase became one of the nineteenth-
century's master narratives, the *Bildungsroman* of the Victorian
author. This narrative was implicit from the start in the tendency
of writers like Moore to cast Byron as a child and themselves
as adult observers of romantic genius. Soon the pattern became
an all-purpose frame though which authors could define their
place in the literary system. In this pattern, Byron, characters
based on him, or characters influenced by him were cast as
promising youths who for various reasons did not achieve their
full potential. Only through their literal or figurative death could
the narrative move forward to achieve a resolution that was
embodied in characters who stood for the author, maturity, and
some vision of a society that had developed beyond Byron's.
Nearly every author that I will examine wrote such a narrative
of transition, and the pattern is latent in the work of authors
whom I do not discuss.

The most interesting writers from the point of view of this
book are those whose narratives were not quite as comfortable
as they might have been. For various reasons, Thomas Carlyle,
Emily Brontë, Alfred Tennyson, and Oscar Wilde were renegades
against both the popular adoration of Byron and the outright
rejection of him on the part of their artistic contemporaries. The
works in which they engaged the Byronic legacy most closely,
Sartor Resartus, *Wuthering Heights*, *Maud*, and *The Picture of Dorian
Gray*, all met with shocked receptions upon their first appearance
partly because they did not fit into established modes of imitating
or rejecting Byron. In the rest of the book, I will explore how
these writers used Byronic clichés to develop works that broke
all the rules. While Byron may have been associated with repetition and reproducibility, work stemming from his took unexpected directions.

CHAPTER 3

Carlyle, Byronism, and the professional intellectual

If Thomas Carlyle, a peasant's son, had been born in 1745 rather than 1795, he would have had no literary career. His success as a major Victorian sage depended on new institutions that allowed writers who otherwise would have been cut off from literary expression to reach a wide audience. Byron the celebrity represented for Carlyle everything opposed to his new class of writer, the professional intellectual. In *Sartor Resartus*, Carlyle writes the professional intellectual into existence as Byron's replacement. Where Byron's success had supposedly depended on rank, the intellectual would depend on "innate" merit; where Byron had supposedly been a casual dabbler, the intellectual would be a serious philosopher. Whether or not Byron was what Carlyle thought he was is not part of my argument. Throughout Carlyle's work, "Byron" represents all that the professional intellectual must overcome.

Carlyle had to represent his role for a public whose taste seemed to have succumbed to the products of Byronism. He did so by developing what I termed in the previous chapter a "narrative of transition." Rather than rejecting Byronism wholly, his writing incorporated and surpassed it so that it could appear as a stage toward the greater goal of the professional intellectual. Carlyle distinguished himself from such writers as Sir Henry Taylor, who asserted his own elite status by spurning Byron because of his popularity. Carlyle had no distaste for large audiences *per se*, since his role as a professional intellectual meant addressing "universal" concerns. Entering the literary system was difficult enough for him that he never had the luxury of writing for a tiny circle of *cognoscenti*. Yet he also could not copy the writings that readers seemed to want, such as novels with Byronic characters or biographies of Byron, because these reinforced Byron's hold over the reading public. *Sartor* rewrote popular Byronic literature in order to redirect public taste toward the professional intellectual's voice.

Charles Richard Sanders and Michael Timko have written usefully about Carlyle's relation to Byron. Sanders counters *Sartor*'s impression of a flat rejection of Byron by describing Carlyle's qualified admiration for some aspects of Byron.[1] Timko supplements Sanders with his discussion of Byron as an apotropaic figure for dangers in authorship for Carlyle, who "sees Byron at various times as either a potential rival [to himself] or as a rival to his one great hero-artist, Goethe."[2] I will develop a different argument from either Sanders or Timko by giving less attention to Carlyle's explicit pronouncements about Byron than to *Sartor*'s more subtle engagement with contemporary forms of Byronism.

Carlyle's animus toward Byron should be understood not as an individual quirk but as the product of a discursive struggle over the definition of the author. Although much of Byron's and Carlyle's success depended on the same institution, the periodical review, the two authors had opposite relations to it. Byron was a poet, not a reviewer. The "Byron" of reviewers was a "genius," almost a supernatural phenomenon, to whom they responded not as fellow geniuses but as critics. Carlyle, in contrast, started as a reviewer. His Diogenes Teufelsdröckh is a reviewer's "revenge" upon Byron, a version of genius that develops from the standpoint of the reviewers; as David Riede notes, "Carlyle is a kind of literary sansculottist, evolving a romantic formulation of the *true* man of letters as revolutionary prophet arising from the lower orders to restore true order."[3] His revenge depended upon unmasking Byron's "genius" as aristocratic snobbery and replacing it with a supposedly more universal perspective.

A revised understanding of Carlyle's access to Byron changes how the relationship between the writers should be interpreted. Sanders and Timko do not distinguish between a nineteenth-century Byron and a twentieth-century one, as if Byron were a stable, ahistorical entity. But in the early 1830s, when Carlyle wrote *Sartor*, "Byron" existed as an area of conflict arising from the numerous manifestations of Byronism. *Sartor* condenses these into three strands: the broad stereotypes of Carlyle's periodical reviews, the Byronism of fashionable novels, and Byron's portrayal in contemporary biographies, especially Thomas Moore's.

Getting behind the image of a monolithic Byron to understand
the levels of mediation at which *Sartor* challenges Byronism should
transform our understanding not only of the Carlyle–Byron
relationship but of *Sartor* itself.

Growing up in Ecclefechan, Carlyle was as far from the literary
centers of the day as possible. Although he eventually became
acquainted with important literary men, he had no easy path to
success. As he wrote to his brother John in 1830, "To my mind
nothing justifies me for having adopted the trade of Literature,
except the remembrance that I had no other"; having chosen it,
he could only "look confidently forward to a life of poverty, toil,
and dispiritment" (*CL*, v: 129). When he wrote this letter, he
had become a prominent translator and interpreter of German
literature in periodicals, but even this position offered no stable
income or satisfaction. Not until *The French Revolution* (1837) did
he really succeed, and when he wrote *Sartor*, this success was
still in the future.

Reading gave Carlyle his chief contact with literary culture.
His early career demonstrates how the dissemination of print in
the early nineteenth century created new intellectual communi-
ties; as Carlyle wrote in 1818, "With none here even to *shew* me
the various ways of living in the world . . . [I am] reduced to
contemplate the busy scene of life, through the narrow aperture of
printed books" (*CL*, i: 143). Periodical reviews were a particularly
important "aperture." Carlyle's letters indicate that he read
periodicals as often as he could. In the 1820s when he became
a writer, he turned first to the periodicals for work. He learned
German literature to capitalize on the interest that periodicals
like *Blackwood's Magazine* had stimulated in the subject, and he
first gained serious public notice from his articles on German
literature in the *Edinburgh Review* and *Foreign Review*.

Carlyle's early work grew out of the social outlook that the
periodicals produced. As I discussed in chapter 2, they created
a new audience of educated, "classless" intellectuals, and fostered
the growth of journalists such as Carlyle. T. W. Heyck has
discussed the "status anxieties" that writing for money created
for these journalists. While literacy raised them above the level
of mere workers, the fact that they sold their labor tainted their
aspirations to be gentlemen.[4] Some accepted their status as hacks,

while others worked to make their profession respectable by becoming serious aestheticians.

Different periodicals reached different audiences. The least prestigious ones kept criticism to a minimum and provided long excerpts from the work reviewed. The more ambitious ones, such as the *Edinburgh Review* and *Quarterly Review*, strove to be popular and elitist at the same time.[5] At their most elite they fostered lengthy, complex reviews characterized by "philosophical criticism." Philosophical criticism in this context had the resonance that "theory" has in the contemporary academy: it was a label fastened to the work of those who regarded themselves as the field's most sophisticated thinkers. From almost the start of his career, Carlyle placed himself among the most philosophical of the philosophical critics.

Twentieth-century critics have often discussed Carlyle's philosophy of literature, which manifested the influence of Coleridge, German idealism, and the reception of both in British periodicals.[6] In essence, he treated literature as a repository of quasi-sacred truths. Writers such as Goethe and Schiller, early versions of the Carlylean hero, became ultimate mediators between man and God. This monumentalization placed the reviewer in an ambivalent relation to artistic genius. At one level, the reviewer was lesser since his or her work was parasitical on the artist's creativity. At the same time, artists depended on critics to understand and interpret their achievements. While reviewers could never equal the sublimity of literature, their ability to appreciate a vision greater than their own and to transmit their appreciation to others at least ennobled them. Carlyle never aspired to be one of his statuesque heroes. Instead, he occupied the seemingly secondary but actually more powerful position of the critic exhorting others to his brand of worship.

Given how important periodicals were to Carlyle, it is not surprising that they molded his reading of Byron. His first surviving mention of Byron concerns not Byron's poetry, but Jeffrey's review of *The Corsair* and *The Bride of Abydos* in the *Edinburgh Review* for April 1814 (*CL*, 1: 24). Until Byron's death in 1824, Carlyle read reviews of his work almost side by side with the poetry, and when he first published in the periodicals, his essays often appeared in the same issue with material relating to Byron. For example, the *London Magazine* for August 1824, in which the

third part of Carlyle's *Life of Schiller* first appeared, had an
article comparing Burns and Byron, which may have influenced
Carlyle's later pairing of the two.

The periodicals developed opinions about Byron to which Carlyle responded even more closely than to Byron's poetry. His
early discussions of Byron imitate commonplaces from the reviews
of Byron's work, and this ventriloquism suggests how he internalized the voice of the reviewers. They were his vehicle for learning
what an aesthetic judgment was. Yet his ventriloquism was never
absolute. Small differences separating Carlyle's discussions from
the general trends arose from the particular place that he occupied in the literary field. His lamentation on Byron's death is
revealing:

> Poor Byron! Alas poor Byron! The news of his death came down upon
> my heart like a mass of lead; and yet, the thought of it sends a painful
> twinge thro' all my being, as if I had lost a Brother! . . . And but a
> young man; still struggling amid the perplexities, and sorrows and
> aberrations, of a mind not arrived at maturity or settled in its proper
> place in life. Had he been spared to the age of three score and ten,
> what might he not have done, what might he not have been! (*CL*, III:
> 68)

He uses the same language as many newspaper tributes to Byron,
with one striking exception: he never mentions Byron's poetry.
Byron the man entirely supplants Byron the poet. When older
critics described Byron's personality, they never completely
excluded more traditional judgments about poetic technique, but
Carlyle places himself with a new generation of critics for whom
poetic technique matters not at all. To use M. H. Abrams's
terms, Carlyle completes the transition from mirror to lamp. His
concentration on Byron's personality marks his alienation from
older forms of criticism and places him with younger, philosophic
critics for whom formal concerns vanish before the all-important
exposition of artistic character.

Carlyle's elegy for Byron also has a defensive edge. Aside from
marking his allegiance to philosophic criticism, his lamentation
for Byron's lost maturity represents an embryonic version of the
narratives of transition that I described in the previous chapter.
According to Carlyle, if Byron had been allowed to reach
maturity, he would have accomplished great things. Since he did
not, those who followed him, such as Carlyle, must achieve the

greatness that he did not. In so doing, they would develop beyond Byron, whom they then could associate with youthful immaturity. Carlyle's silence about Byron's extensive poetic output functions as a defense against his own slender achievement. He was twenty-nine in 1824, and Byron had achieved far more at twenty-nine than he, as he was well aware. His letter suggests that although he has been less productive, he is more mature than Byron was at thirty-six and will eventually create more mature work.

This narrative of transition away from Byron is present implicitly in the review essays that first made Carlyle's name. Since British culture in the 1820s offered no obvious counters to Byron, Carlyle turned to German literature for an entire pantheon of alternatives. His advocacy of such writers as Goethe, Richter, and Schiller inevitably pitted them against Byron. Reducing Byron to stereotypes from the reviews allowed him to magnify the Germans in contrast. Typically, Carlyle suggested that the German authors were less Byron's opposite than Byrons who had grown beyond Byronic stereotypes: "Our Byron was in his youth but what Schiller and Goethe had been in theirs: yet the author of *Werter* wrote *Iphigenie* and *Torquato Tasso*; and he who began with the *Robbers* ended with *Wilhelm Tell*" (*CW*, xxvi: 69).

"Goethe" (1828) makes Byron the end-point of sentimentalism:

Byron was our English Sentimentalist and Power-man; the strongest of his kind in Europe; the wildest, the gloomiest, and it may be hoped the last. For what good is it to "whine, put finger i' the eye, and sob," in such a case? Still more, to snarl and snap in malignant wise, "like dog distract, or monkey sick"? Why should we quarrel with our existence, here as it lies before us, our field and inheritance, to make or to mar, for better or for worse? (*CW*, xxvi: 219)

In 1816, Walter Scott had written a similar indictment of Byron in a review: "To narrow our wishes and desires within the scope of our powers of attainment . . . seem[s] the most obvious and certain means of keeping or regaining mental tranquillity."[7] But whereas Scott in 1816 politely dissents from Byron's egotism, Carlyle in 1828 faces the greater burden of writing after Byron's death and defining alternatives to him. Scott writes as a Johnsonian moralist who acknowledges that ridding oneself of Byronic attitudes entails diminishment. Carlyle is far more ambitious because he addresses the full implications of Byron's career. He is also far more nervous than Scott, and the violence of his questions undercuts his stated desire for tranquillity. His tone recalls Nietzsche's famous characterization of Carlyle's "continual passionate dishonesty towards himself."[8] In "Goethe," this "dishonesty," Carlyle's characteristic disjunction of tone and content, signals the lack of a fully realized alternative to Byron's rebelliousness. This lack attests less to a failure of Carlyle's imagination than to Byronism's dominance in British culture. No institutional position existed from which a would-be professional intellectual such as Carlyle could seriously challenge what seemed to be Byron's omnipresence.

A few months after "Goethe," Carlyle returned to the motif of Byron's immaturity in his essay on Burns (1828):

> Surely, all these stormful agonies, this volcanic heroism, superhuman contempt and moody desperation, with so much scowling, and teeth-gnashing, and other sulphurous humour, is more like the brawling of a player in some paltry tragedy, which is to last three hours, than the bearing of a man in the business of life, which is to last threescore and ten years. Perhaps *Don Juan*, especially the latter parts of it, is the only thing approaching to a *sincere* work, he ever wrote; the only work where he showed himself, in any measure, as he was; and seemed so intent on his subject as, for moments, to forget himself. Yet Byron hated this vice; we believe, heartily detested it: nay, he had declared formal war against it in words. So difficult is it even for the strongest to make this primary attainment, which might seem the simplest of all: to *read its own consciousness without mistakes*, without error involuntary or wilful! (*CW*, xxvi: 269)

Parallels to everything Carlyle says can be found in earlier reviews of Byron's poetry, but, as in "Goethe," the essay arranges the commonplaces of Byron's reception into a narrative of a foreshortened development.[9] Byron failed to overcome the lure of affectation, even though he hated it and "had declared formal war against it in words." Carlyle refers to a particular moment in *Don Juan*: "And I will war, at least in words (and—should / My chance so happen—deeds) with all who war / With Thought;— and of Thought's foes by far most rude, / Tyrants and Sycophants have been and are" (ix.24). Characteristically, Carlyle reduces Byron's war against "Tyrants and Sycophants" to one against his own affectation. The problem that he finds in Byron is not, as in "Goethe," that he was too self-conscious, but that he was not self-conscious enough, or at least not in the right way: "So difficult is it even for the strongest . . . *to read its own consciousness without mistakes.*" He constructs Byron as a naive artist and himself as the more sophisticated philosophical reviewer who can evaluate Byron's flaws because of his greater self-consciousness.

While such essays demonstrate how Carlyle assimilated the opinions of other reviews, other essays suggest how his social and economic background as the son of a peasant gave his treatment of Byron a more distinctive edge. For him as for Hazlitt, Byron's success as an aristocrat represented the upper-class domination of literature that threatened the careers of writers who were not gentlemen, like themselves. In "Burns," for example, he notes how Byron's rank hindered him from achieving his full potential: "Both poet and man of the world he must not be; vulgar Ambition will not live kindly with poetic Adoration" (*CW*, xxvi: 315). A running polemic in all his essays of the 1820s is that "with the culture of a genuine poet, thinker or other artist, the influence of rank has no exclusive or even special concern" (*CW*, xxvi: 42). He praises the philologist Heyne because his career disproves the notion that "to make a scholar and man of taste, there must be cooperation of the upper classes, society of gentlemen-commoners, and an income of four hundred a year" (*CW*, xxvi: 353). While many professional reviewers shared this enmity toward moneyed authority, he was more outspoken than others in proportion to the greater lowliness of his social origins.

The bitter "Jean Paul Friedrich Richter Again" (1829) develops his most detailed class critique of Byron. In his review, Carlyle mentions having seen letters by Byron and goes on to discuss them from memory. The letters appeared in Lockhart's review of Hunt's Byron biography, but when Carlyle describes them, he misremembers their content so as to heighten Byron's class snobbery. According to Carlyle, Byron believed that "the great ruin of all British Poets" sprang from "their exclusion from High Life in London" and that all rules for poetry " 'were not worth a d—n' " (*CW*, xxvii: 134). While the opinions actually expressed in Byron's letters are quite different from what Carlyle describes, the important point is that Carlyle's misrememberings turn Byron into a representative of aristocratic dilettantism. Because of writers such as Byron, according to Carlyle, Britain witnessed "a degree of Dapperism and Dilettantism, and rickety Debility, unexampled in the history of Literature" (*CW*, xxvii: 131). Journalists such as Carlyle could always be suspected of dilettantism and amateurishness, since they had no obvious professional credentials. Carlyle, by accusing Byron of dilettantism instead, suggests that philosophical critics like himself were the true professionals.[10]

Yet Carlyle was never entirely satisfied with periodical reviews as his vehicle. His class background made him a permanent outsider to the norms of polite culture that men such as Lockhart or Jeffrey were creating in the reviews. Although advocacy of German literature allowed him to be inside the British literary system and outside of it at the same time, his reviews rarely fit the periodical format comfortably. Jeffrey, for example, revised Carlyle's essay on Burns extensively to make it conform to his review's stylistic and critical norms.[11]

Remaining in literary criticism was impossible for Carlyle because its concerns were too narrow. Even for a philosophic critic, writing only about literature came too close to the dilettantism that he rejected in Byron. Successfully turning away from Byron meant abandoning literature. His essays in the 1820s expanded beyond the traditional review to address larger social concerns. By the 1829 "Signs of the Times," these larger concerns had become the focus of the review, which denounced the present age as "mechanical" and pleaded for a more organic and spiritual awareness. The essay was both the climax of the positions developed in Carlyle's reviews and the sign that he was moving away from their format.

Carlyle's letters in the late 1820s announce his dissatisfaction with reviewing and his desire to write a book of his own that would allow him to elaborate his views. As he wrote to his brother, "In the valley of the shadow of Magazine Editors, we shall not always linger" (*CL*, v: 202). *Sartor* resulted from his dissatisfaction. Yet having written a book that exploded the established bounds of the review, Carlyle could not find a publisher for it. It at last appeared in the format that he had hoped to avoid, the periodical review, when it was serialized in *Fraser's Magazine* in 1833–34. *Sartor*'s fate suggests how periodicals such as *Fraser's* were for Carlyle the best among bad alternatives. He was an intellectual needing a mode of institutional support that did not become available until later in the century: the academy. *Sartor* prophetically imagines as fiction the role in the academy that later Victorian sages would actually play as charismatic critics. But when Carlyle wrote *Sartor*, no such role existed. Carlyle could not look to institutions such as the academy to help him differentiate his voice from that of the reviewers.

Without such institutional support, Carlyle found other strategies through which to achieve distinction. One was his style. If his opinions about Byron owed much to earlier reviewers, the language in which he expressed them was as far as possible from their tepid English. Carlyle polemically enlisted German authors in support of his style and maintained that the British had not accepted Goethe because his work was not "written in the style of what we call a *gentleman*" (*CW*, XXVI: 204). His style was distinctly not that of a gentleman: it was a perpetual reminder that he wrote as an outsider even when he worked within the limits of the reviews. It marked his difference not only from the reviewers' bland prose but also from Byron's loftily careless English. Through his style alone Carlyle distinguished himself from other contemporary writers.

Style marked Carlyle's writing as distinctively "literary" even when he was not necessarily writing about literature. In writing as he did, he helped to rearrange the traditional hierarchy of poetry and prose that valued poetry because more education was needed to produce it. Although the outrage greeting Wordsworth's experimental poetry suggests how seriously critics took this hierarchy, the development of standards for polite prose threatened to disrupt it. The English of George Crabbe or Samuel Rogers was not strikingly different from that of Jane Austen or Sir Walter Scott: all conformed to the norms of polite English. As a result, a new standard arose to distinguish literary writing from other, implicitly less elevated forms: authorial style.

Writers who at first were most stylistically distinctive tended to be those who did not come from privileged classes, such as John Keats or Charles Lamb. They used literary English to assert their place against the users of polite English. Literature's growing autonomy depended on this linguistic development. In the hands of writers such as Carlyle, literature employed language that, rather than conforming to "correct" norms, manifested the author's individual style, his or her self-consciously manipulated

words. Keats's failure during his life and subsequent success
registers the shift from polite English to individual style as the
marker of literary language.

   If style defined literary language, poetry lost its priority as the
most literary of genres. Highly stylized prose might compete with
it because both could be considered art if they manifested an
author's particular style. As a result, a "literary" writer might
attempt to supplant a poet such as Byron because both were
occupying the same ground, as opposed to the absolute distinction
between Byron and his earlier reviewers. In moving from his
review essays to *Sartor*, Carlyle left behind literary criticism but
not literature, since his style marked his writing as "art." In his
hands, the professional intellectual distinguished his writing from
that of ordinary reviewers partly because his was literature, while
theirs was another version of an increasingly dated polite English.
Carlyle's style tried to establish a form of authority that as yet
had no institution through which to realize itself. As I will argue,
Sartor dramatizes the birth of this authority from Byronism's
ashes.

Carlyle's disenchantment with the periodicals coincided with the
loss of public interest in German literature. He worked for a
year on a history of it only to have a publisher tell him, "I . . .
would be proud to publish for you again, upon almost any
subject but German Literature."[12] One of the only journals still
interested in him was the literary monthly *Fraser's Magazine*. It
had started up in 1830, and its publishers were eager to secure
the services of a prestigious reviewer. The journal modeled itself
closely on *Blackwood's* with its German philosophy, mock-learning,
outrageous pseudonyms, stylistic extravagance, and arrogant self-
assurance. Like *Blackwood's*, it provided a forum for authors
fashioning a self-consciously literary style.

   Writing for *Fraser's* initially seemed to be a step down from
the heights of the philosophical review. Carlyle's first impression
was that the journal was "a hurlyburly of rhodomontade, punch,
loyalty, and Saturnalian Toryism as eye hath not seen . . . a
kind of wild popular Lower-Comedy" (*NB*, p. 170). Yet its
"hurlyburly" qualities allowed him to experiment with alternative, more "popular" modes than the review. In August of 1830,
he sent *Fraser's* some poetry and fiction that he had not dared

to send elsewhere. In response, the publisher sent him the first six issues of the magazine to interest him further. These arrived in September, near the time that he began *Sartor*'s first draft. These six issues of *Fraser's* were a vital influence on the form of *Sartor*, and they also shaped its treatment of Byron.[13] For Carlyle, a particularly important Byron critic was *Fraser's* prolific editor William Maginn, who included more discussion of Byron in *Fraser's* than any comparable journal of the early 1830s. Although earlier in the 1820s John Murray had asked Maginn to write the official biography of Byron that eventually was written by Thomas Moore, Maginn's attitudes toward Byron had become relentlessly hostile.[14] As an Irish schoolteacher's son, he, like Carlyle and Hazlitt, was a member of a new class of writers for whom the aristocratic Byron represented all that blocked their success.

I will first look at *Sartor*'s most mediated relationship to Byronism in terms of its response to Maginn's 1830 review of Bulwer Lytton's fashionable novels.[15] Bulwer Lytton's career forms part of the subject of chapter 6, so I will emphasize here only that his novels, as contemporary reviewers recognized, directly responded to Byron's life and work.[16] *Pelham* (1828), one of his greatest successes, translated Byronic types into a tale of fashionable society, complete with a brooding poet and a witty dandy. Critics have often discussed Maginn's review of *Pelham* as an important influence on Carlyle's "The Dandiacal Body," in which Teufelsdröckh mentions having read in "some English Periodical . . . something like a Dissertation on this very subject of *Fashionable Novels!*" (*SR*, p. 278). Teufelsdröckh also paraphrases a section from *Pelham* about rules for fashionable dress, which Maginn had printed and ridiculed. Yet critics have not discussed the article's significance in the context of Byronism and Carlyle's struggle to define the professional intellectual.

Maginn's "Mr. Edward Lytton Bulwer's Novels; and Remarks on Novel Writing" attacks Bulwer Lytton and *Pelham*, which it treats as unregenerate dandyism. The essay excerpts enough of Bulwer Lytton's work to make its Byronic tendencies clear; it quotes a remark from *Pelham* on the excellence of *Childe Harold*, and, in reference to *Paul Clifford*, notes "the Lara or the Corsair of Byron" as a model for Bulwer Lytton's portrayal of passion.[17] Although Carlyle never associated Byron with dandies before reading this article, he repeatedly did so afterward. For example, in his brief "Schiller, Goethe, and Madame de Staël," written in the spring of 1831, he mentioned that Byron's letters were written "not with philosophic permanent-colours, but with mere dandyic ochre and japan" (*CW*, xxvi: 503), and in his notebook that December he wrote, "Byron we call 'a Dandy of Sorrows, and acquainted with grief.' That is a brief definition of him" (*NB*, p. 230). The dandy was a useful image that could stand for the critique of Byron's dilettantism that Carlyle had made in "Jean Paul Friedrich Richter Again." Figuring Byron as a dandy connected his rank with an ambiguously gendered status against which Carlyle could offer his more "manly" stance as a philosopher.

Yet the relevance of Maginn's article to Carlyle goes beyond its association between Byron, Bulwer Lytton, dandies, and fashionable literature. Maginn has much to say about Bulwer Lytton as a philosopher. *Pelham* includes many conversations on abstract, philosophical topics, which give it an air of intellectual seriousness not characteristic of other fashionable novels. For writers such as Carlyle and Maginn, Bulwer Lytton's appropriation of philosophic discourse, which had been a distinctive characteristic of the serious reviewer, threatened to undermine the distinction between popular genres such as the novel and the philosophical review's supposedly more sophisticated work. Maginn trounces the amateurishness of *Pelham*'s philosophy: "With this pretension to metaphysical science, and this real ignorance as to its elementary principles, it is not extraordinary that Mr. Bulwer's novels should be so deficient in arrangement and unity."[18] In particular, he blames Bulwer Lytton for being ignorant of German idealist philosophy and relying on Reid, who merely "had an indistinct perception of a system of philosophy which has since been perfected by Kant and Schelling in Germany, and by Stewart and Coleridge in England."[19] Bulwer Lytton did not know the very systems that Carlyle had popularized throughout the late 1820s and whose ideas had influenced his approach to literary criticism. Maginn reasserted the superiority of the philosophic critic in the face of the upstart ignorance of Bulwer Lytton.

For Maginn, Bulwer Lytton's philosophic failure leads to class snobbery: "[I]t is a favourite notion with our fashionable novelists, to sacrifice the middle classes equally to the lowest and highest," although "it is from the middle classes that men of genius have in general risen."[20] Bulwer Lytton had "failed to prove his capacity to paint the lower and truly philosophical orders of mankind."[21] If Bulwer Lytton had portrayed the middle classes, he might have written real philosophy, but since he did not, his work was worthless. Maginn's class animus against Bulwer Lytton resembles that of Carlyle against Byron. Although novels were not an aristocratic genre, Bulwer Lytton's novels about fashionable aristocrats represented another facet of the aristocracy's perceived domination of literature that Carlyle and Maginn deplored in Byron's success.

Maginn's review gave Carlyle a precedent for treating fashionable novels as a target mediating his complaints about Byron. Even more usefully, Carlyle could parody the genre of the fashionable novel in his search for a literary form embodying the viewpoint of the professional intellectual. In *Sartor*, he wrote an unfashionable novel about fashion, adapting the Byronic form of Bulwer Lytton's novels and turning them against themselves. Rather than featuring dandies and Byronic heroes who were incapable of serious philosophy, his work foregrounded a far more ambitious philosopher who properly belonged to no class except that of the professional intellectual.

Sartor took for its nominal subject one of the fashionable novel's most common motifs: the significance of clothes. Maginn's review had emphasized the importance of clothes to fashionable novels, and the passage from *Pelham* quoted by Maginn that Carlyle paraphrases in *Sartor* describes rules for a dandy's dress. At the end of September 1830, Carlyle wrote an essay on clothes, *Sartor*'s first incarnation (*NB*, p. 176). He had contemplated the metaphor of clothes in his notebooks and essays before this time, so Maginn's discussion of fashionable novels cannot be treated as the exclusive spur to *Sartor*'s Clothes Philosophy.[22] But in terms of *Sartor*'s relation to contemporary forms of Byronism, the clothes imagery in fashionable novels gave Carlyle the possibility of presenting himself as a successor to Byron by appropriating the clothes metaphor as a path to transcendent truth, thereby winning over the fashionable novel to the side of philosophic criticism. Rather than presenting his philosophy straight, Carlyle manipulates tropes of fashionable Byronic literature for higher ends and thereby presents his writing as a successful development away from them.

In the "Adamitism" chapter, clothes for Teufelsdröckh represent the arbitrary hierarchies of society that disguise true equality:

> Often in my atrabiliar moods, when I read of pompous ceremonials, Frankfort Coronations, Royal Drawing-rooms, Levees, Couchees; and how the ushers and macers and pursuivants are all in waiting; how Duke this is presented by Archduke that, and Colonel A by General B . . . on a sudden, as by some enchanter's wand, the—shall I speak it?—the Clothes fly-off the whole dramatic corps; and Dukes, Grandees, Bishops, Generals, Anointed Presence itself, every mother's son of them, stand straddling there, not a shirt on them; and I know not whether to laugh or weep. (pp. 60–61)

Novels such as *Pelham* offered readers a view of high life, as Byron's poetry had offered a view of an aristocrat's mind. When Teufelsdröckh presents his version of penetrating the secret interiors of the aristocracy, he undoes any fascination that aristocratic privacy might possess. There is no secret erotic charge to this imagined display of nakedness, only a leveling emphasis on the fact that men are "bound by invisible bonds to *All Men*" (p. 60). Such a passage counters the allure with which entrepreneurs such as Murray and writers such as Byron and Bulwer Lytton surrounded aristocratic interiors.

Having dismissed class as an effect of clothes, Teufelsdröckh in the "Pure Reason" chapter reveals that clothes, metaphorically conceived, are the garment of the spirit: "The thing Visible, nay the thing Imagined, the thing in any way conceived as Visible, what is it but a Garment, a Clothing of the higher, celestial Invisible?" (p. 67). He offers not dilettantish philosophy but his version of the German idealism supposedly unknown to Bulwer Lytton, so that the Byronic fashionable novel appears philosophically impoverished beside the greater wisdom of Carlyle's text about clothes. The Clothes Philosophy undercuts Byron and Bulwer Lytton by providing a different perspective on clothes: rather than being emblems of high society, they are emblems of high spiritual truth.

While the fashionable novel provided a generic context for *Sartor*'s Clothes Philosophy, a different mode of fashionable literature, the Byron biography, provided its plot. Three major biographies of Byron appeared in 1830: James Kennedy's *Conversations with Lord Byron*, John Galt's *Life of Lord Byron*, and, most important, Moore's biography, discussed in chapter 2. In "Signs of the Times," Carlyle had announced that Byron "already begins to be disregarded and forgotten" (*CW*, XXVII: 78). Even *Sartor* maintained that "the very Byron, in some seven years, has become obsolete" (*SR*, p. 47). The outpouring of material about Byron in 1830 proved Carlyle wrong.[23] All three biographies, particularly Moore's, were widely reviewed; in many cases, the reviewers' comments marked the beginning of the Victorian rejection of Byron. In all cases, the reviewers used the opportunity to scrutinize the origin and definition of the artistic character because Moore had used "genius" as the central analytical category of his discussion of Byron.

In *Fraser's*, Maginn reviewed the first volume of Moore's biography in March, Kennedy's in August, and Galt's in October. The Galt review is particularly interesting with regard to *Sartor*'s genesis because it seems to have been written for Carlyle. Galt's biography had received poor reviews, but Maginn defended it against its critics, particularly those at the *Athenaeum*. Nevertheless, he attacked Galt, like Bulwer Lytton, for his incompetent philosophy: when Galt "ventures into the stream of philosophy," he "soon gets out of his depth and flounders woefully."[24] What Galt failed to give and what was really needed was "a full development of [Byron's] character—a metaphysical analysis of his mental qualities, his idiosyncratic complexion."[25] Maginn described the style of biographical analysis that Carlyle had already perfected. Maginn's review also seems to have had Carlyle in mind when it objected to Byron's selfish complaining, dilettantism, and incoherence in terms that paraphrased Carlyle's in "Goethe." Maginn even acknowledged Carlyle explicitly when he said that "Göthe [*sic*] would have taught him [Byron] differently," quoted lines by Goethe as "they are translated by his friend, Mr. Thomas Carlyle," and echoed the phrase "snarl and snap like dog distract," which Carlyle had used in "Goethe."[26] His review of Galt's *Life of Byron* implicitly invited Carlyle to write a "metaphysical analysis" of Byron.[27]

This invitation worked, but not for *Fraser's*. In November 1830, Carlyle wrote to the editor of the *Edinburgh Review* asking to write about Byron:

Occasionally of late I have been meditating an Essay on *Byron*; which, on appearance of Mr Moore's Second Volume, now soon expected, I should have no objection to attempt for you . . . My chief aim would be to *see* him and show him, not, as is too often the way, (if I could help it) to write merely "about him and about him" . . . Dilettantism, and mere toying with Truth, is, on the whole, a thing which I cannot practice: nevertheless real Love, real Belief, is not inconsistent with Tolerance of its opposite . . . For *Byron*, no Books were wanted except Mr Moore's two vo[lumes] to which Galt's might be added: except the *Plays* and *Don Juan*, which also would be needed, all his poems are already here. (*CL*, v: 196–97)

Macvey Napier, the editor, turned Carlyle down, because the review of Moore had already been given to Macaulay; instead, he sent him William Taylor's *Historic Survey of German Poetry* (1828) to review. Nevertheless, Carlyle read the first volume of Moore's biography by late 1830 or early 1831.[28] In January, he asked his brother to retrieve his essay on clothes from *Fraser's* because he wanted to give Teufelsdröckh more biography (*CL*, v: 215). It is no coincidence that Carlyle decided to revise *Sartor* to give Teufelsdröckh more biography near the same time he was reading the first volume of Moore's biography. Byron's life as told by Moore became a decisive negative model for the biography of Teufelsdröckh in the second volume of *Sartor*.

For Carlyle, whose philosophic criticism had led him to discuss Byron as a man, not a poet, Moore's best-selling biography gave him a more detailed image than he had ever had before of Byron as a powerful but unphilosophical aristocratic genius against which he could pose his ideal of the classless philosopher. Yet Carlyle framed his rejection of Byron not as a flat refusal but as a development out of Byron's immaturity. Moore's book allowed him to expand the implicit narrative of transition that he had always associated with Byron into a full-fledged plot that would trace the origins of genius. Diogenes Teufelsdröckh's life rewrites the first half of Moore's biography until Teufelsdröckh at last breaks the Byronic mold to become Carlyle's ideal. Where Moore describes the growth of Byron's haughty and impulsive genius, Carlyle uses Moore as a model to narrate the development of an alternative form of genius, the professional intellectual.

Carlyle's project of representing Teufelsdröckh's growth beyond Byronism meant that Teufelsdröckh would have to be enough like Byron that his life could be recognized as a version of

Byron's. To begin with, the name "Diogenes Teufelsdröckh" (God-born Devil's dung) suggested an array of Byronic stereotypes. The reviewers of Moore's biography saw in Byron an archetypal embodiment of man's duality, perhaps applying to Byron his own description of Napoleon as "antithetically mixt." For example, Lockhart noted that Byron's comment on Burns, "What a strange compound of dirt and deity!" might better have been applied to himself.[29] Carlyle's own essays had been divided between representating Byron as a divine prophet, as in "Burns," and as a howling animal, as in "Goethe." The reviewers' version of Byron provided Carlyle with a particularly modern instance of the ancient topos of man's duality, and the division in Teufelsdröckh implied by his name conformed to all the stereotypes of Byronic genius.

Teufelsdröckh's name also associates him with the Satanic stereotypes that clustered around Byron, as in Southey's tag for Byron's school of poetry, the Satanic school. Carlyle associates Teufelsdröckh's Satanism partly with his humor; the Editor says that his perverse and satirical qualities make one "look on him almost with a shudder, as on some incarnate Mephistopheles" (*SR*, p. 32). The Editor finally gives up his biography because of the "painful suspicion" that Teufelsdröckh, with his "humouristico-satirical tendency," has written autobiographical documents that "are partly a mystification!" (*SR*, p. 202). Byron's satirical mystifications were often commented on in writings about him, especially in Moore's biography, which noted that he succumbed to the temptation "of displaying his wit at the expense of his character" because he liked "to astonish and *mystify*" (*M*, 1: 135). Moreover, it was "difficult, in unravelling the texture of his feelings, to distinguish at all times between the fanciful and the real" (*M*, 1: 201).[30] Such clues linked Teufelsdröckh to characteristics associated in Moore and in the reviews with Byron's personality.

The Editor justifies the need for Teufelsdröckh's biography in terms of the Byronic equation between man and author. Like Byron, Teufelsdröckh cannot be understood "till a Biography of him has been philosophico-poetically written, and philosophico-poetically read" (*SR*, p. 75). His language recalls Maginn's desire in his review of Galt's biography for a "metaphysical analysis of [Byron's] mental qualities, his idiosyncratic complexion." *Sartor's*

Book II is the review of Moore's biography that Carlyle never actually wrote; he casts it as a competing biography of a supposedly truer genius than Byron. Carlyle even hints at his debt to Moore's biography near the end of the "Sorrows of Teufelsdröckh" chapter when the Editor explains the need for Teufelsdröckh to pass through a stage of passionate suffering akin to Byron's: "For what is it properly but an Altercation with the Devil, before you begin honestly Fighting him? Your Byron publishes his *Sorrows of Lord George*, in verse and in prose, and copiously otherwise" (*SR*, pp. 156–57). Previous critics have not commented on the reference to Byron's prose, which is puzzling if applied to the prose published during Byron's life. Carlyle must refer to the letters published in Moore's biography, which, according to reviewers such as Macaulay, revealed the "sad and dark" story of Byron's early unhappiness.[31] Carlyle's small reference to Byron's prose points to a larger debt to the letters published by Moore and to Moore's interpretation of them throughout this section of *Sartor*.

Like the novels of Bulwer Lytton, Moore's biography was a piece of fashionable literature, another example of how Byron's career allowed the aristocracy to maintain the cultural dominance that it had lost in the economy. Teufelsdröckh's unfashionable life begins as a point-by-point reversal of the young Byron's; its events are written against Byron's early experiences as told by Moore to create Carlyle's competing history of the origins of genius. The revision's overall effect is to emphasize the effects of class, which becomes the symbolic ground for Carlyle's attack on Byron. Both Byron and Teufelsdröckh are only children, but they come from radically different backgrounds. Moore devotes several pages to Byron's illustrious ancestry; Teufelsdröckh is an orphan given to the Futterals by a mysterious stranger. Carlyle underscores that Teufelsdröckh's origins are not noble because Teufelsdröckh has looked "through all the Herald's Books, in and without the German Empire" and found no record of his name (*SR*, p. 86). Teufeldröckh maintains that his humble origins have benefited his spiritual character: "Wouldst thou rather be a peasant's son that knew, were it never so rudely, there was a God in Heaven and in Man; or a duke's son that only knew there were two-and-thirty quarters on the family-coach?" (*SR*, p. 99). Moore notes the bad effect that Byron's early elevation to nobility had on him: "Had he been left to struggle on for ten years longer, as plain George Byron, there can be little doubt that his character would have been, in many respects, the better for it" (*M*, 1: 20). Carlyle, in contrast, creates the first of the long series of Victorian orphan heroes, whose lack of family emphasizes that their successes depend not on patronage but on their "innate" abilities.

The image of the highly moral peasant family that adopts Teufelsdröckh counters the family structure that turned Byron into a selfish aristocrat. Though Teufelsdröckh's lack of a father during childhood parallels Byron's, he at least has a strong substitute in his foster-father, Andreas Futteral. Like Byron's father, Andreas is a military man, but he has retired and become "Cincinnatus-like" (*SR*, p. 82), unlike the wild and irresponsible Captain Byron. Their mothers present a similar contrast. Both are religious: Mrs. Byron "was of a very religious disposition" and taught Byron "while yet an infant, to repeat a great number of the Psalms" (*M*, 1: 9); Gretchen teaches Teufelsdröckh "less indeed by word than by act and daily reverent look and habitude, her own simple version of the Christian Faith" (*SR*, p. 99). Carlyle's emphasis on Gretchen's deeds reflects back unfavorably on Mrs. Byron, who, despite her piety, was a woman "full of the most passionate extremes" (*M*, 1: 11). Moore describes her as a violent, often uncaring mother whose passions, arising from her aristocratic haughtiness, were responsible for flaws in Byron's character. The differences between the children reflect those of the parents. Teufelsdröckh as an infant "seldom or never cried" and felt that "he had other work cut-out for him than whimpering" (*SR*, p. 89); Byron "[e]ven when in petticoats . . . showed the same uncontrollable spirit with his nurse, which he afterwards exhibited, when an author, with his critics" (*M*, 1: 8).

Carlyle does not simply reverse Moore's biography, but suggests that Teufelsdröckh is a redeemed Byron who fulfills the potential ruined in the real one. Despite their social disparity, traits indicating unusual poetic sensitivity quickly develop in both. They are obsessive readers. Teufelsdröckh recalls that "what printed thing soever I could meet with I read" (*SR*, p. 101), and Moore quotes a letter by Byron in which he writes, "I read eating, read in bed, read when no one else read, and had read all sorts of reading since I was five years old" (*M*, 1: 40). Byron spends

much of his childhood in Scotland, as had Carlyle, and develops
a love for mountains at sunset: "After I returned to Cheltenham,
I used to watch them every afternoon at sunset, with a sensation
which I cannot describe" (*M*, 1: 17). Though Teufelsdröckh is
supposed to grow up in Germany, the landscape that he describes
looks suspiciously like Carlyle's Scotland and Byron's Cheltenham: "There, many a sunset, have I, looking at the distant
western Mountains, consumed, not without relish, my evening
meal" (*SR*, p. 93).

   Both undergo a crisis of identity in their early adolescence
when they are suddenly alienated from all that has been familiar.
Gretchen and Andreas pretend that Teufelsdröckh is their grand-
nephew, but after Andreas's death, Gretchen tells him "that he
was not at all of this kindred" (*SR*, p. 107). Suddenly, Teufelsdröckh feels set apart from humanity: "A certain poetic elevation, yet also a corresponding civic depression, it naturally
imparted: *I was like no other*" (*SR*, p. 107). When Byron is ten,
the fifth Lord Byron dies; Byron, his grand-nephew, becomes the
sixth Lord Byron. Though he asks his mother "whether she
perceived any difference in him since he had been made a lord,
as he perceived none himself," Moore notes that "the child little
knew what a total and talismanic change had been wrought in
all his future relations with society, by the simple addition of
that word before his name" (*M*, 1: 20). Byron is unable to answer
to his name in school when *dominus* is prefixed to it for the first
time; like Teufelsdröckh, he suddenly feels that he is "like no
other." Characteristically, however, Carlyle uses class as a means
of moral distinction. Byron's alienation comes from a move up
the social ladder that had catastrophic results for his moral
development, as Moore suggests. Teufelsdröckh's "civic
depression" emphasizes that he has none of Byron's worldly
advantages; his achievements will be the result of his merits
alone.

   Carlyle suggests similar comparisons between the unsatisfactory
education of Byron and Teufelsdröckh and their loss of faith: in
both cases, he presents Teufelsdröckh's experiences as more profound and deeply felt than those depicted in Moore. Yet an even
more critical moment in the development of both men is their
first disappointment in love. Byron's lost love is Mary Chaworth;
his attachment to her "sunk so deep into his mind as to give a

colour to all his future life" (*M*, 1: 53). Carlyle revises this
episode when Teufelsdröckh falls in love with a woman whom
he calls Blumine. She loves Teufelsdröckh, but is encouraged by
her "Duenna Cousin" (*SR*, p. 144) to break off the relation
because of his lack of prospects. He plunges into despair:
"Through the ruins as of a shivered Universe was he falling,
falling, towards the Abyss" (*SR*, p. 146). Teufelsdröckh's disaster
arises from his economic hardships, whereas Moore presents
Byron's merely as a result of Mary Chaworth's coquettish dislike
of Byron's lameness. In every aspect of life, Teufelsdröckh confronts experiences that Carlyle designs to make the aristocratic
upbringing of Moore's Byron look shallow by comparison.

Teufelsdröckh's disappointment brings him to his most
explicitly Byronic phase. According to the Editor, he can do only
one of three things: "Establish himself in Bedlam; begin writing
Satanic Poetry; or blow-out his brains" (*SR*, p. 146). To the
editor's surprise, he chooses none: "He quietly lifts his *Pilgerstab*
(Pilgrim-staff) . . . and begins a perambulation and circumambu-
lation of the terraqueous Globe" (*SR*, p. 147). Carlyle is here at
his trickiest. We are supposed to understand that Teufelsdröckh
has rejected the Byronic alternative of writing Satanic poetry,
but Carlyle could not have referred more explicitly to Byron
than by sending Teufelsdröckh on a pilgrimage. Yet even as
Teufelsdröckh becomes a later incarnation of Childe Harold,
Carlyle preserves a few marks of difference from Byron's stereotypical storminess by praising Teufelsdröckh's combination of
"intensity of feeling" with "stoicism in external procedure" (*SR*,
p. 147). The Editor marvels that Teufelsdröckh "was meek,
silent, or spoke of the weather," while underneath "a whole
Satanic School [was] spouting, though inaudibly, there" (*SR*, p.
148). Teufelsdröckh may be living up to the Satanism of his
name, but he maintains a stiff upper lip. Moore's Byron also
masks his pain and his "bursts of vivacity on the surface [were]
by no means incompatible with a wounded spirit underneath"
(*M*, 1: 188). Yet Teufelsdröckh does not resort, like Byron, to
vivacity, but to "meek, silent" stoicism. Still resembling the baby
who would not whimper, the adult Teufelsdröckh hides his pain.

Teufelsdröckh's pilgrimage is not fully underway until he sees
Blumine and his English friend Herr Towgood in a "gay
Barouche-and-four" attended by servants and postilions wearing

wedding-favors (*SR*, p. 151). At this sight, the Satanic School in
him at last wins out: "Life has become wholly a dark labyrinth;
wherein, through long years, our Friend, flying from spectres,
has to stumble about at random, and naturally with more haste
than progress" (*SR*, p. 152). In case we miss the connection here
between Teufelsdröckh and Byron, the Editor notes, "From which
is it not clear that the internal Satanic School was still active
enough?" (*SR*, p. 155).[32] Like Teufelsdröckh, Byron sees his
beloved Mary Chaworth and her husband immediately before
he sets off on his pilgrimage, and the sight plunges him into
despair: "His passions had, at the very onset of their career,
forestalled the future; and the blank void that followed was by
himself considered as one of the causes of that melancholy, which
now settled so deeply into his character" (*M*, 1: 182). Carlyle
closes the chapter on the "Sorrows of Teufelsdröckh" with the
reference to the *Sorrows of Lord George* discussed above.
Teufelsdröckh is undergoing the same "Altercation with the
Devil" as Byron, but from which he emerges victorious, as Byron
did not.

The shock of rejection leads Teufelsdröckh and Byron to the
nadir of their spiritual journey. Carlyle again presents
Teufelsdröckh's "Everlasting No" as having far purer depth than
Byron's. Moore describes Byron's bitterness as arising out of
revenge and impatience: "Baffled . . . in his own ardent pursuit
of affection and friendship, his sole revenge and consolation lay
in doubting that any such feelings really existed . . . What others
would have bowed to, as misfortunes, his proud spirit rose
against, as wrongs" (*M*, 1: 186). Though Moore maintains a
distanced tone, he treats Byron's despair as petty and self-
indulgent. Teufelsdröckh, in contrast, does not feel revenge or
scorn so much as cosmic emptiness: "It is all a grim Desert,
this once-fair world of his; wherein is heard only the howling of
wild-beasts, or the shrieks of despairing, hate-filled men" (*SR*,
p. 161). Far from being upset by worldly disappointments, as
Byron is, Teufelsdröckh feels the vast hollowness of a world
without faith, in which a mechanistic philosophy has turned all
into "one huge, dead, immeasurable Steam-engine, rolling on, in
its dead indifference" (*SR*, p. 164). Yet Teufelsdröckh's despair
is only a stage "wherefrom, the fiercer it is, the clearer product
will one day evolve itself" (*SR*, p. 158). Unlike Byron's aimless

bitterness, Teufelsdröckh even at his most forlorn is growing toward greater spiritual strength.

At the end of "The Everlasting No," Teufelsdröckh realizes that a needless fear of death has crippled him because he has the ability to suffer "all that the Devil and Man may, will or can do" against him (*SR*, p. 167). He rejects the Everlasting No and emerges from despair, yet he has not fully overcome Byron because no new faith yet replaces his emptiness. During this interim, the "Centre of Indifference," Teufelsdröckh undergoes many adventures that the Editor does not describe: "—But at this point the Editor recalls his principle of caution, some time ago laid down, and must suppress much ... Of Lord Byron, therefore, of Pope Pius, Emperor Tarakwang, and the 'White Water-roses' (Chinese Carbonari) with their mysteries, no notice here!" (*SR*, p. 178). This passage is particularly rich in allusions to the reception of Moore's biography. The editor's elaborate disclaimer pokes fun at the ones made by Moore, whom reviewers nevertheless criticized sharply for divulging the more unsavory sides of Byron's life, especially his Italian mistresses. Byron's appearance in Carlyle's list functions as an "in-joke" through which he signals the beginning of the end of Teufelsdröckh's Byronic phase. Byron is now only an exotic worthy whom Teufelsdröckh meets on his pilgrimage, just as Byron described exotic worthies in *Childe Harold's Pilgrimage*. The humor lies in the fact that the Editor does not need to dwell upon Teufelsdröckh's adventures because readers already know their general shape from having read *Childe Harold* and Moore's biography. For example, the reference to Chinese Carbonari may be a barely disguised allusion to Byron's involvement with the Italian Carbonari. Since Byron's career had made such episodes familiar, *Sartor*'s Editor can recall principles of caution that he has no real need to employ.

Until this moment, Teufelsdröckh's career parallels Byron's, although it contains numerous implicit differences. In the "Centre of Indifference," however, Carlyle's narrative must demonstrate that its hero can move away from all that Byron represents and realize his potential as a full-fledged professional intellectual. Carlyle accomplishes this shift with an exceptional event involving a complex revision of an episode in Moore associated with origins of Byron's creative genius. Teufelsdröckh, alone "in the solitude of the North Cape," muses on a promontory over the ocean, while viewing "nothing but the granite cliffs ruddy-tinged, the peaceable gurgle of that slow-heaving Polar Ocean" (*SR*, p. 179). Although Carlyle moves Teufelsdröckh geographically northward, his position recalls that of Moore's Byron in Greece, who "when bathing in some retired spot, [used] to seat himself on a high rock above the sea . . . lost in that sort of vague reverie, which, however formless and indistinct at the moment, settled afterwards, on his pages, into those clear, bright pictures, which will endure forever" (*M*, 1: 254). Carlyle revises a moment in Moore's text locating Byron in a scene describing the origins of creative genius. The interest of Moore's text, beyond its details about Byron's life, was that it offered a coherent narrative of the development of genius, and in revising this moment, Carlyle fastens on the most provocative aspect of Moore's biography in order to present a counter-narrative of the origins of creativity.

Sartor rewrites Moore's scene as a setting not for artistic inspiration but for the professional intellectual's triumph. Teufelsdröckh is visited not by poetic visions but by "a man, or monster, scrambling from among the rock-hollows; and, shaggy, huge as the Hyperborean Bear" who assails him "with his importunate train-oil breath" (*SR*, pp. 179–80). When the man will not go away despite Teufelsdröckh's courteous request for privacy, Teufelsdröckh draws a gun and says, "Be so obliging as retire, Friend (*Er ziehe sich zurück, Freund*), and with promptitude!" The Hyperborean, whom Teufelsdröckh fears is a Russian smuggler, leaves "with apologetic, petitionary growl" (*SR*, p. 180).

Just as Carlyle translates Teufelsdröckh from Byron's Greece to the North Cape, so the Hyperborean represents a northward movement from Byron's exotic Greek corsairs to a Russian smuggler. With this geographic dislocation comes a parodic debasement of traits that he used to characterize Byron. The Hyperborean's savagery recalls Carlyle's association of Byron with savage wildness in his early essays, as when in "Goethe" he wonders what good it does Byron "to snarl and snap in malignant wise, 'like dog distract, or monkey sick' " (*CW*, XXVI: 218). Moore's biography emphasizes Byron's violent, potentially murderous nature, as when he is "heard to say, in an under voice, 'I should like to know how a person feels, after committing a murder!' " (*M*, 1: 235). Moreover, Teufelsdröckh's rejection of the Hyperborean recalls Jesus's "Get thee behind me, Satan," thus connecting the Hyperborean with the Satanic aspects of both Byron and Teufelsdröckh.[33] The Hyperborean is a burlesque of the savage, Satanic characteristics that Carlyle typically associated with Byron, as well as a parodic projection of the Byronic wildness in Teufelsdröckh himself.

Teufelsdröckh becomes a purified version of Byron after he dismisses the Hyperborean as a parodically debased one. For Teufelsdröckh, rejecting the Hyperborean becomes an emblem of rejecting the Satanic school. Immediately after the episode, the Editor notes that "the Satanic School, was now pretty well extirpated and cast out" (*SR*, p. 181). While Moore presented Byron as drawing poetic inspiration from his elevated outlook over the sea, Teufelsdröckh produces not poetry but a gun. He draws the moral that gunpowder "makes all men alike tall"; because of it, "savage Animalism is nothing, inventive Spiritualism is all" (*SR*, p. 180). Byron too had a high regard for guns, according to Moore, and he always had arms about him because "the mortification which he had . . . to endure at school, from insults . . . hazarded on the presumption of his physical inferiority, found consolation in the thought that . . . the law of the pistol would place him on a level with the strongest" (*M*, 1: 27). Like Teufelsdröckh, Byron believes that guns make all men alike tall. Yet his allegiance to guns is one more marker of his aristocratic status; Moore describes Byron as being always on the point of a duel. Through Teufelsdröckh, Carlyle redefines the significance of possessing firearms as a characteristic of the philosopher. Guns rather than poetry mark inventive spiritualism's triumph because the truly inventive can translate their ideas into technologies that secure superiority.

Although Teufelsdröckh never actually fires the gun, his praise of gunpowder is one of Carlyle's most disturbing moments because of its association between the intellectual and violence. We might have expected that Teufelsdröckh would have demonstrated his "inventive spiritualism" by some quick-witted maneuver to avoid the Hyperborean. Instead, he links spirituality with gunpowder. In part, the gun allows Carlyle to emphasize the practical effectiveness of Teufelsdröckh's spirituality. Yet the episode is almost pathetically incapable of sustaining the allegory of brute force versus inventive spirituality that Teufelsdröckh fastens onto it, since the Hyperborean merely leaves when threatened with superior violence. Teufelsdröckh's gun may suggest that Carlyle has few models for describing the effectiveness that a professional intellectual might possess. Teufelsdröckh hardly presents a real alternative to the early ninteenth-century Byron: his dismissal of the Hyperborean retains much of the Byronic violence that he is supposedly rejecting. His spiritualization of gunpowder is a violent fiction, a dark underside to Carlyle's desire to make unspiritual objects, such as clothes, fashionable novels, or the biography of Byron, into spiritual ones.

The "Everlasting Yea" diffuses the violence of this encounter, though it does not dissipate it, by translating it from plot to rhetoric:

I asked myself: What is this that, ever since earliest years, thou hast been fretting and fuming, and lamenting and self-tormenting, on account of? Say it in a word: is it not because thou art not HAPPY? Because the THOU (sweet gentleman) is not sufficiently honoured, nourished, soft-bedded, and lovingly cared-for? . . . Art thou nothing other than a Vulture, then, that fliest through the Universe seeking after somewhat to *eat*; and shrieking dolefully because carrion enough is not given thee? Close thy *Byron*; open thy *Goethe*. (*SR*, pp. 191–92)

The final statement suddenly translates moral problems into a choice between authors. The struggle over the author's role is so serious in *Sartor* that "Byron" and "Goethe" stand for whole networks of literary practices, moral codes, and institutional affiliations. Within them, Carlyle emphasizes the class element of his cultural warfare; the Byronic Teufelsdröckh is a "sweet gentleman" who expects to be "honoured, nourished, soft-bedded, and lovingly cared-for." The passage suggests that underneath the sweet gentleman is the shrieking vulture; gluttony for happiness reduces him to another version of the Hyperborean's savage animalism. Yet the savagery does not seem to be Byron's alone. This moment revises the scene in which Teufelsdröckh's pistol forces the retreat of the monstrous Hyperborean. As there, Byron has been "closed" with a ferocity that is not as far from savage animalism as it would like to pretend.

Teufelsdröckh, having rejected Byron, can at last emerge a professional intellectual by telling himself, "Produce! Produce! Were it but the pitifullest infinitesimal fraction of a Product, produce it, in God's name!" (*SR*, p. 197). Yet there is an odd falling-off from his ringing affirmation of potential to his actual fate. His use of Byron and Goethe to define himself creates the expectation that once he closes his Byron, he will become Goethe. Instead, he becomes Professor of Things-in-General at the university in Weissnichtwo, where he gives occasional orations in the coffee-house, though no formal lectures. Rather than being a creative artist, he becomes an academic bearing startling resemblances to the charismatic "theorist" of the twentieth century; he is the first absent-minded professor in English literature. In the academy, Carlyle imagined an institution where the professional intellectual could flourish. The university appeared to be a haven that would foster intellectual development untainted by the marketplace's demands, unlike the periodicals. *Sartor* writes into being the careers of influential academics, regardless of discipline: the vatic, eccentric personality; the difficult body of often fragmentary work that needs translation by disciples; and the tense relation to the rules of the institution. These characteristics signal that the professional intellectual's work resists the economic pressures which for Carlyle were exemplified by the marketing of such authors as Byron.

When Carlyle was writing, English universities were hardly such havens, and his portrayal of his own university in *Sartor*'s Book II does not suggest that the Scottish schools were much better. Yet his experience with the periodicals would have encouraged him to connect reviewers and academics. John Wilson, the guiding force behind *Blackwood's*, was Professor of Moral Philosophy at the University of Edinburgh; Carlyle had inquired about applying for the same position at the University of London in 1827, and actually applied unsuccessfully for a similar job at St. Andrews a few months later. The university offered a stable source of income and prestige not available from the periodicals. For all the comedy of Teufelsdröckh as an academic, he represents a serious fantasy for Carlyle of the possibility of lodging professional intellectuals in a supportive institution that would give them a free space to develop their philosophies.

Although not a reviewer, Teufelsdröckh demonstrates close ties between his work and the periodical reviews. He sits at the Weissnichtwo tavern "reading Journals" (*SR*, p. 19); "Periodical Literature" (*SR*, p. 24) litters his room; and he announces that "the Journalists are now the true Kings and Clergy" (*SR*,

p. 45). The Editor hopes to publish articles on Teufelsdröckh in
"widely-circulating Critical Journals" (SR, p. 10). G. B. Tennyson notes how the structure of Sartor itself represents an expansion
of the structure of Carlyle's earlier periodical reviews.[34] Sartor
subjects the philosophic review to a less hostile version of its
treatment of Byronism by incorporating and surpassing it to
celebrate its new man, the professional intellectual.

Sartor's role for the professional intellectual has a political as
well as a creative component, which becomes explicit in "The
Dandiacal Body" in Book III. Dandies represent one facet of
Byron's career that fashionable novels like Pelham intensified and
popularized. By putting the chapter late in the book, Carlyle lets
the dandies appear as one more incarnation of the aristocratic
Byron who was rejected in "The Everlasting Yea." I have already
argued that Carlyle's trope of clothes revises the characteristic
motif of the fashionable novel, and the Editor confesses as much
when he notes, "The all-importance of Clothes, which a German
Professor, of unequalled learning and acumen, writes his enormous Volume to demonstrate, has sprung up in the intellect of
the Dandy without effort, like an instinct of genius" (SR, p. 272).
Yet Byronic dandies also have a political edge for Carlyle. They
are not merely an unusual social group; they represent a political
development with disastrous implications. The chapter's light-
hearted tone, in which Teufelsdröckh describes the dandies and
fashionable novels as a religious sect of which he disapproves,
darkens tremendously when he contrasts the dandies with the
wretchedness of "Poor-Slaves" (SR, p. 285), the Irish peasantry
whose condition is spreading beyond Ireland. He concludes by
predicting that the sects are "two bottomless boiling Whirlpools"
that will overflow England until "we have the true Hell of
Waters, and Noah's Deluge is outdeluged" (SR, p. 286). This
outcome seemed threateningly possible in the troubled years
immediately preceding the 1832 Reform Bill. As Carlyle wrote
in his notebook, "Hay-stacks and corn-stacks burning over all
the South and Middle of England! Where will it end? Revolution
on the back of Revolution for a century yet?" (NB, pp. 178–79).

Dividing England into Dandies and Poor-Slaves excludes
the position of the professional intellectual represented by
Teufelsdröckh. The chapter implicitly poses him as the only
possibility for staving off the apocalyptic consequences of the

increasing division between rich and poor, because only he sees the coming danger. Carlyle wrote in his notebook, "Not that we want *no* Aristocracy, but that we want a *true* one" (*NB*, p. 179). The true aristocracy consists of professional intellectuals of intrinsic merit, such as Diogenes Teufelsdröckh, rather than dilettantish aristocrats, such as Byron, whose merit is judged by birth. In the hands of the true aristocrats lies not only the future of literature, but England's political salvation.

Yet Carlyle also confronts in Teufelsdröckh the questionable political efficacy of the professional intellectual. As an intellectual, Teufelsdröckh seems as isolated from the "real" world as Byron had been and never demonstrates the practical force supposedly characteristic of a hero like Goethe. As long as Teufelsdröckh does not become Goethe, he retains residual traces of Byron, which are particularly evident in the editor's reminiscences of him. His initial appearance suggests that if he has moved beyond Byronic despair, he has not conquered Byronic solipsism. When he looks out from his window onto the town, he observes, "All these heaped and huddled together, with nothing but a little carpentry and masonry between them ... But I, *mein Werther*, sit above it all; I am alone with the Stars" (*SR*, p. 23). The Editor calls Teufelsdröckh's room his "speculum or watch-tower" (*SR*, p. 20); Carlyle mistakenly uses "speculum," mirror, for "specula," watch-tower. The mistake is overdetermined in its suggestive confusion of internal and external because when Teufelsdröckh looks out, he does not quite see himself as in a mirror, but he sees a vision of the world that bolsters his sense of his own specialness. A similar confusion of internal and external occurs when Teufelsdröckh calls the Editor "*mein Werther.*" He treats the Editor as a younger, sentimental version of himself, although the Editor never gives hints of having undergone experiences resembling the "Sorrows of Teufelsdröckh."

Only at *Sartor*'s end does Teufelsdröckh abandon this solipsism for a more active, Goethian ideal of heroism. He mysteriously disappears from Weissnichtwo, and the Editor tries to reconstruct the last days before his disappearance. When Teufelsdröckh learned of the Paris Revolution of 1830 shortly before his disappearance, he commented "*Es geht an*" (It is beginning); as Harrold notes, the words translate the French "Ça ira," the song of the French Revolution (*SR*, p. 296). The Post-Director reports that Teufelsdröckh has corresponded with the Saint-Simonians, a radical French sect (*SR*, p. 296). Certain alarmists blame him for having caused an uprising of tailors in Berlin. The Editor's private theory is that he has come to London, which in 1831 was rocked by tensions over reform. Although the Editor never says that Teufelsdröckh is actually intervening in these tensions to foment revolution, these events strongly hint that he has become involved in revolutionary activities.[35] Given the consistency with which Teufelsdröckh's life mirrors Byron's, his final activities suggest a revision of Byron's departure from Italy to fight for Greek independence. In "Goethe" and "Burns," Carlyle spoke of the last stage of Byron's life as his best, the one in which he was beginning to achieve spiritual victory. The most fitting fate he can imagine for his professional intellectual is to return to the Byronic model at its best, having rejected it at its worst. Goethe never went off to fight for freedom. The final pages of *Sartor* suggest that Teufelsdröckh has closed his Goethe and reopened his Byron. Presumably, he will be able to accomplish the victory that Byron was able only to glimpse.

Thus far I have treated Teufelsdröckh on his own terms, with little reference either to *Sartor*'s editorial apparatus or to its humor. I will suggest that both aspects arise from Carlyle's situation as a man projecting a role that as yet does not exist. The Editor's relation to Teufelsdröckh presents Carlyle's transformations of the relation of a biographer, such as Moore, to an original "genius," such as Byron; of a reviewer to a professional intellectual; and of an English man of letters to the seemingly less cultivated voice of Scotland. By foregrounding the Editor's role, Carlyle criticizes Moore's seemingly objective stance, which produced a superficial version of Byron by overlooking all that made him significant. The contrast between the Editor's blandness and Teufelsdröckh's wild prose reworks the contrast between Moore's tepid Johnsonian style and the witty verve of Byron's letters. When the Editor notes that his style has become contaminated by Teufelsdröckh's, "Thus has not the Editor himself, working over Teufelsdröckh's German, lost much of his own English purity?" (*SR*, p. 293), his loss suggests that he has sympathized with the importance of his subject in a way unavailable to Moore. His description of digging for the truth beneath

Teufelsdröckh's "printed and written Chaos" (*SR*, p. 80) masks
Carlyle's more profound "editing" of Moore's text. It is as if he
were trying to delve beneath Moore's perceived superficialities
to get at a core of vital potential latent in the subject that was
not developed. Teufelsdröckh's life is the life that should have
been written about Byron if Byron and Moore had been all that
they might have been.

Yet Carlyle's Editor is not merely Teufelsdröckh's greatest
admirer; he is also his harshest critic. If Teufelsdröckh is the
apotheosis of the professional intellectual, the Editor, with his
fussy concern for the reactions of the British reader, is a parodic
version of a magazine hack. While Carlyle was writing *Sartor*,
Jeffrey insisted that he would never find an audience: "No man
who despises and contemns educated and intelligent men, at the
rate you do, will ever have any success among them ... I wish
I could persuade you that you are not an inspired being, and
never will be the founder of a new religion."[36] Jeffrey criticized
Carlyle from the standpoint of the periodical reviews: he asked
Carlyle to adopt a polite style that would appeal to a community of "educated and intelligent men." In the tension between
Teufelsdröckh and the Editor, Carlyle relocates the tension between Jeffrey's older version of the reviewer and his new ideal
of the professional intellectual. The Editor treats Teufelsdröckh
as Jeffrey treated Carlyle by pointing out his failings: "Thus
does the good Homer not only nod, but snore" (*SR*, p. 46);
"Beware, O Teufelsdröckh, of spiritual pride" (*SR*, p. 100); "Does
your Professor take us for simpletons?" (*SR*, p. 287). Next to
Teufelsdröckh, the Editor, and implicitly men such as Jeffrey,
dwindle into small-minded pedants.

Yet the Editor's criticisms prevent Teufelsdröckh's philosophy from being taken too seriously, an effect heightened by
Teufelsdröckh's stylistic excess. The Editor's comments foreground the importance of the act of interpretation itself, although
we are not always asked to agree with his interpretations. Understanding, judging, and responding to Teufelsdröckh properly are
as important as Teufelsdröckh himself. The humorous distance
from Teufelsdröckh's voice that Carlyle develops permits him to
avoid the crudity of seeming to preach in his own person. Without
subverting Teufelsdröckh, the device of the Editor lets Carlyle
suggest that he himself subscribes to more temperate versions of

Teufelsdröckh's doctrines. His version of the professional intellectual is as yet only experimental and not to be taken too seriously.
Given the enormous power that Byron still exercised in 1830–31
and the unlikelihood that Carlyle would ever become what he
envisioned, he offers his ideal less as a blueprint for the future
than as a seriocomic fantasy. In proportion to his later success
in actualizing Teufelsdröckh's role, the humor with which he
surrounded it decreased until he took himself with grim
seriousness.

When the Editor comments on the extent to which Teufelsdröckh's German has corrupted his English purity, his words
hint at a nationalist aspect of the relation between him and
Teufelsdröckh. Germany in the text stands, among other things,
as a code for Scotland. Teufelsdröckh's outrageously "German"
language enacts Carlyle's challenge to the canons of polite English
represented by gentleman authors such as Byron, Moore, Bulwer
Lytton, and Jeffrey. Even though Moore and Jeffrey were not
natives of England, they had made their careers by conforming
to models of good English. As I suggested earlier, Carlyle's style
marked a transition from polite English as a shared norm for
educated writers to literary English as the sign of an author's
individual genius. Nominally, Teufelsdröckh's prose is German,
but it also stands as a kind of "Scottish" redeemed from the
contempt heaped on that language by the users of polite English.
Specifically, it represents a rebellion against the power of polite
English to maintain social hierarchies by a man who grew up
speaking quite a different language. Teufelsdröckh's literary Scottish manifests all the prophetic verve and ferocity that Carlyle
suggests has been drained from modern English. The sign that
Teufelsdröckh has conquered polite English is the degree to which
his style and the Editor's become indistinguishable. Carlyle's
nationalist struggle associates the professional intellectual's genius
with his access to a peculiarly literary language. His precedent
ultimately made non-fictional prose possible as a distinct category
of literature.

The Editor allows Carlyle to dramatize both the tentativeness
of his vision and the significance of Teufelsdröckh as a movement
away from reviewers, biographers, and users of polite English.
Yet the question still remains of how Byron shaped the actual
content of Teufelsdröckh's philosophy. Although Carlyle invests

the role of the intellectual with tremendous significance, the status of philosophy in *Sartor* is uneasy. Many of Teufelsdröckh's dogmas, such as his insistence on the value of production and the need to avoid self-consciousness, are truisms of Calvinist morality, disguised in electrifying vocabulary. Others, such as the ideality of space and time, may bear a vague relation to German transcendentalism, but attempts to read *Sartor* as a serious exposition of German philosophy usually conclude that it is highly diluted or simply inaccurate.[37]

Sartor's philosophic peculiarities arise less from Carlyle's incompetence than from his almost impossible position as an author. He broke with the reviews and wrote *Sartor* when he found himself with almost no audience at all, and when such influential voices as Francis Jeffrey's maintained that he never would have one. In contrast, the unphilosophical Byron dominated the audience at which Carlyle aimed, as had such products of Byronism as *Pelham* and Moore's biography. The success of Byronism was a continual reminder of Carlyle's limited power as an intellectual before the broader appeal of all that Byron represented.

Byron's success put Carlyle in a paradoxical position. He had made his reputation by posing the philosophic seriousness of his reviews against Byron's dilettantism. Yet a detailed exposition of German idealism was never going to reach the audience that Byron had held enthralled. Carlyle could not simply replace Byronic falsehoods with philosophic truths imported from Germany. In Book II, as I have argued, he appropriated a Byronic text and rewrote it as a narrative of transition from one kind of author to another. In Books I and III, he developed a brilliant fiction, the Clothes Philosophy, that mediated between a vision of romantic philosophy and the actuality of literature in the 1830s. It pointed to the needs to which philosophy, and theology before it, used to provide answers, and to which Byronism had been supposedly inadequate. The violent assertiveness of this mock-philosophy countered Byron's lack of "philosophic permanence." Carlyle's text overflows with insistently dogmatic statements about man, nature, and the divine. These statements involve less the exposition of ideas than virtuosic rhetorical displays, which impose order on chaos as if they were asserting ideas. *Sartor*'s spiritualization of the material world is less an insight than a grand principle through which Carlyle's rhetoric

orders the perceived heterogeneity of experience. Natural super-
naturalism is a spectacular cliché through which *Sartor* rejects
what it constructs as Byron's emptiness for the seeming fullness
of its philosophy.

The nearly hysterical tone with which Teufelsdröckh asserts his
philosophy, like the text's humor and its complicated interaction
between Editor and hero, all signal the extent to which, in 1830–
31, Carlyle was writing in a vacuum. *Sartor* attempts by sheer
force of rhetoric to mark the end of one kind of author, represented by Byron, and the creation of a new one. When Carlyle
went to London to interest publishers in *Sartor*, he even concentrated on John Murray, as if he wanted to mark this transition
by having his book published by the same man who published
Byron. Neither Murray nor any other publisher was interested,
and when he eventually serialized it, subscriptions to *Fraser's*
plummeted, and utter bewilderment greeted its first publication
in book form. These difficulties reveal how alien Carlyle's fantasy
was in the early 1830s and how thoroughly authorship after the
model of Byron, Moore, and Bulwer Lytton dominated
expectations.

Only long after its publication did *Sartor* achieve fame, once
the success of *The French Revolution* and *Past and Present* had proven
that Carlyle could occupy the position that his earlier text had
projected. After having achieved this position, Carlyle no longer
needed Byron as a figure to be overcome. Yet he never fully
made the transition from Byron to Goethe that he envisioned in
Sartor, partly because his position as a professional intellectual
was never as secure as it was for later writers. For Carlyle as
for Teufelsdröckh, not being Goethe meant retaining traces of
Byron, albeit involuntarily. Although *Sartor*, after its initial failure,
was taken seriously as an alternative to Byronic despair, Carlyle's
insistence on the need to close Byron itself became Byronic to
his contemporaries. John Morley wrote that "Carlylism is the
male of Byronism," and Roden Noel thought "that Carlyle did
most of his cursing and swearing in private, and Byron a good
deal of his in public. That was, on the whole, the difference
between them."[38] For them, Carlyle had not quite made the
transition projected by *Sartor*; like Nietzsche, they recognized
that Carlyle's dishonesty against himself was his most distinctive
quality.

The function of "Byron" in *Sartor* has little to do with Carlyle's reading of Byron's poetry or with what Byron means to an academic audience in the late twentieth century. Rather, "Byron" and Byronism were for Carlyle emblems of a literary system hostile to all that he represented. Influence, in this case, involved far more than an intersubjective relation between two authors. It involved Byronism as a cultural movement that seemed to prevent a man with Carlyle's background from succeeding as a writer. In this context, *Sartor* looks less like an odd translation of German philosophical ideals than a polemical appropriation and redirection of the modes of authorship dominating the British literary marketplace in the early 1830s.

CHAPTER 4

Byron at the margins
Emily Brontë and the fate of Milo

The Brontë children's cultural isolation in Haworth was even more extreme than Carlyle's in Scotland. By their contemporaries' standards, nothing happened to them; as Elizabeth Gaskell noted, "There were no events to chronicle in the Haworth letters."[1] While the other Brontë children eventually attained some social identity, Emily's life was largely without incidents that the world beyond Haworth would have found worth recording. It avoided events and relations that usually formed a woman's history in nineteenth-century England. In particular, at a time when women were defined in relation to men, Emily was little more than the unmarried daughter of the Rev. Patrick Brontë.

This lack of history is itself the most important historical fact about Brontë's work. I emphasize it to question a frequent assumption about her. Critics treat the scarcity of information about her as an accident of history, as if more would be known if more documents had survived. Yet the lack of information is itself symptomatic of her position as a non-person. Not only did her gender almost automatically marginalize her, she did none of the things that a woman was supposed to do to gain an identity: get married and have children, or at least fall in love. Even Emily Dickinson left records of erotic attachments to her sister-in-law and to her "Master"; no such material survives for Emily Brontë.

Byron was a hard act for anyone to follow, but for someone in Brontë's position, he was particularly challenging. His success had depended on his representation of a soul tormented by passions so deep that they supposedly could have belonged only to the author himself. While everything had happened to Byron, nothing happened to Brontë. She had no comparable personal history on which to draw, and as a woman, had few means of attaining one. Unlike many other women in her situation, she did not use the conventional discourse of Protestant spirituality to write an inner history that could compensate for the lack of an outer one. She remained a woman without history.

Her alienation from experience constituted what was recognized from the start as the peculiar "originality" of her writing, a characteristic whose fetishization by Emily and by her later readers I will be exploring throughout this chapter. Her writing seemed to come from nowhere precisely because there was no "life" to be reflected in it. If she had had what her contemporaries considered to be a life, her writing would have been far more conventional because social relationships would have guided her, like most women writers, toward established literary modes. The absence of such relationships and her consequent distance from any conventional authorial stance made her work unlike that of any other writer. In the nineteenth century, most writers as far from literary centers as Brontë did not produce strikingly innovative work. Instead, they were as derivative as possible to demonstrate their familiarity with the major literary trends of the day; their goal was to compensate for their isolation, not to emphasize it.[2] Brontë created a radically different authorial role by using her work to emphasize her position as an outsider. "Originality" distinguished her voice at the margins because it fitted no recognized categories.

Brontë's canon has two sides: poetry, written from her childhood almost to the end of her life, and *Wuthering Heights*, probably written in the mid-1840s. In both, the family mediated her relationship to writing. Critics do not often treat the family as an institution for literary production, but in the case of the Brontës, it assumed a role comparable to that of the periodicals in Carlyle's career or the Apostles in Tennyson's. Brontë's early work belonged to a tiny manuscript culture restricted entirely to the Brontë family. The family provided a context for the work that has since been lost, and the challenge for later interpreters is to understand the work in the face of this absence.

The Brontë children received just enough education to know how unimportant and isolated they were. They used the family as a site of literary production partly to compensate for their powerlessness. Writing had to substitute for many gaps. Their mother was dead; their father, aloof, distant, and possibly drunk;

except for Charlotte, they had no friends of their age or class; their time at school was brief. With no other way to form any relation to a world outside Haworth, they turned to authorship. Their juvenilia were not charming pastorals separated from social or political relevance, but attempts to insert themselves imaginatively into a world from which they were otherwise cut off. Their father had become a political figure of some importance in Yorkshire from the letters that he submitted to the local newspapers: he gained stature entirely from writing.[3] The children similarly used their juvenilia to write themselves into importance, at least within the walls of the Brontë parsonage.

For them, finding a literary voice was tantamount to finding a personal identity. They manifested early an intense sense of what Lawrence Stone has called "affective individualism," the need to assert a unique sense of self.[4] The pressure on authors, especially after Byron, to manifest their original voice blended for the Brontës with the family's role as a social structure fostering the development of individual identities. For the Brontës, the signs of this developing individualism were their intense sibling rivalries in life and in writing. These reflected a fundamental paradox of the bourgeois family: it was supposed to create different identities for children in externally similar circumstances. Sibling rivalry was one method for establishing difference in the face of such similarity.

The few records we have of the children's behavior suggest that their rivalries were intense. One of Charlotte's early stories describes their "furious fights where tooth nail feet and hands were employed with equal fury."[5] Their father remembered them quarreling over "the comparative merits of him [the Duke of Wellington], Buonaparte, Hannibal, and Caesar."[6] They performed noisy and violent plays, which so frightened their servant Tabby that she thought they had gone mad.[7] Although we know little about Emily as a child, the characteristic most often noted about her was a stubborn sense of independence, which let her define herself against her siblings. She never liked to admit that she was influenced by them or by anyone else. Charlotte claimed that "on that mind time and experience alone could work; to the influence of other intellects she was not amenable."[8] Charlotte's description is double-edged, for it suggests that Emily's resistance to influence demonstrated an intense susceptibility to others' opinions, since she set herself against them so resolutely. Emily's dogged "originality" never existed in a vacuum. It depended not on indifference but on defining herself in opposition to potential roles that others created for her.

In the Brontë juvenilia, sibling rivalries became textual ones. Quite early, the children split into two camps: Charlotte and Branwell invented the sagas of Angria; Emily and Anne, those of Gondal. In analyzing Charlotte's juvenilia, Christine Alexander has demonstrated how Charlotte used her work to write herself into individuality. Charlotte's versions of Angrian events differ from Branwell's, and she makes fun of events and characters in Gondal.[9] For Charlotte, and presumably for the other children, these kingdoms let them create their difference from one another.

Their juvenilia also let them address political and cultural events from which they were otherwise isolated. Charlotte and Branwell, for example, took leading political figures for their heroes. Their interest in Byron was inevitable, given their eagerness to assimilate major trends in contemporary culture. Like Carlyle, they learned about Byron through periodical reviews, particularly *Blackwood's Magazine* and *Fraser's Magazine*. In 1829, Charlotte noted that the family received several newspapers and *Blackwood's*, which she called "the most able periodical there is."[10] In 1835, Branwell wrote that "while a child 'Blackwood' formed my chief delight."[11] Charlotte also mentioned in 1831 that Aunt Branwell had "consented to take in '*Fraser's Magazine.*' "[12]

For the Brontës as for Carlyle, periodicals were beacons of culture to those far from Britain's cultural centers. In them, they would have found much material on Byron, including long reviews of Byron biographies, and would have learned critical opinions about Byron, especially that Byron had portrayed himself in his heroes. Most importantly, in 1833, the Rev. Brontë acquired Murray's handsome, seventeen-volume edition of Byron's poems. It included Moore's biography and engravings by the Finden brothers, which the Brontë sisters copied to practice their drawing.[13] In 1834, when Charlotte gave Ellen Nussey a reading list, she demonstrated her knowledge of this material by recommending Moore's biography and by responding to Ellen's doubts about reading Byron with the advice, "Omit . . . the '*Don Juan,*' perhaps the '*Cain,*' of Byron, though the latter is a magnificent poem, and read the rest fearlessly."[14] The presentation of *Don Juan* and *Cain* in Murray's edition, which introduced them with several pages of warning excerpts from reviews, probably influenced her opinion.

Just as the Brontës made political figures their heroes, they imitated Byron in order to participate in a culture that otherwise ignored them. Branwell, as the eldest and the only male, led their games and writings, and the sisters all responded to his Byronic imitations. He would have known several different Byrons, including the witty gossip of the letters, Moore's man of mobility, or the self-absorbed complainer that *Fraser's* described. Yet the Byron whom he most admired was the one who seemed to have had the greatest cultural effect: the clichéd hero with one virtue and a thousand crimes. The children's fascination resulted less from childishly melodramatic imaginations than from their tendency to imitate trends that newspapers and periodicals represented as important. If their juvenilia today seem derivative, we should remember that they were supposed to be: the Brontës were not separating themselves from contemporary artistic trends, but showing how well they knew them.

The Byronic clichés that the Brontës imitated most were elegiac ones, especially moments when a hero mourned his beloved. Elegy may have been particularly vivid for them since they lost their mother and older sisters when they were quite young, and grew up surrounded by graves at Haworth Parsonage. Yet it also may have been a compensation for their youth. Just as they used writing to overcome their cultural isolation, they also used it to combat their immaturity, since their age, like their isolation, was another sign of unimportance to be overcome. They aimed to write not as children but as adults. This striving for maturity guided them to elegy as their dominant genre.

Byronic elegy is most transparent in Branwell's and Charlotte's poetry. A characteristic Byronic effort by Branwell is the long poem "Misery," which opens with an imitation of the Giaour's wild ride as the hero, Lord Albert, rushes to the bed of the dying Maria.[15] Inevitably, he arrives too late to save her, and he witnesses her last breath in a scene modeled on Conrad's arrival at Medora's deathbed in *The Corsair*:

> But where's the Rider gone?
> Up that high turret staircase sped
> With gladdened haste alone.
> The Ante Room looks hushed and still
> With lattice curtained close.   ("Misery," 1.194–99)

He reaches his turret door—he paused—no sound
Broke from within; and all was night around.
He knocks and loudly—footstep nor reply
Announced that any heard or deem'd him nigh.
(*The Corsair* III.581–84)

Byron briefly describes Conrad's agony and concludes with an elegy upon his blasted life. Branwell takes the motif of the mourning hero to an extreme, so that Byron's conclusion is only the midpoint of "Misery." Maria dies at the end of Part I, and Part II opens with Albert, defeated in battle, lying near death on the field. He has dying visions of Maria, recollects his past happiness, and despairs of being reunited with her in heaven. After more than 200 lines, he dies at last when a wounded horse collapses on him. Unlike Byron's Turkish Tales, Branwell's poem is not concerned with plot: he imitates solely elegiac moments. He isolates what periodical reviews taught him was most Byronic, the tormented male psyche, and expands it to the point of ignoring all else.

Charlotte's Angrian poetry largely copies Branwell's, at least with regard to Byronic motifs. Her poem "Each, sound of woe has dyed [*sic*] away upon the summer air" is typical in its treatment of Alexander Percy and his mourning for his dead wife and daughter.[16] Percy is an obvious imitation of Byron's Conrad; Charlotte even calls him a "Corsair": "But yet at times the Corsair had far other moods than these / He still within his bosom held some human sympathies / His heart yet answered to the thrill of loves all conquering power" (78–80). As in Branwell's "Misery," Charlotte's poetic females are idealized visions projected by the male elegiac consciousness. In the poem Percy recollects his first meeting with a maiden "so young so mildly fair" (112) on a rock by the sea, who has since died; she is not even named. Charlotte's and Branwell's poetry exaggerates Byronic gender roles to the point where the chief male activity is remembering lost women. Whereas Byron's Turkish Tales flirted with the possibility that the inner self might belong to a woman as much as to a man, Charlotte's and Branwell's Byronic mode gave it exclusively to men.

Knowing how much Byronic fiction the Brontë children read is difficult. While novels with stereotypically Byronic heroes had been written even before Byron, Caroline Lamb gave the genre new life when she translated her affair with Byron into the

notorious *Glenarvon* (1816). Novels with Byronic heroes prolifer-
ated at the beginning of the century, such as Charles Maturin's
Melmoth the Wanderer (1820) and Mary Shelley's *The Last Man*
(1826). The one example of such fiction mentioned in a Brontë
birthday fragment was Bulwer Lytton's *Eugene Aram* (1832).[17]
Heavily as such novels depended on Byronic clichés, his precedent
was less overwhelming in prose than in poetry. Although novels
were filled with confessions, novelists could create heroes with
Byronic characteristics who would not be taken as versions of
themselves. As a result, it was easier for them than for poets to
adopt a critical or ironic attitude toward a Byronic type even
when they glorified it.

Whether or not she knew contemporary Byronic novelists,
Charlotte's Byronic fiction is like theirs in having a self-
consciously critical edge to it, especially when she describes her
Angrian hero, the Duke of Zamorna.[18] Before 1833, he is kind
and gentle, but after 1833, when the Brontës acquired Byron's
complete works, his personality changes startlingly. Charlotte has
found new models for a hero: "All his usual insufferableness or
irresistibleness, or whatever the ladies choose to call it, surrounding him like an atmosphere, he stands as if a thunderbolt could
neither blast the light of his eyes nor dash the effrontery of his
brow. Keen, glorious being! . . . All here is passion and fire
unquenchable . . . Young duke—Young demon!"[19] The passage
is striking less for how Byronic rhetoric influences it than for
how the Byronic hero looks ridiculous when translated from
poetry to prose. Charlotte's mocking phrase, "insufferableness or
irresistibleness, or whatever the ladies choose to call it," assumes
an urbane, mocking perspective on Zamorna. This hero has
already become a little clichéd for her, as her reference to the
"ladies" suggests.

Nevertheless, Charlotte's mocking perspective has little effect
on her plots, which follow the conventions of novels such as
Glenarvon or *Eugene Aram* in describing the hero's fatal effects on
women who love him. In *Caroline Vernon*, one of the last Angrian
pieces, the heroine is a passionate, impulsive girl raised by
Zamorna, who believes that "reading Lord Byron has half-turned
[her] head."[20] His comment is an in-joke, since Caroline's head
is turned not by reading Byron but by living with a character
modeled on Byron, Zamorna himself. He is a scrupulous guardian

while she is a child, but once she grows and develops a quasi-
incestuous passion for him, he changes abruptly: "Hitherto we
have seen him rather as restraining his passions than yielding
to them . . . but he is going to lay down the last garment of
light & be himself entirely."[21] His eyes beam "with a spark from
the depths of Gehenna," the narrator calls him "Satan's eldest
Son," and he cries "Crede Zamorna!" when Caroline trembles
in his embrace, paraphrasing Byron's motto "*Crede* Byron."[22] She
succumbs to him and disappears; the fragment ends shortly
afterwards.

Although Charlotte's writing earlier in *Caroline Vernon* is not
particularly indebted to Byron or his followers, as soon as sexual
passion appears, stereotypes of Byronism proliferate. Whereas in
the rest of the fragment Charlotte shows considerable skill at
creating psychologically complex portraits, Zamorna and Caroline
assume stereotypical Byronic roles of predator and prey once
overt sexuality erupts. In Byron's poems gender relations are
quite complex, but in the clichéd Byronism of Charlotte and
Branwell they are simple: dominating men annihilate women.
For Charlotte as for Branwell, keeping abreast of Byronic literary
trends meant sacrificing female characters.

The individuality fostered by the family as a site of literary
production invited Emily to distinguish herself from her older
siblings' writing. She and Anne invented a different kingdom,
Gondal. Less is known about it than about Angria because no
Gondal prose survives. What remains is a substantial body of
poetry, much of it fragments, belonging to a lost context.
Although Emily seems to have distinguished between Gondal
and non-Gondal poems, we often do not know if a given poem
was part of the saga. We also know nothing about the relation
between Gondal prose and Gondal poetry. Characters in the
poetry may have been different from those in the prose or, if
they were the same, they may have had different experiences in
the different modes.

Yet having more information about Gondal might not matter.
The temptation with Emily's poetry is to divide it into lyrics
that stem from the imaginary world of Gondal and those that
supposedly reflect the reality of her experience. Yet such a division arbitrarily designates certain lyrics as expressing feelings

that Emily is supposed to have had, while claiming that others reflect only an imaginary life. It ignores the fact that apart from the imaginary world of Gondal, she had no personal "experience," especially not the kind that usually formed the material for lyric poetry. Writing itself constituted the bulk of her experience, so that the pretended division between imaginary and real experience collapses when examining her work.

If the context of the Gondal prose has been lost, the larger context of the Brontë family has not. The Brontës' characteristic intertwining of sibling and textual rivalry meant that Emily had to set herself against Charlotte's and Branwell's Byronic work. As critics have often noted, her poetry did so through its representation of gender. In Gondal, Emily reinvented for female characters the language of Byronic passion. It is hard to know exactly why she foregrounded gender; her choice cannot be attributed simply to her sex, since neither Charlotte nor Anne chose similarly. Moreover, Emily would have had few contemporary models for feminizing Byronic passion. I suspect that she chose gender because it initially provided the most direct means of distinguishing herself from her siblings: Gondal would be to Angria as female was to male. She established her originality not by ignoring Charlotte's and Branwell's writings but by systematically inverting their gender patterns.

Yet her strategy was not as simple as it might seem because female and male were not commensurate terms for Emily. Although she replaced Zamorna, she did not revise her siblings' patriarchal assumptions that defined a woman's history only in relation to men. Instead, she demonstrated how barren female subjectivity became as a result of such assumptions. Since in Byron, especially as filtered through her siblings, women existed to die and be remembered or annihilated by men, her poetry used Byron's work to represent women remembering men. While for Charlotte and Branwell copying Byronic prototypes made it easy to write about the contents of their heroes' memories, Emily had no obvious model for the contents of female memory. Rather than invent one, her poetry emphasized why she had none: if women are excluded from history or experience except in relation to men, then they will have little of their own to remember. Memory and remembrance are obsessive topics for Gondal's women, but they remain eerily without content except as sources of woe. The distinctive blankness of memory in Emily's work ensures the impossibility of any reconstruction of her saga's events. While Byron's work shrouds the heroes' pasts in mystery, Emily gestures to her heroines' pasts but rarely offers specifics about why they are so miserable.

The character most closely associated with Emily's feminization of Byronic memory is Gondal's queen, Augusta Geraldine Almeda (A.G.A.). Most Byronic echoes occur in poems involving A.G.A., whose first name recalls that of Byron's half-sister.[23] In "There shines the moon, at noon of night" (H 9), the first poem in Emily's notebook entitled "Gondal Poems," A.G.A. remembers the death of Lord Elbë.[24] The situation reverses the gender roles of her siblings' work, in which a man idealizes a dead woman. As A.G.A. speaks, her language reveals traces of Byron's, particularly of *Childe Harold's Pilgrimage*:

There shines the moon, at noon of night
("There shines the moon," 1)

How in the noon of night that pibroch thrills
(*Childe Harold* III.26)

My weary feet return at last.
("There shines the moon," 10)

The pilgrim rested here his weary feet.
(*Childe Harold* II.64)

How wildly Time has altered me!
("There shines the moon," 16)

Yet Time, who changes all, had altered him.
(*Childe Harold* III.8)

When A.G.A. speaks about Lord Elbë, rather than becoming a female Harold, her voice disappears as his grows stronger, even in her memory. She stops speaking about herself and instead reconstructs Elbë's dying words and thoughts, until his voice takes over for hers entirely. A.G.A. proves Elbë's fears of her forgetfulness to have been wrong; "years have past," but she still remembers him and his death. She remembers them so well that they block her memory of her own past, or at least substitute for it.

Lyn Pykett notes that "in recalling Elbë's death A.G.A. does not simply tell its story, but rather appropriates his dying consciousness and makes it sing a song which prefigures and echoes her own song in the poem's dramatic present."[25] Yet if A.G.A. describes her past only through the voice of a man, her own perspective is necessarily curtailed. Instead of the instability of gender roles that Byron represents in *The Corsair*, Brontë's treatment of memory is absolutely divided: A.G.A. speaks of the past only by reproducing a man's voice. At the poem's beginning, she emphasizes how much she has changed, and we expect that she will later explain what those changes are and why they occurred. Yet the poem gives no explanation. The gaps highlight how Emily represents female memory as an impossibility except as a reflex of male memory.

Brontë repeats the pattern of "There shines the moon" throughout the Gondal poetry. In "A.G.A." (H 60), A.G.A. begins by asking, "Why do I hate that lone green dell?" and, once again, we expect a history that will explain her hatred. Instead, she announces, "None but one can the secret repeat / Why I hate that lone green dell" (7–8). The "one" is the "noble foe" whom she addresses in the rest of the poem, a man who comforted her in the past but from whom she has been alienated. Only the "foe" can "the secret repeat"; in her own voice, A.G.A. cannot describe her past. The image of the past as a secret to be told by men, not by a woman, epitomizes female alienation from mythic history in Brontë's saga.

Insofar as A.G.A. has a past, only men such as her imprisoned lover, Ferdinand De Samara, reveal it; he bitterly laments her treachery in "Written in the Gaaldine Prison Caves to A.G.A." (H 133), a poem modeled on Byron's "Fare Thee Well!" Like Byron, De Samara recalls the circumstances that have forced him to part from his beloved. In so doing, he remembers a scene of A.G.A.'s past, when she asked him to sing for her; he hopes that its memory will grieve her: "Does memory sleep in Lethean rest? / Or wakes its whisper in thy breast? / O memory, wake! Let scenes return / That even her haughty heart must mourn!" (53–56). A.G.A. is never described as remembering these "scenes"; we know of them only because De Samara mentions them. Although his imprisonment suggests that he has been subordinated to her rule, even in prison he still maintains rhetorical power over her because only he, as a man, describes her past. As in the Byronic poetry of Emily's siblings, female history is articulated only as the product of a male voice and consciousness. We might expect that in the climactic poem, "The Death of A.G.A." (H 143), in which A.G.A. is brutally murdered, she would at last be allowed a retrospect of her own life. Instead, a soldier who mourns her loss speaks her elegy. Even in her final moments, A.G.A.'s past is not hers to tell. By giving the summation of her life to a man, Emily's poem allows A.G.A. to retain the aura of a woman who haunts the imagination of others. Yet it does so only by turning her into a figure whose history is an image projected by male characters. Even the history itself seems dominated by men because, as described by the soldier, it imitates the clichés of Byron's career. Like Byron, she is "adored" and "deified" (380), and has a "comet-like" youth that is "quenched far too soon" (325, 328). When she died, she seemed to be reaching maturity: "Thy passionate youth was nearly past, / The opening sea seemed smooth at last" (337–38); numerous critics had made similar remarks about Byron when he died in 1824.[26] Brontë does not alter the commonplaces about Byron's life to fit a female character, but transfers them wholesale. The soldier's description suggests in miniature the problems for a female poet in relation to a romantic tradition. At her death, A.G.A. finally gets a history, but it is the derivative history of a male "genius," not a distinctively female one.

Emily's critical position in relation to her siblings' Byronic work made her poetry unusual for someone as far removed from centers of literary production as she was. Typically, the poetry of those in such a position resembled Charlotte's and Branwell's in being heavily derivative. From the beginning, Emily's voice set itself against received trends by demonstrating how a Byronic mode underscored female alienation from history, especially when a female character like A.G.A. was at the center of attention. For Emily, unlike for most other writers in her position, being an outsider meant not taking for granted the assumptions of those on the inside.

Although Emily later resurrected A.G.A., the poem about her death marked a subtle change in her work's direction. By 1839, Branwell, Anne, and Charlotte had largely put their juvenilia behind them, left home, and confronted the need to make a living. Southey had even told Charlotte to give up writing after she had sent some of her poetry to him. She did not do so, but she did abandon Angria, and around 1839 wrote her her last Angrian piece. It seemed that even Emily might have to work to support herself. After some unpleasant jobs as a teacher and governess, Charlotte planned to open a school with Emily's help; in 1841, Emily wrote of it, "I hope and trust it may go on and prosper and answer our highest expectations."[27] In 1842, she embarked on one of the few events of her life when she accompanied Charlotte to Brussels, where both went to improve their French. Even this endeavor was too drastic a change for her, perhaps because becoming a teacher would have meant conforming too much to conventional female behavior. Unhappy and ill, she soon came home, and in 1843 lived alone with her father at Haworth.

While the world of Emily's siblings expanded, hers contracted. In coming home to her father, she guaranteed that her exclusion from history continued. Almost nothing is known about her time alone because she did nothing that anyone considered worth recording in a form that would last. Yet her seclusion was not merely a negative retreat from the world. It was also a positive strategy whereby she guaranteed that her "originality" would last. Alone at Haworth, she was seemingly immune from having to confront any influence outside herself. Her poetry became increasingly private, and she seems to have stopped showing it to anyone.[28] It came more to resemble the diaries that other nineteenth-century women kept as a material means for producing an inner life by recording it.

Yet Emily's work differed from that of other women. Most writing about the inner life by women in the first half of the nineteenth century was heavily didactic, usually concerned with domestic and religious topics. This didacticism located the writer's inner life in relation to a specific audience and social context. Emily's work entirely lacked such a connection. The avoidance of any didactic impulse in her work emphasized how cut off it was from any audience or context beyond Emily herself. Her poetry was original because it in itself constituted whatever context her life may have had.

While Charlotte, Anne, and Branwell were seeking their futures in the world outside of Haworth, Emily's future became a topic for her poetic exploration. Since her station remained much as it had, her poetry was the only realm where she might compete with her siblings by inventing a future of her own. Doing so meant refashioning her relation to Byron's poetry as well. Since her earlier poetry was so invested in Byronic modes, writing about the future involved defining it against a past associated with Byronic language. Like so many other Victorian authors, she developed a transition away from Byron, which took the form of poems that described the future as an escape from or transcendence of Byronic modes.

Emily's poetics of ambivalence explored different possibilities without fully endorsing any. This ambivalence was not a sign of indecisiveness, but of her freedom as an author from a context that mandated a univocal message. In her poems about the future, she explored two chief possibilities. The first was the traditional consolation of death and transcendence; the second, associated with the Gondal character of Rosina, demanded leaving behind the past to achieve success. From the point of view of the first, the second looked vain and worldly; from the point of view of the second, the first looked like cowardice. In creating and criticizing both, Emily's poetry emphasized how her solitude let her be at once inside and outside conventional modes.

In "A.G.A. to A.S." (H 169), A.G.A. bids farewell to A.S. and imagines what the future holds. When she describes her past behavior, she speaks like a more repentant version of Byron in "Fare Thee Well!": "I know that I have done thee wrong—/ Have wronged both thee and Heaven—/ And I may mourn my lifetime long / Yet may not be forgiven" (9–12). Like Byron, she presents herself as the guilty party in a failed relationship, although she is more willing to take the blame. As in the earlier poetry, no specifics are given about what her terrible deeds might have been, only her assertions that she indeed has some history with A.S. But the poem's final stanza turns away from Byron and from Emily's earlier poetry: "Till far beyond earth's frenzied strife / That makes destruction joy, / Thy perished faith shall spring to life / And my remorse shall die" (21–24). Whereas in the earlier poetry, A.G.A.'s memory had brought with it pain so overwhelming that it halted her discourse, here she envisions for her and A.S. the promise of transcendence. While the heaven she imagines is not Christian, it offers her a version of Christian consolation. A.S. will experience the resurrection not of his faith in Christ but of his faith in A.G.A., and her remorse will die not because she will be purified of her sins but because A.S. will love her. Beyond the torments of her Byronic past, A.G.A. projects a future that is more promising.

Yet other poems undercut this hope. In "The Philosopher" (H 181), the speaker longs for an escape from tormenting, Byronic desire:

> *"O for the time when I shall sleep*
> *Without identity,*
> *And never care how rain may steep*
> *Or snow may cover me!*
>
> *No promised Heaven, these wild Desires*
> *Could all or half fulfil;*
> *No threatened Hell, with quenchless fires,*
> *Subdue this quenchless will!"*   (7–14)

Her "quenchless fires" echo *Childe Harold*'s famous stanza beginning "But quiet to quick bosoms is a hell," with its description of the "fire . . . quenchless evermore" that cannot "tire / Of aught but rest" (III.42). In Byron, those with such fire become "Conquerors and Kings, / Founders of sects and systems" (III.43). In contrast, the "quenchless will" of Brontë's Philosopher looks forward only to "sleep / Without identity" (7–8). Unlike in "A.G.A. to A.S.," death offers no positive consolation, only a cessation of pain.

The speaker longs for death because she cannot reach the future that she wants. The imaginary fulfillment of her quenchless desires appears as a male muse, whose gaze unites three streams into a vision of unity: "The glad deep sparkled wide and bright—/ White as the sun; far, far more fair / Than the divided sources were!" (38–40), an image that may stem from Byron's portrayal of the ocean as "boundless, endless, and sublime—/ The image of Eternity" (*Childe Harold* IV.183). The Philosopher is frustrated because she has never attained whatever this muse represents. If she had, she "ne'er had raised this coward cry / To cease to think and cease to be—" (47–48). Brontë here demystifies the death-wish of poems like "A.G.A. to A.S." as nothing more than a "coward cry," even though the Philosopher cannot imagine any resolution other than death for her Byronic "quenchless fires."[29] The poem questions the effectiveness of transcendence as a genuine turn away from a present filled with Byronic fire. Just as Emily's early poetry suggested the past's emptiness for female subjectivity, so her later poetry suggests the similar emptiness of the future. Such poems distance her equally from Christian faith and from clichés of romantic transcendence. Neither set of conventions is adequate as an alternative to Byronic passion, destructive though it is.

"Remembrance," one of Emily's best poems, offers a different possibility for moving away from a Byronic past by representing female ambition not as otherworldly transcendence but as political power. The poem has been controversial because it is difficult to decide how sincere its speaker is. Christine Gallant sees her as surrendering entirely to grief: "Her ultimate rejection of the present rewards her with the emotion uncorrupted by 'the empty world.' "[30] Nina Auerbach, in contrast, describes memory in the poem as "a dark call like suicide, denying fullness of being and promise."[31] Like Auerbach, Pykett sees the speaker as eventually overcoming the dangerous lure of memory to reach "a tentative reconciliation to a life of 'change and suffering.' "[32] Irene Tayler offers a third view by describing the speaker as torn between impulses to remember and to forget. Her ambivalent attitude produces "opposing elements of denial and impulsion" that develop "a vivid sense of a structure strained just to the point of explosive but welcome collapse."[33] This critical conflict highlights the difficulty of interpreting how Emily positions her female speaker's relation to her past and future.

Originally, "Remembrance" was entitled "R. Alcona to J. Brenzaida" (H 182); in the Gondal context, it is Rosina of Alcona's lament for the dead Julius Brenzaida. Since the critics cited above have ignored its Gondal context, it is useful to examine Gondal to find what light it casts on who Rosina is and why she, alone among Brontë's female speakers, explicitly desires political power. Her few appearances elsewhere suggest that she is a morally questionable character associated with scheming self-advancement. In "Rosina" (H 151), she cannot sleep while waiting for news of Julius because "dark Ambition's

thwarted pride / Forbade her lids to close" (43–44). She appears
again in "From a Dungeon Wall in the Southern College" (H
178), spoken by a prisoner whose relation to her is similar to
that of De Samara to A.G.A. He describes how any tenderness
in Rosina's eyes "fades faint and wan / Before Ambition's scorch-
ing sun" (57–58). Whereas A.G.A. was already in a position of
power as queen of Gondal, Rosina is Gondal's Becky Sharp, a
woman scheming for power.

Although Emily's language in "R. Alcona to J. Brenzaida" is
not indebted to Byron, her setting is, especially when viewed in
the larger context of her poetry. Rosina's situation of remembering her dead beloved directly parallels that of A.G.A. in
"There shines the moon." Yet what makes the later poem so
different is that Rosina, unlike A.G.A., provides a coherent narrative about her past development and envisions an earthly future,
not a heavenly one. This poem rejects Emily's earlier revision
of Byron by projecting a woman who gains her future because
she can do what A.G.A. could not: imagine agency for herself
apart from men.

Yet just as poems such as "The Philosopher" critiqued conventions of romantic transcendence, so "R. Alcona to J. Brenzaida"
does not present a woman who takes on conventionally masculine
ambition as entirely admirable. Lines such as "Faithful indeed
is the spirit that remembers / After such years of change and
suffering!" (11–12) acquire a suspiciously self-congratulatory tone.
Rosina lingers proudly on the fact that she survived the death
of Julius and notes that "even Despair was powerless to destroy"
her (22). Part of her seems relieved that "fern-leaves cover /
[His] noble heart for ever, ever more" (7–8); her repetition of
"ever" is telling, as if she lingers over the impossibility of his
reappearance. Although she tells him, "All my life's bliss is in
the grave with thee" (20), she has found alternate modes of
sustaining herself: "Sterner desires and darker hopes beset me"
(15). The verb "beset" suggests that the desires and hopes have
come to her unbidden, although her later description of checking
"tears of useless passion" (25) and weaning "her young soul
from yearning" (26) suggest that she does not passively suffer
events to unfold.

Rosina is more dedicated to the "empty world" (32) than she
tells the spirit of Julius directly. Her elaborate rhetoric of grief

comes increasingly to seem like a mask for a woman filled with ambition's pride. The intensity with which she speaks of her love suggests not that she still loves Julius but that she has a command of language powerful enough to achieve some of her "sterner desires." "R. Alcona to J. Brenzaida" sets femininity, love, and memory against masculinity, ambition, and forgetting. In Emily's previous poems, memory overwhelmed female characters. In this poem, a female character uses forgetting as a weapon through which to leave behind her femininity and assume what the poem presents as masculine ambition and determination.

In so doing, Rosina also moves beyond the Byronic mourning of A.G.A. Emily poses Rosina's ambition against the nostalgia associated with Byron. Yet "R. Alcona to J. Brenzaida," like "The Philosopher," avoids treating its alternative to Byron as necessarily superior. Few female poets of the first half of the century sustained such ambivalence; Emily's poem reads more like one of Browning's dramatic monologues. Emily's poetics of ambivalence countered not only her siblings but also an entire range of didactic writings in the 1830s and 1840s defining normative female behavior. Her insistent ambivalence is a reminder of her removal from history. It marked her status as someone not part of a community that prescribed her relation to Byron. She used it to sustain her "originality," her distinctive voice from the margins as one that fitted into no conventional categories.

In 1845, after Charlotte's plans for a school collapsed, the Brontë sisters' circumstances altered. They inherited enough money after Aunt Branwell's death in 1842 to prevent their absolute poverty and to make the need to earn a living less pressing, although Anne and Branwell continued to work at Thorp Green until Branwell's disgrace. After having been separated for several years, the siblings reunited at Haworth. The family had changed because its members met as individuals with different experiences of the world and different relations to writing. Charlotte described them as strangers; their "habit of communication and consultation had been discontinued" and they were "mutually ignorant of the progress [they] might respectively have made."[34] The family no longer defined their writings' boundaries, as it had in their juvenilia. Since their work was not directed solely for themselves, the possibility arose that they might reach a wider audience.

As usual, Branwell led such attempts. Although his experiences with the Robinsons had broken him, he had been more adventurous than his sisters in submitting his work for publication, and in 1842 some of it had even been published.[35] For the sisters, isolated at Haworth, few occupations were available other than teacher or author. Since they had failed as teachers, they turned to authorship. Charlotte, having found Emily's poems, persuaded her to select some for publication. Anne, not wanting to be left out, also contributed her poems, and the sisters together paid Aylott and Jones to print *Poems by Currer, Ellis, and Acton Bell.*

Although the volume sold only two copies, it changed their relations to the literary system because they were at last writing for a public. They had to find a publisher, edit their poems, and learn to prepare a manuscript. In editing their poetry, the sisters removed all marks of Gondal and Angria to make their poems closer to the polite verse of their female contemporaries. Even Emily edited twenty-one of her poems to wrench them from Gondal and make them appropriate for a general audience. In so doing, the sisters eliminated the most original aspect of their poetry, its mythography, and presented to the world a far more conventional façade. They did what authors at the margins usually did: they conformed.

The sole unusual aspect of their first effort was that it was a complete book. A more conventional path would have been to imitate Branwell and submit individual lyrics to reviews. Instead, they conceived of their authorship as a family unit, even though doing so probably made their first appearance in print more difficult than it otherwise would have been. While their pseudonyms were ambiguously gendered to hide the fact that they were women, they still drew attention to the fact that they were related and were publishing as family members. This insistence on the family perhaps resulted from their collective unfamiliarity with publication and consequent unwillingness to venture upon it alone. Instead, they imported a setting that they knew, the family, into more impersonal relations of publication.

Perhaps predicting the failure of their poetry, the sisters, having gained some experience, turned to the potentially far more lucrative genre of the novel.[36] At roughly the same time, Charlotte wrote *The Professor*, published posthumously; Anne, *Agnes Grey*, which had been begun earlier; and Emily, *Wuthering Heights.*

Gaskell describes how they relied on one another during the composition of these works: "At this time, they talked over the stories they were engaged upon, and described their plots. Once or twice a week, each read to the others what she had written, and heard what they had to say about it."[37] Although Charlotte thought that these meetings had little influence on her writing, Gaskell's description suggests that the novels can be seen as reciprocal commentaries on one another. Whereas in the juvenilia the children's antagonistic relations appeared overtly, by the mid-1840s the sisters seemed to have gone their separate ways. Nevertheless, the novels, like the juvenilia, reveal competition as well as cooperation. The sisters still used their writing to create distinctions between three women in ostensibly similar circumstances. The difference between the juvenilia and the novels was that this competition occurred within books designed for the general public.

Writing for this public meant situating themselves in relation to novelistic trends of their day, which once more led them to Byronism. As the oldest sister, Charlotte assumed leadership, and, as in the 1830s, her writing conformed to what seemed to her to be dominant literary fashions. While in the early 1830s those involved imitating Byron in poetry, by the 1840s they involved rejecting him in prose. For Charlotte, to move from poetry to the novel was to move from romance to realism, private to public, feminine to masculine, and Byronism to anti-Byronism.

Her earlier writing had anticipated this movement. Southey had suggested that she give up writing entirely because, as he told her, "The day dreams in which you habitually indulge are likely to induce a distempered state of mind."[38] In a fragment, Charlotte followed Southey's advice: "Still, I long to quit for awhile that burning clime where we have sojourned too long . . . the mind would cease from excitement and turn now to a cooler region where the dawn breaks grey and sober."[39] Yet her division of realism from romance participated in a larger debate about novels in the 1840s. Although these terms had been central from early in the history of novel criticism, they had acquired particular resonances when Charlotte wrote *The Professor*. Popular novels of the 1830s, such as those of Bulwer Lytton, depended heavily on conventions of Byronic romance, even when the novels implicitly criticized them. Theoretical criticism of the novel in the 1840s reacted vigorously against this dependence. In 1845, for example, Archibald Alison, after noting the "prodigious success and widespread popularity" of the "new school of romance," condemned it for its "degrading tendency."[40] Instead, the decade saw an increasing interest in contemporary social realism: "Whereas in 1838 Harriet Martineau had trouble finding a publisher for *Deerbrook*, because its hero was a surgeon, and its heroine came from Birmingham, by 1851 a reviewer in *Fraser's Magazine* welcomed a novel precisely because 'it is perfectly quiet, domestic and truthful . . . there is nothing irreconcilable with every day experience.' "[41] Writers on the novel in the 1840s often associated Byron with romance and the rejection of him with realism. For example, Sarah Ellis hoped in her best-selling *The Daughters of England* (1841) that "readers could be persuaded to reject the Corsairs of Byron and the Isles of Greece . . . for alternative attractions in 'the page of actual life.' "[42] She associated feminine propriety with the rejection of one literary mode for another, romance for realism. The shift toward realism that Ellis requests implied a movement away not only from Byron's poetry, as she specifies, but also from Byron's imitators, such as Bulwer Lytton. Although Bulwer Lyttonesque romance never vanished, in the 1840s novels such as Charles Dickens's *Dombey and Son* (1848), William Makepeace Thackeray's *Vanity Fair* (1848), and Elizabeth Gaskell's *Mary Barton* (1848) provided an alternative associated with domestic realism.

One reason for the trend away from Byronic romance was that by the 1840s, entrepreneurs such as Murray had saturated the market. Byron had become easily available in cheap editions to nearly all who could afford to buy books. Novels imitating his heroes reached an even wider audience, so that the specificity of Byron's poems was lost in the larger, more general phenomenon of imitators. The greater the market for Byron the celebrity, the less he could serve as the vehicle for cultural distinction. While a small group of writers during Byron's lifetime had scorned him to demonstrate their superior discrimination, by the 1840s such a position was becoming available to many. Although the movement toward realism that Ellis demanded was a later version of Carlyle's "Close thy *Byron*; open thy *Goethe*," Carlyle's decree was so radical in the early 1830s that no one would publish it; by the early 1840s it had become conduct-book advice.

Not coincidentally, Ellis demanded that Byron be abandoned at the moment that he was being adopted most fervently by radical members of the working classes. Once the Chartists turned Byron into a hero, Byron became less desirable as an aesthetic model for those in more privileged cultural positions.

Ever attuned to contemporary trends, Charlotte in *The Professor* followed Ellis to the letter: "Novelists should never allow themselves to weary of the study of real Life—if they observed this duty conscientiously, they would give us fewer pictures chequered with vivid contrasts of light and shade; they would seldom elevate their heroes and heroines to the heights of rapture—still seldomer sink them to the depth of despair."[43] In dedicating herself to this program, Charlotte gave the public what a writer like Ellis suggested that it should want: the attractions of "actual life" as opposed to those of Byronic romance. The effect on her writing was a strong polarization between realism and romance, as if they were necessarily antagonistic modes. *The Professor* rejected Byronic romance as enthusiastically as Charlotte's juvenilia had imitated it. Both reactions stemmed from the position of an author on the fringes of the literary system who overcompensated for her marginality by aggressive conformity. Charlotte's novel drew upon her painful experiences with Héger in Belgium, yet it avoided suggesting a Byronic equation between characters and author. Faithful to an anti-romantic program, Charlotte distanced herself from her story by using as her narrator and hero a male figure, William Crimsworth, marked by his matter-of-fact complacency. The object of his desire was not a romantic Caroline Vernon but the plain Frances Henri, who is as far removed from the passionate abandon of Angrian ladies as Crimsworth is from Zamorna.

Yet Frances is not quite as timid as she seems, and, in a telling passage, Charlotte uses her character's romantic side to embody her novel's message about the transition from Byronic romance to realism. Frances is capable of flashes of wit and passion that both attract and annoy Crimsworth. After their marriage, whenever she teases him, he "doses" her with Wordsworth:

She had a difficulty in comprehending his deep, serene, and sober mind; his language too was not facile to her; she had to ask questions; to sue for explanations; to be like a child and a novice and to acknowledge me as her senior and director. Her instinct instantly penetrated and possessed the meaning of more ardent and imaginative writers; Byron excited her; Scott, she loved; Wordsworth, only, she puzzled at, wondered over, and hesitated to pronounce an opinion upon.[44]

The scene's gender relations allegorize Charlotte's program as a narrative of transition away from Byron, who is lumped together with Scott. She aligns masculinity, Wordsworth, Crimsworth, and realism as superior to femininity, Byron/Scott, Frances, and romance. In reading Wordsworth, Frances must "be like a child and a novice" and recognize Crimsworth "as her senior and director." His enjoyment of infantilizing Frances suggests how Charlotte uses her novel to associate Byron with mere juvenilia.

At one point, Crimsworth comments about his relation to another character that "A change had come over the spirit of our intercourse."[45] Although not noted by modern editors, his line echoes the refrain of Byron's "The Dream": "A change came o'er the spirit of my dream." Charlotte's deflation of "dream" to "intercourse" can stand for her novel's banishment of romance. Any such banishment brings an almost inevitable nostalgia because what is offered rarely looks as inviting as what is abandoned. The harshness of the scene of Frances's instruction suggests that Charlotte's repudiation of romance for realism did not occur without regret: Crimsworth could use someone to teach him Byronic dreams. Yet the more seductive Charlotte's writing made romance, the more heroic it was in endorsing Crimsworth's realism. Only if the novel makes Byronic romance attractive could its rejection carry weight as a programmatic choice of realism.

Although we have no details about the relative chronologies of the composition of *Wuthering Heights* and *The Professor*, Emily's novel answered Charlotte's. Even if it did not respond to Charlotte's completed novel, it responded to the general direction that Charlotte took. As in the juvenilia, the family as a site for producing individual identities created an intertwining of sibling and textual rivalry and, once again, Emily established her originality against Charlotte's obedience to convention. Yet the sisters' circumstances had altered. By the time she wrote *The Professor*, Charlotte had had more of what counted as "experience" for women, especially her unrequited love for Héger, while Emily remained a woman without a history. While Charlotte wrote an autobiographical novel, as did Anne in *Agnes Grey*, Emily had guaranteed that she had no such life on which to draw.

Emily's outsider status did not mean that she did not participate in debates over romance and realism, only that her work was not as invested in taking sides as Charlotte's was. If the hierarchical binarisms of Charlotte's novel represented the effect of moving to the popular literary market, Emily's work set itself entirely against Charlotte's obedient didacticism. Like Emily's juvenilia, *Wuthering Heights* produces the marginal voice not as one that supports convention but as one that refuses it. The novel systematically confounds Charlotte's binarisms: realism versus romance, male versus female, and anti-Byron versus Byron. More largely, it takes the perspective of a *spectator ab extra* on contemporary novelistic modes, so that its originality stems not from its avoidance of them but its refusal to situate itself in any one.

Most strikingly, Emily again turns the weakness of her position as a writer, her status as a non-person, into a strength. The novel has an extraordinarily complicated narrative structure to avoid any voice that might be associated with her. Insofar as it succeeds in divorcing the author from the characters, it departs radically from Byron's precedent of self-revelation, no matter how much Heathcliff may remind us of Byron's heroes. Emily ostentatiously exiles herself from the novel, and *Wuthering Heights* ensures that her voice remains that of a woman with no identity. As a writer on the margins, she demystifies other modes without having to bias her critique by claiming her own allegiance.

Gender relations are the chief marker of the novel's unconventionality. Charlotte's didactic rejection of Byron in *The Professor* endorsed the primacy of Crimsworth's reason over Frances's imagination. If the goal of *Wuthering Heights* were simply to counter Charlotte, it would have presented the wildly Byronic adventures of a passionate woman modeled on A.G.A. Yet such a celebration would have simply reversed hierarchies, not subverted them. It also would have meant regressing to the Byronic romances of the 1830s and, more to the point, copying Charlotte's Angrian fiction. *Wuthering Heights* is no straightforward celebration of Byronic romance, although it has often been misread as one. Instead, it uses its portrayal of gender relations to critique the entire debate in which Charlotte's work was participating.

Although psychological and materialist approaches have enriched readings of *Wuthering Heights*, I have a few hesitations about some points that have achieved the status of near-orthodoxy. First, a familiar critical tradition idealizes the love between Catherine Earnshaw and Heathcliff as a privileged realm of freedom battling the constraints of society: "Both the kind and the degree of intensity which they bring to their passion make it impossible to sustain in any of the given social roles."[46] Looking at Catherine and Heathcliff's relationship to Byronic models demands understanding their love with considerably more suspicion. Most of the novel describes not their mutual identification but the violent power struggles through which they destroy one another. I will argue that these struggles arise from the demystifying posture that Emily takes toward Byronic romance.

Second, several materialist critics have described the historical ramifications of *Wuthering Heights* in terms of its relation to events such as the growth of Victorian capitalism, the expansion of the empire, and the rise of the domestic sphere.[47] These accounts assume that the novel's place in history is visible in its plot, which is supposed to endorse a conservative social vision since it ends with the marriage of Catherine Linton and Hareton. Fredric Jameson has attacked traditional criticism of the novel for misreading the significance of Heathcliff's ambiguity; Heathcliff's character "has remained an enigma for intuitive or impressionizing, essentially 'representational,' criticism, which can only seek to resolve the ambiguity in some way (for example, Heathcliff as 'Byronic' hero)."[48] He reads Heathcliff less as a traditional character than as an "actantial locus" whose aging "constitutes the narrative mechanism whereby the alien dynamism of capitalism is reconciled with the immemorial (and cyclical) time of the agricultural life of a country squiredom."[49] For Jameson, Heathcliff is the "locus of *history* in this romance." When critics invoke the archetype of the "Byronic hero" to describe him, according to Jameson, they replace his particular historical significance with a cliché of literary history.

I share Jameson's impatience with the sloppiness with which critics invoke "the Byronic" because the term does little other than dissolve Heathcliff into stereotypes of Romanticism. Yet I question the confidence with which he locates Heathcliff's historical significance within the realm of economics, because he thereby elides the history surrounding the composition and reception of *Wuthering Heights* as literature. His approach cannot explain the novel's outsider status in the 1840s and the shocked reactions that greeted its first appearance. It also privileges the social order represented at the plot's conclusion as one that the novel endorses, even though *Wuthering Heights* is unusual among Victorian novels for the degree to which it refrains from authoritative judgments. Although Jameson's assumption that the novel underwrites the conclusion may react against an older interpretation emphasizing the novel's refusal to choose one side or another, I want to historicize its often noticed moral detachment. The compelling historical question about *Wuthering Heights* is not which side it is on, but how it produces a new side by so skilfully avoiding a choice.

The novel takes characters and motifs from contemporary literary genres and dislocates them so as to puncture the conventions associated with each. Lockwood, who narrates the opening chapters, comes out of the fashionable novels that Carlyle critiqued in *Sartor*. He could have been a minor character in *Pelham*, although his priggish self-satisfaction may also parody Charlotte's insufferable Crimsworth. Yet the novel places him not in high life but in a situation resembling that of one of Scott's heroes: he is a civilized young man from the south who travels north to meet its more "primitive" inhabitants. Lockwood's disappointment upsets the novelistic conventions of describing the picturesque ways of northern "folk." Instead, Lockwood encounters exactly what writers like Charlotte and Ellis were trying to keep out of the 1840s novel, Byronic romance.

After Lockwood's introduction, Nelly Dean's viewpoint dominates the narrative and her conventional judgments heighten sympathy for the characters that she criticizes. She is an embodied conduct book with no use for Byronic romance. Her limited perspective, like Lockwood's, distances the novel's treatment of Byron by containing it within a humdrum perspective. Lockwood and Nelly are Emily's version of the "page of actual life" that Charlotte had produced in *The Professor*, and her novel uses them to heighten the allure of the Byronic passion that they cannot understand. Straightforward Byronic romance would have appeared hopelessly dated in the 1840s, but when seen from the perspective of Nelly and Lockwood, the older mode loses its familiarity and appears incomprehensibly new.

The novel dramatically highlights the Byronic mode's first appearance. Having had a nightmare in which he brutalizes a shivering specter calling itself Catherine Linton, Lockwood yells with terror and awakens Heathcliff, who orders him out of bed. Before Lockwood leaves, he witnesses what he regards as "a piece of superstition" from Heathcliff:

> He got on to the bed, and wrenched open the lattice, bursting, as he pulled at it, into an uncontrollable passion of tears.
> "Come in! come in!" he sobbed. "Cathy, do come. Oh do—*once* more! Oh! my heart's darling! hear me *this* time—Catherine, at last!"
> The spectre showed a spectre's ordinary caprice; it gave no sign of being; but the snow and wind whirled wildly through, even reaching my station, and blowing out the light.   (p. 35)[50]

Heathcliff tries desperately to let in what Lockwood tried to keep out. Though Catherine does not appear, the romance of "uncontrollable passion" that dominates *Wuthering Heights* does. If Lockwood's narrative is a deliberate false start, the novel begins here, with the dramatic return of the Byronic romance that Charlotte had repressed.[51]

Although by the 1840s writers such as Bulwer Lytton had converted Byron's poems into stereotypical motifs, I will concentrate less on the novel's obvious imitations of these than on Emily's uses of particular Byronic texts and the ways that these are illuminated by her access to Byronism.[52] In this scene, as Winifred Gérin and Margiad Evans have demonstrated, the novel draws on *Manfred*, the most fantastic of Byron's poems, as its alternative to Charlotte's sober realism.[53] The allusion to Byron's play shatters the most pressing of Charlotte's binarisms, romance versus realism, when Heathcliff's actions introduce an alternative literary mode into Lockwood's narrative. Heathcliff's plea to the ghost of the dead Catherine derives closely from Manfred's plea to the ghost of the dead Astarte to speak to him, which I discussed in chapter 1: "Speak to me! though it be in wrath;— but say—/ I reck not what—but let me hear thee once—/ This once—once more!" (II.iv.148–50). The similar situations of ·Heathcliff and Manfred, the spectralization of Catherine and Astarte, and the incestuous nature of their relationships suggest the prominence of Byron's work in Emily's novel. Not coincidentally, given the dynamics of sibling rivalry in the Brontë family, *Manfred* confronted most directly of all Byron's works the challenge of defining identity against that of family members who were at once similar and different. Emily used Byron's drama about incest among siblings to mediate her own relations to her siblings' texts.

Yet the novel does not simply copy *Manfred*. Heathcliff is an even more passionate Manfred, as if, in response to Charlotte's abandonment of romance in Crimsworth, Emily takes her hero to the opposite extreme by outdoing even one of Byron's. Heathcliff cannot sever his relation to Catherine as Manfred does with Astarte because he is at once a more faithful and a more narcissistic lover. The difference between Manfred's "let me hear thee once" and Heathcliff's "Hear me *this* time" suggests the difference between the two. Manfred's gropings after knowledge in his questions to Astarte have an unacknowledged selfishness: "Am I forgiven?," "Say, shall we meet again?," "Say, thou lovest me" (ii.iv.153, 154, 155). Astarte's presence is not enough; Manfred insists that she talk about him. Heathcliff's relation to Catherine, in contrast, is not qualified by linguistic communication. For him, merely to see her again would suffice. The pathos of her non-appearance, which Lockwood cruelly calls "a spectre's ordinary caprice," intensifies the stark simplicity of Heathcliff's plea, as opposed to Manfred's insistent questions.

The end of *Wuthering Heights* draws on *Manfred* to sharpen the distinction that this scene develops between the passion of Heathcliff and Manfred. Manfred's concluding fantasy of autonomy stems from the extinction of Astarte's hold over him, while Heathcliff's feverish bliss stems from the power of his devotion to Catherine. Manfred rejects the Abbot's Christian consolation because Christianity is unable to comprehend his isolation; Heathcliff rejects Nelly's Christianity because his heaven is a reunion with Catherine. The Abbot speculates on Manfred's fate only to reassert the fact of his death: "He's gone—his soul hath ta'en its earthless flight—/ Wither? I dread to think—but he is gone" (iii.iv.152–53). In contrast, a shepherd boy tells Nelly that he has seen "Heathcliff and a woman, yonder, under t'Nab" (p. 412), and the country people say that "he *walks*." No reunion occurs for Manfred and Astarte, but Heathcliff's union with Catherine is allowed a spectral existence among the lower class, whose closeness to the earth seems to allow them nearer access to the primitive energy of Heathcliff's love. Next to Heathcliff's love for Catherine, Manfred's love for Astarte seems a poor thing.

The novel also strips Manfred's class and blood from Heathcliff to prevent his love for Catherine from seeming to arise from socially predetermined conditions. Emily writes as if Byron's "naked heart" were not autonomous enough. Like Teufelsdröckh, Heathcliff is an orphan, and as in Carlyle's text the absence of origin figures a lack of social relations biasing the character's future. Although Mr. Earnshaw's discovery of Heathcliff in Liverpool has several possible historical resonances, Heathcliff's lack of a family underscores how thoroughly his love for Catherine alone determines his development. In contrast, Manfred's character arises in opposition to his father, who was "proud,—but gay and free,—/ A warrior and a reveller" (iii.iii.19–20). His love for Astarte has an aura of fatal necessity because she is his sister, so that Manfred does not find her; she is given to him. In contrast, biology does not predetermine the love between Heathcliff and Catherine. When Nelly returns after having been sent out of the house, Catherine and Heathcliff have suddenly become "very thick" (p. 46). The symbolic incest of their relationship is more shocking than the actual incest of the relation between Manfred and Astarte because it is not conditioned by ties of blood. It is as if the only true incest in the novel involves relations between selves that resemble one another not from mere heredity, but from deeper bonds.

Although in Heathcliff's character Emily defies the chilly realism of *The Professor* by intensifying and "correcting" Manfred's passion, the novel hardly presents Heathcliff as a romantic ideal. Doing so would align it too closely with a single literary mode, and it consistently avoids such alignment. While its treatment of *Manfred* pushes against the restrictions of realism, it does not idealize Byronic romance. Instead, Heathcliff's story suggests the consequences of taking Manfred's narcissism to an extreme within a realistic setting. Underneath Heathcliff's greater fidelity to Catherine lies an egoistic violence far more aggressive than that of Manfred, Zamorna, or Crimsworth.

The critique of Byronic romance is most evident in Heathcliff's behavior toward Isabella, whom he treats with relentless savagery. Isabella's mistake was to imagine that Heathcliff really was one of Byron's heroes; he says, "She abandoned [her friends] under a delusion ... picturing in me a hero of romance, and expecting unlimited indulgences from my chivalrous devotion" (p. 183). Like most characters in the novel, Isabella can be understood as a character dislocated from an alternative literary mode. Her situation in *Wuthering Heights* revises that of heroines destroyed by their love for the hero in Byronic romances, as imitated in Charlotte's *Caroline Vernon*. Just as Caroline succumbed to the Byronic Zamorna because of an overactive imagination stimulated by reading romances, so Isabella mistakes Heathcliff for a Byronic "hero of romance." Her fate is essentially Caroline's: annihilation. Although she escapes from Heathcliff, her exit from the narrative is equivalent to her death as a character. Her story allows Emily's novel to glance backward at the cruder Byronism of Angria and Charlotte's novelistic models by rewriting the sexual allure of figures like Zamorna as mere sadism.

Yet even Heathcliff's ruthless treatment of Isabella is more conventional than the novel's central erotic relationship, his love for Catherine. The extent to which later adapters have tamed the plot into a stormy romance reflects how odd the original is, because Heathcliff's narcissism is far more apparent in his treatment of Catherine than in his treatment of Isabella. Once Catherine returns from her adventure at Thrushcross Grange, their conflicts are incessant. His relationship to her improves only after her death, as she predicts when she asks bitterly, "Will you be happy when I am in the earth?" (p. 195). Only then can Heathcliff believe that she obeys his command to haunt him: "No! she has disturbed me, night and day, through eighteen years — incessantly — remorselessly" (p. 349). As a figment of his imagination, she is more faithful than she is in life.

His stance in much of the book's second half, as he remembers the dead Catherine, repeats the motif of Byronic men mourning dead women that Charlotte and Branwell portrayed in their Angrian poetry. Yet his desire for a reunion with her becomes grotesquely literal. Because her spirit will not appear to him, he forces the sexton to unearth her coffin, and he opens the lid to see her face. He tells Nelly how he had planned to do the same immediately after her death: " 'If I can only get this off,' I muttered, 'I wish they may shovel in the earth over us both!'

and I wrenched more desperately still. There was another sigh, close at my ear . . . I knew no living thing in flesh and blood was by—but . . . I felt that Cathy was there, not under me, but on the earth" (p. 350). Heathcliff is closer to Catherine here than he is while she is alive, because after her death he projects an ideal version of her, a Catherine who pursues him with an enthusiasm that the real Catherine does not have. His visions always remain merely visions: no one else imagines that Catherine follows him as he imagines she does. Manfred's ability simply to forget Astarte almost seems preferable to Heathcliff's devotion to a Catherine who exists only in his mind.

His necrophilia is the novel's figure for narcissism driven to an extreme because he exercises over Catherine's body the power he did not have over her mind. Catherine in her madness even predicts his behavior: " 'They may bury me twelve feet deep, and throw the church down over me, but I won't rest till you are with me' . . . She paused, and resumed with a strange smile. 'He's considering . . . he'd rather I'd come to him!' " (p. 154). She begins by imagining his scenario, in which she restlessly pursues him, but Emily's masterstroke is to have her recognize his second thoughts. All his visions after her death are his way of making her come to him, as are his plans for their mingling after death. Emily's novel foregrounds the narcissism of Heathcliff's fidelity; his most attractive trait is also his most solipsistic.

The novel's representation of Heathcliff's desire is particularly telling in terms of the collapse of *The Professor*'s opposition between romance and realism. Initially, when Lockwood witnesses Heathcliff calling to Catherine's ghost, the scene presented the eruption of romance into a realistic mode. Heathcliff's passion is entirely "other" from the literary modes to which Lockwood and Nelly belong. Yet as the novel progresses, it becomes apparent that Heathcliff operates skilfully to achieve his ends. If he is a Byronic hero, he is one with a far greater ability to manipulate social structures than Byron's heroes have. Part of what makes his treatment of Isabella so appalling is that it is thoroughly legal, as is his treatment of his son and Catherine Linton. When he breaks the law, no disciplinary force punishes him because he effectively controls the law; he even bribes the lawyer, Mr. Green. The novel demystifies the narcissism of the Byronic hero in part by suggesting that, far from departing from societal norms, it works fully in accord with them. Nothing in the novel is more representative of the "page of actual life" than Heathcliff's brutality.

Nevertheless, Heathcliff cannot realize his greatest desire, a reunion with Catherine, despite his skill in manipulating the social structure. If during the novel's middle Emily demonstrates how comfortable Heathcliff is in a realistic literary mode, by the end, when his desire for Catherine has become obsessive, the novel's imitation of *Manfred* restores him once more to its adaptation of Byronic romance. This final oscillation underscores the difficulty of judging him in terms of any single literary mode. He seems *sui generis*, as Nelly suggests when she realizes that nothing can go on his tombstone except for his name. When Inga-Stina Ewbank declares Heathcliff to be "a Byron with the glamour gone, with cruelty and torture, physical and mental, seen from the point of view of the tortured ones as well, and hence seen for what they are,"[54] she registers an aspect of Heathcliff overlooked surprisingly often by critics, but she still gives a partial view by emphasizing only his cruelty. Through Heathcliff, Emily's novel presents the Byronic lover at his best and at his worst, and reveals that the two are the same.

In Gondal, Emily's adaptation of Byron distinguished itself from her siblings' simply by replacing a male figure with a female one. *Wuthering Heights*, in contrast, differentiates itself from *The Professor* by countering its representation of sexual relations. In part, it recuperates the Byronic romance that Charlotte rejects. Yet while Heathcliff's relation to this Byronic element is obvious, Catherine Earnshaw does not seem like any heroine either in Byron or in *The Professor*. Emily's revision of *Manfred* early in the novel underscores this difference. Catherine's ghost does not appear when her lover calls, unlike Astarte's. In the Byron edition that the Brontës owned, the scene that Emily imitates is glossed by John Wilson: "We think of Astarte as young, beautiful, innocent—guilty—lost—murdered—buried—judged—pardoned; but still, in her permitted visit to earth, speaking in a voice of sorrow, and with a countenance yet pale with mortal trouble."[55] For Wilson, Astarte is an extreme example of the Byronic heroine as helpless victim. In Catherine Earnshaw, Emily rewrites Astarte to make her heroine far more than Wilson's sentimental wisp.

Yet this rewriting's irony is that Catherine, for all her strength, remains as much a victim as Astarte. The unsettling of anti-Byronic realism and Byronic romance that characterizes Heathcliff works quite differently for a female character. In particular, the social structures that Heathcliff masters make Catherine's life impossible. As in Emily's juvenilia, when she foregrounds female experience, she emphasizes the extent to which men determine it. In both the realistic and romance writings of her contemporaries, especially Charlotte's, female characters eventually submit themselves to men. Emily's writing sets itself against these conventions by suggesting that the only way for a female character not to submit to a male one is to be split between two men at the same time. Catherine's relation to contemporary literary modes appears as a choice between two equally problematic men: Heathcliff, romance, and Byronism are set against Edgar, realism, and anti-Byronism. If in Heathcliff's story, the novel represents the hero's power to move between literary modes, Catherine's story reveals how unavailable such oscillation is to a female character.

Wuthering Heights uses Byronic subtexts to represent the difficulty of Catherine's position as a conflict between realism and romance. A telling moment juxtaposes Moore's biography (realism) with Byron's "Ode to Napoleon Buonaparte" (romance) to characterize the conflicts in Catherine's situation. As Gérin has suggested, Moore gave Emily a model for representing the choice of realism over romance in terms of a rejection of Byron when he describes how Mary Chaworth spurns Byron. Moore notes that

a circumstance mentioned in [Byron's] "Memoranda," as one of the most painful of those humiliations to which the defect in his foot had exposed him, must have let the truth in, with dreadful certainty, upon his heart. He either was told of, or overheard, Miss Chaworth saying to her maid "Do you think I could care anything for that lame boy?" This speech, as he himself described it, was like a shot through his heart. Though late at night when he heard it, he instantly darted out of the house, and scarcely knowing whither he ran, never stopped till he found himself at Newstead.[56] (*M*, 1: 55–56)

Like Byron, Heathcliff runs away from Wuthering Heights after overhearing Catherine explain to Nelly, "It would degrade me to marry Heathcliff, now" (p. 100). While so much contemporary fiction represented the Byronic hero as irresistible to women,

Emily found in Moore himself the evidence that a woman could reject Byron. Moore merely presents Byron's disappointment as a sentimental episode in the life of a sensitive aristocrat. Emily rewrites it from the woman's point of view and makes it a far more serious event by exposing the economic constraints that underlie what looks like feminine coquetry. Catherine's painful choice of Edgar over Heathcliff suggests that her story will be neither an Angrian romance nor a tale of fashionable life like Moore's. Instead, she makes the choice that she is supposed to make as the daughter of Yorkshire gentry.

Although Heathcliff understands Catherine's rejection to be cruel caprice, her decision depends on social relations beyond her control. She is quite clear-sighted about the degree to which love is not enough; marriage to Heathcliff would deprive her of money and all social agency. Absurd as her fantasy of helping Heathcliff with Edgar's money may appear, it suggests how thoroughly her lack of economic power constrains her choices. She perhaps underestimates Heathcliff's ability to raise himself by his own efforts, but little in the novel has given any evidence of his ability to do so. Only her rejection provides him with the incentive to become a gentleman. The real winner of the scene is Edgar's money. Catherine recognizes that it has power to create change in a way that she does not.

In choosing Edgar over Heathcliff, Catherine closes her Byron. From the point of view of realists such as Charlotte and Sarah Ellis, her choice ought to lead to a happy conclusion. Marriage should mature her from a passionate adolescent to a sober adult. Emily's novel counters this myth of progress by emphasizing that Catherine's heart remains with Heathcliff. Its most explicit allusion to a poem by Byron occurs when Catherine suggests how much more Heathcliff means to her than Edgar does. Immediately after Heathcliff runs away, she protests violently to Nelly the impossibility of ever separating from him: " 'We separated!' she exclaimed, with an accent of indignation. 'Who is to separate us, pray? They'll meet the fate of Milo! Not as long as I live, Ellen—for no mortal creature' " (p. 101). Her reference to Milo is odd. In terms of her character, it is uncharacteristically erudite, since she is proud of her lack of book-learning. It is also uncharacteristic in a novel where few characters refer to myths and certainly not to ones as obscure as that of Milo. It stands out as a moment in which an alternative discourse disrupts the "realistic" representation of a character.

As the editors of the Clarendon *Wuthering Heights* note (pp. 422–23), Emily probably learned the Milo myth from Byron's "Ode to Napoleon Buonaparte":

> He who of old would rend the oak,
>   Dreamed not of the rebound;
> Chained by the trunk he vainly broke—
>   Alone—how looked he round?
> Thou in the sternness of thy strength
> An equal deed has done at length,
>   And darker fate hast found:
> He fell, the forest-prowlers' prey;
> But thou must eat thy heart away!   (46–54)

Although Milo is not named in Byron's poem, the 1832–33 Murray edition glossed the passage with this excerpt from Byron's diary: "Like Milo, he would rend the oak; but it closed again, wedged his hands, and now the beasts—lion, bear, down to the dirtiest jackall—may all tear him."[57] In Byron's poem, Milo is another Prometheus, a striving man punished for his audacity. His fate has the neat symmetry of a fairy-tale: he who tore, is torn himself. The greatest Prometheus, Napoleon, has done an "equal deed" (51) to Milo's, but his torment will be even worse because it will be self-inflicted: "But thou must eat thy heart away!" (54). For Byron, the comparison of Napoleon to Milo assimilates Napoleon's fate to legend; social and political aspects of Napoleon's career fade before the spectacle of the suffering, isolated individual punished for his transgressions. Byron's passage underscores the grand but fatal effect of Romantic will, which alone determines the self's victories and punishments.

When *Wuthering Heights* adapts this passage, it again revises a Byronic text from a female character's point of view. At first, it seems as if the spirit of the allusion is close to that of Byron's poem. Catherine does not compare herself to Milo; instead, her allusion suggests that she and Heathcliff are like the oak that cannot be torn, as well as like the beasts who would rend any potential Milos having to separate them. Her allusion puts her relationship with Heathcliff in the same mythic world where Byron located Napoleon, one that the autonomous will determines, not the force of social or political circumstance.

Yet there is an ironic undercurrent to her speech, because Catherine has already played the role of Milo by separating Heathcliff from her. Brontë underscores this irony with the storm that breaks out a few pages after this speech, in which a tree is actually rent: "There was a violent wind, as well as thunder, and either one or the other split a tree off at the corner of the building" (p. 105). Catherine describes her relation to Heathcliff in mythical terms only after it has been destroyed, as if her ability to verbalize it signaled its death. Her seeming to give herself up to absolute unity with Heathcliff is a rhetorical fiction to mask the reality of her conscious separation from him.

The pathos of Catherine's desperate assertion of unity unmasks the delusions of autonomy in Byron's ode by reversing the relevant gender roles. Byron takes the most politicized figure of his generation, Napoleon, and treats him in sublime isolation from all structures that might determine his behavior except the autonomous self. When in *Wuthering Heights* a female character makes similar claims to transcend culture, the claims operate chiefly as a cruel delusion: the more violently Catherine protests the autonomy of her love for Heathcliff, the more absolutely she reveals her powerlessness to sustain it. If she has been her own Milo in separating herself from Heathcliff, her act has not derived from mere hubris, like that of Byron's Napoleon, but from an impossible social situation.

Yet money alone does not determine Catherine's decision to play her own Milo. Her reference to the Milo myth rewrites the Byronic image to associate it with natural unity between a man and a woman. As I argued in the first chapter, Byron's poems, especially *Manfred*, explore this unity by suggesting the dangerous effects for a male hero of identifying too closely with a female figure. Emily's novel, in contrast, suggests the dangers for a female character of identifying with a male one. Such a fate reproduces too exactly the fate of her siblings' heroines in their work, as well as the unquestioned subordination of women to men in the literary modes of the 1840s. Emily's novel develops a considerably more ambivalent picture of sexual relations.

Tellingly, Heathcliff never assumes that he and Catherine are as inseparable as an oak, despite his conventional references to her as his soul. Catherine alone voices the fantasy of Byronic romance, that male and female souls might be identical:

If all else perished, and *he* remained, I should still continue to be; and
if all else remained, and he were annihilated, the Universe would turn
to a mighty stranger. I should not seem a part of it . . . my love for
Heathcliff resembles the eternal rocks beneath—a source of little visible
delight, but necessary. Nelly, I *am* Heathcliff—he's always, always in
my mind—not as a pleasure, any more than I am always a pleasure
to myself—but, as my own being. (pp. 101–02)

Catherine's identification with Heathcliff is not as unambiguously
positive as it is often taken to be. She claims to have surrendered
herself to a masculine presence as thoroughly as the most conventional heroine of the 1840s. "I *am* Heathcliff" does not imply
"Heathcliff is me," and Heathcliff never claims to be Catherine.
Rather than celebrating equality, Catherine's speech suggests the
subordination lurking in the romance of identity. Far from being a
sexual radical, Catherine here seems more like one of Charlotte's
Angrian heroines succumbing to Zamorna. As Gérin notes, her
words echo those of Charlotte's most clinging Angrian heroine,
Mina Laury, who describes her absolute obedience to Zamorna:
"He was sometimes more to me than a human being—he superseded all things—all affections, all interests, all fears or hopes
or principles—Unconnected with him my mind would be a
blank—cold, dead, susceptible only of a sense of despair."[58]
Catherine's words suggest that even when a female character
takes on a Byronic strength of passion, she still subordinates her
identity to a male one as completely as any heroine in the
Byronic tradition.

What prevents Catherine from manifesting such subordination
is that her actions do not live up to her words. Rather than
being Heathcliff, she spends much of her time working at being
as distinct from him as possible. Her actions make sense less as
a demonstration of spiritual kinship with Heathcliff than as a
means of preserving autonomy next to his overwhelming narcissism. Her marriage to Edgar, for example, gives her an identity
as someone other than Heathcliff, Mrs. Edgar Linton, although
she works at maintaining her independence from Edgar as well.
For Catherine, to be with either Heathcliff or Edgar exclusively
is to have no story. She exists as a character only because the
conflict between the two gives her some possibility for voice,
even if it is ultimately self-destructive. In terms of literary modes,
Emily's novel suggests that both Byronic romance and anti-

Byronic realism give the heroine little identity apart from a male figure; she exists only by setting them against one another.

While Catherine's struggle against Edgar's authority is obvious, her need to maintain herself against Heathcliff has received less attention. In her death scene, she claims to have internalized him: " 'That is not *my* Heathcliff. I shall love mine yet; and take him with me—he's in my soul . . . I'm wearying to escape into that glorious world, and to be always there . . . I shall be incomparably beyond and above you all. I *wonder* he won't be near me!' She went on to herself. 'I thought he wished it. Heathcliff, dear! you should not be sullen now. Do come to me, Heathcliff' " (p. 197). This passage is difficult to follow because of its sharp changes of direction. Catherine begins by turning against her earlier claim to be Heathcliff. Instead, she has internalized him to the extent that Heathcliff himself does not matter. Suddenly, she moves to a passage whose claims for visionary autonomy echo those of Brontë's poetry; she will be "incomparably beyond and above [them] all." At this moment, she comes closer to the autonomy that Manfred claims for himself in his final moments than Heathcliff ever does, for it is not certain that her heaven even has room for him. Yet her jump from "I shall be incomparably beyond and above you all" to "I *wonder* he won't be near me!" is startling, and suggests that her immortal longings are insincere. Her speech has an ulterior motive: she is angling for Heathcliff's attention, and when he does not respond, she throws off her claims to have internalized him and to be "above them" all. Instead, she pleads that he will come to her, as he will later plead for her to come to him. Yet even as she pleads, it is too late: physical proximity cannot close the gaps between them. As in her previous speech, she is torn between her desires to be Heathcliff, to be beyond him, and to be close to him.

Catherine finally is driven to slow but determined suicide by the impossibility for a woman to do what Heathcliff does so well: manipulate the social structure. With no ability to affect anyone's behavior except her own, she plays her own Milo by destroying herself. Unlike Rosina, she cannot forget her past; in the end, she resembles A.G.A., tormented by the overwhelming power of memory. In her mad scene, she describes to Nelly the forces that she thinks are driving her insane:

I thought . . . that I was enclosed in the oak-panelled bed at home; and my heart ached with some great grief which, just waking, I could not recollect . . . and most strangely, the whole last seven years of my life grew a blank! I did not recall that they had been at all. I was a child; my father was just buried, and my misery arose from the separation that Hindley had ordered between me and Heathcliff . . . I wish I were out of doors—I wish I were a girl again, half savage and hardy, and free! (pp. 152–53)

Like A.G.A., memories invade her mind to cancel out her present identity, so that "the whole last seven years of [her] life grew a blank." She glimpses a time when no Milo had split the oak representing her love for Heathcliff; the wood of the "oak-panelled bed" in which the two slept together may even carry a hint of the Milo myth. Having been separated from Heathcliff and from her former self, she longs only for a return to her girlhood. This return does not seem to include Heathcliff's company, as if she longed for a time when she was wholly herself, prior to both Heathcliff and Edgar. As Nelly says, "her latest ideas wandered back to pleasant early days" (p. 204), as if her only escape is to separate herself from them entirely.

In its representation of Catherine, Emily's novel avoids the standard fate whereby heroines submit themselves to men in both the anti-Byronic mode of *The Professor* and the Byronic one of Bulwer Lytton or the Angrian fiction. Yet *Wuthering Heights* still emphasizes the terrible effects that result from either because in both the history of women depends entirely on their relations to men. The first half of *Wuthering Heights* ultimately reveals that the choice posed by *The Professor* between realism and romance is, for a female character, no choice at all. Catherine's independence is not a positive quality but one that arises from an impossible choice between two suitors embodying Byronic and anti-Byronic modes. She succumbs to neither, but the struggle kills her. The second half of the novel takes up the challenge of creating a heroine whose story reworks the binarisms that collided so violently in the first half of *Wuthering Heights*.

As Stevie Davies has stressed, Catherine Earnshaw's death is Catherine Linton's birth, and the conjunction of the two events suggests that the daughter will be antithetical to the mother.[59] At least with respect to a Byronic presence, the second Catherine shares nothing with the first. Whereas Emily represented the first Catherine's struggle in terms of a conflict of realism and romance, the second fits squarely into realism. At first glance, Catherine Linton is more like Frances Henri or Agnes Grey than her mother. The absence in her of all that Byronic romance signified in the first half of the novel accounts in part for the near-universal disdain with which critics treat her.[60] Gilbert and Gubar see her as little more than an allegory of domesticity: "Because she is a dutiful daughter, moreover, Catherine II is a cook, nurse, teacher, and housekeeper. In other words, where her mother was a heedless wild child, Catherine II promises to become an ideal Victorian woman, all of whose virtues are in some sense associated with daughterhood, wifehood, motherhood."[61] For them, the second Catherine fits as securely in realism as the first fit in romance.

Yet this polarization of the mother as "wild child" versus daughter as "ideal Victorian woman" oversimplifies both. Emily's novel consistently disrupts such neat categorizations and the stereotypes of feminine behavior associated with them. If the story of the first Catherine revealed how completely both Byronic romance and anti-Byronic realism involved male domination of women, that of the second demonstrates what a female character must become in order to survive this domination. Where her mother fought against male control, Catherine uses relations with several men to guarantee that no single bond dominates her life. In particular, she counters the power that the men of the older generation, Edgar and Heathcliff, have over her through her relations to men of the younger generation, Linton and Hareton.

The novel gives us several hints that Catherine is not as yielding as Nelly, and Gilbert and Gubar, make her out to be. Lockwood maintains, "She does not seem so amiable . . . as Mrs. Dean would persuade me to believe" (p. 362), and Zillah dislikes her. Most significantly, her pursuit of Linton Heathcliff leads her almost from her first appearance to chafe against Edgar's restrictions. Although Linton is one of the most disagreeable characters in fiction, his weakness allows her to dominate him easily and to escape from her virtual imprisonment by Edgar. Yet for all the narcissism of her love for Linton, she turns her relationship to him into a source of strength. The irony of Heathcliff's plotting in the novel's second half is that he wastes his violence in forcing Catherine to do what she would do anyway.

She even tells him, "I promise to marry Linton—papa would like me to, and I love him—and why should you wish to force me to do what I'll willingly do of myself?" (p. 332). Although she is wrong in thinking that her father would approve, and Nelly vehemently objects to the marriage, her ambition to stay with Linton proves more than a match for Heathcliff's violence.

When Heathcliff taunts her with the prospect of her wretched union with Linton, she turns on him with a surprising intensity: "I know he has a bad nature . . . he's your son. But I'm glad I've a better, to forgive it . . . Mr. Heathcliff, *you* have *nobody* to love you; and, however miserable you make us, we shall still have the revenge of thinking that your cruelty arises from your greater misery! . . . *Nobody* loves you—*nobody* will cry for you, when you die! I wouldn't be you!" (p. 348). Although Gilbert and Gubar find in this passage evidence of Catherine's "patriarchal Christianity," her power comes not from piety but from her ability to fashion her relation to Linton into more than it is worth.[62] Nothing in the novel separates her more from her mother than her parting shot, "I wouldn't be you!", which reverses her mother's "I *am* Heathcliff." For all Heathcliff's violence, her remark effectively silences him, and he immediately afterwards talks to Nelly about digging up the first Catherine's grave, as if to counter the daughter's charge of his loneliness. Against Heathcliff's financial scheming she asserts the primacy of her ability to form attachments.

Yet even as she does so, she also reveals that her relation to Linton is hardly selfless. It gives her a chance to demonstrate her better nature, and she usually treats Linton as a pet; she enjoys him only while she can dominate him. The first Catherine, for all her passion, had little ability to control the men in her life, while the second, who is far less overtly domineering, has a better ability to assert power, even against Heathcliff. When she loses one man, she quickly finds another with whom she can demonstrate her better nature. For example, when she first appears, her dedication to her father is unswerving: "I love him better than myself, Ellen" (p. 282). Yet during his final illness, she goes to meet Linton and shows signs of forgetting Edgar: "[H]er poor little heart reproached itself for even that passing forgetfulness of its cares" (p. 323). Though she may feel guilty, her forgetfulness aids her against Heathcliff, because she transfers her love for Edgar to Linton: "Linton is all I have to love in the world" (p. 347). After Linton's death, she locks herself in her memories, complaining that she is "*stalled*" (p. 363) and that "her life was useless" (p. 377). For a few pages, Emily raises the specter of the first Catherine, and it seems that the second Catherine also will become a victim of the past. Given all she has suffered, her ability to forget her wrongs seems almost like insensibility, particularly when compared with her mother's intense suffering. Nevertheless, she soon turns to Hareton: "I was miserable and bitter at everybody; but, now I thank you, and beg you to forgive me, what can I do besides?" (p. 380). Her attitude spreads to those around her; Joseph says that because of Catherine, Hareton has "forgotten all E done for him, un' made on him" (p. 388). Catherine is determined to have a happy ending.

In the first Catherine, the novel countered Charlotte's didactic account of the transition from romance to realism by suggesting how both were equally problematic for female characters. In the second, the novel instead presents an eerily unsinkable heroine. She moves from one man to another with a forgetfulness that is absolute: she hardly mentions her father after his death or Linton after his. Especially after her mother's behavior, her ability to rise so completely above the tragedies she has suffered, like Gondal's Rosina, is slightly chilly. While not an overt parody of Frances Henri, she is almost too good at accommodating herself to men, although always to ones who do not oppose her. Heathcliff claims that the first Catherine is relentless, but the adjective may apply better to the daughter.

The coldness that allows Catherine to achieve greater happiness than her mother also prevents the novel from endorsing her. Although materialist critics often take her happy marriage to Hareton to represent the domestic relations supported by the novel, as if Emily Brontë were Nelly Dean, the novel's presentation is considerably more equivocal. By putting the description of Catherine and Hareton in Lockwood's voice, Emily gives it a near-parodic tone through his description of Catherine's voice "as sweet as a silver bell" (p. 371) and her face's "smiting beauty" (p. 372). In addition, though Lockwood's vision of them occurs chronologically at the end of the story, Nelly's far more powerful narrative of Heathcliff's death dominates the novel's conclusion. After hearing it, Lockwood cannot stomach looking at the young lovers and instead visits the tombs of Heathcliff, the first Catherine, and Edgar. His gesture pointedly averts the novel's gaze away from Catherine and Hareton to a different version of erotic relations. The juxtaposition of both present and past rejects the tidy conclusions of Charlotte with a carefully unsettled ending, which encapsulates the larger unsettlings that Emily's novel has created throughout in its persistent avoidance of contemporary categories for fiction.

It is interesting to speculate whether or not the first readers of *Wuthering Heights* would have been as baffled if, instead of appearing in 1847, it had appeared in 1827, when Byronic modes were more popular. I suspect that they would have been, if only because *Wuthering Heights* departed from conventions of earlier Byronic romance as much as it did from those of the 1840s realistic novel. The novel uses and critiques Byronism and anti-Byronism at the same time and revises contemporary literary possibilities without announcing a program of its own. It is little wonder that its first critics were so nonplussed. While the family as a site of literary production encouraged Emily's anomalous stance, the utter novelty of *Wuthering Heights* depended on her status as a writer completely cut off from the business of literature as usual. Her reaction to Byron and Byronism permitted the voice from the margins to be the voice of innovation.

CHAPTER 5

The flight from vulgarity
Tennyson and Byron

Tennyson's career seems the reverse of Byron's. Tennyson was a respectable, conservative, middle-class sage; Byron was a scandalous, radical, aristocratic transgressor. H. A. Taine noted of Tennyson in 1864, "[H]e does not rebel against society and life; he speaks of God and the soul, nobly, tenderly, without ecclesiastical prejudice; there is no need to reproach him like Lord Byron; he has no violent and abrupt words, excessive and scandalous sentiments; he will pervert nobody."[1] Taine sounds almost disappointed: his Tennyson needs some Byronic spice. Yet his description captures Tennyson as a Victorian cultural monument. He stood for the clichés of Victorianism as Byron had stood for those of Romanticism.

Maud is the striking exception to Taine's generalizations. Far from being bland or comforting, it is filled with "violent and abrupt words" and "excessive and scandalous sentiments." From its first appearance, it has troubled readers because it does not seem to come from the same pen that published *In Memoriam* only five years earlier. The poem's first readers knew why it seemed peculiar: it was Byronic. George Eliot labeled the hero a "modern Conrad," and a reviewer in *Blackwood's Magazine* maintained that the poem recalled "a certain *Childe Harold* who once set the world aflame."[2] These readers did not expect Byronic heroes from Tennyson, who had a reputation for rejecting Byronic excess. If Victorian writers were supposed to put Byron behind them at the beginnings of their careers, it was odd that Tennyson returned to Byron in the middle of his.

Making sense of *Maud*'s relation to Byron demands looking at Tennyson's career from the beginning. The young Tennyson's position at the Somersby rectory resembled that of the Brontës in Haworth and Carlyle in Ecclefechan. Admiring and imitating

Byron allowed him to participate in seemingly distant cultural
events. Later in life, Tennyson enjoyed describing how he carved
the words "Byron is dead" on a rock when he learned of Byron's
death, "a day when the whole world seemed to be darkened for
[him]."[3] Critics have often noted imitations of Byron in the 1827
Poems by Two Brothers, which included his brother Charles's elegy
for Byron. Like Branwell and Charlotte Brontë, the Tennysons
imitated Byron because his work seemed to define what poetry
was supposed to be in the early nineteenth century. Morse
Peckham even suggests that the brothers wrote their volume to
satisfy public taste.[4] Whether or not he is right about their
intentions, the young Tennyson confidently imitated contemporary trends in poetry.

Despite the importance of Byron to the 1827 volume, Tennyson
avoided Byron's characteristic genre of the verse romance.[5] The
poems in the 1827 volume were all lyrics. Lyric, not verse
romance, increasingly dominated poetry in the late 1820s and
after. At issue in this dominance was the status of literary
language itself. If, as Byron's career had demonstrated, poetry
was supposed to express individual genius through a unique
style, its political or social content became relatively unimportant;
refined literary expression was all. Since novels and plays were
implicitly "lower" forms, the lyric, a genre as unlike them as
possible, best represented poetry as a higher art. In addition,
publishers could most easily commodify refined literary expression
through the lyric. The popularity of annuals and anthologies
featuring lyrics or lyrical excerpts suggests how lyrics represented
high culture for newly literate classes wanting to acquire it
quickly.

Since lyricism's value depended on being as unlike ordinary
speech as possible, the more "literary" it was, the better it could
stand for high culture. As a result, poets made their lyrics poetic
by highlighting how much their language owed to that of previous
writers. Tennyson's early derivativeness marked not his inexperi-
ence, but the demand for poetry as "pure lyricism." Although
Tennyson later wrote better poetry than anything in the 1827
volume, his derivativeness remained his most interesting characteristic. No personal experience of Tennyson's, not even the loss
of Hallam, mattered for his poetry so much as his reading.
Despite the critical desire to read Tennyson's life in his art, no

other poet's biography ever told so little about his poetry and no other poet's letters are so unrevealing. As Henry James remarked after meeting him, "Tennyson is not personally Tennysonian."[6] Tennyson himself insisted that his poems were not autobiographical; he remarked about "Locksley Hall," for example, *"There is not one touch of biography in it from beginning to end."*[7]

After the 1827 volume, Tennyson's poetry altered when he went to Cambridge because he found new models. He claimed that his interest in Byron stopped: "My 'schwärmerei' for Byron entirely ceased when I was eighteen, and I have scarcely ever looked into him since then."[8] Like most Victorian writers, he abandoned Byron as a way of marking a perceived transition from artistic adolescence to maturity. In Tennyson's case, the incentive for this transition came from the Cambridge Apostles, the highly selective club that he joined. Its members fashioned themselves as an intellectual elite, a Coleridgean "clerisy."[9] Their self-appointed position at the cutting edge of culture led them to scorn those whom they regarded as merely popular artists, such as Byron. The *Athenaeum*, a weekly paper that they initially staffed and funded, gave them a highly public forum.[10] In it, F. D. Maurice, the club's moral and spiritual guide, wrote sneeringly that Byron was "the favourite of pious Reviewers, the drawing-room autocrat, the boudoir deity."[11] To him, Byron's cardinal sin was his histrionic self-dramatization, which seemed designed solely to titillate the popular audience. The message for Tennyson was that a great poet should avoid the confessionalism that supposedly marred Byron's art.

Byron's popularity with Cambridge students sharpened the Apostles' distaste. One maintained that at Cambridge it was "not only fashionable, but almost indispensable, for every youth to be Byronic," but the Apostles saw in Wordsworth and Shelley something that satisfied what they "knew to be [their] better and higher aspirations."[12] In 1829, three leading Apostles went to Oxford to take the pro-Shelley side of a debate over whether Byron or Shelley was greater. The winning speaker, a pro-Byron man from Oxford, argued that Byron was, because "we have all of us read Byron; but ... if Shelley had been a great poet, we should have read him also; but we none of us have done so."[13] For him, Byron's popularity demonstrated his greatness; Shelley's obscurity, his lack of worth. The Apostles reversed this scale of values and chose the unpopular for their heroes. Despising Byron allowed them to constitute themselves as elite *literati* within an already elite population.

As this debate suggests, the Apostles' poetic hero was Shelley. For them, he paralleled Carlyle's Goethe as a model alternative to Byron. The *Athenaeum* praised him for "his constant inculcation of man's capacity for a higher condition than the present."[14] Arthur Henry Hallam thought that his poem "Timbuctoo" would justify itself if its imitation of *Alastor* drew attention to Shelley.[15] Tennyson, however, experienced some tension with the Apostles over their admiration for Shelley. For them, Shelley was important as much because of his moral ideals as because of his style. He was a model because "a great poet . . . ought to consider contemporary problems rather than being content with a rapt, self-searching lyricism."[16] Yet Tennyson knew better than they how dated the Shelleyan connection between poetry and politics had become. The collapse of the poetry market in the 1830s meant that it became a luxury for a few. Although working-class readers continued to obtain Shelley's radical work, especially *Queen Mab*, Mary Shelley's editions guaranteed that he survived for higher-class readers not as a political poet but as a polite lyricist.[17] Although Ebenezer Elliott might versify the Corn Laws, a more elite poet like Tennyson inherited a medium in which content had become secondary to the demands of refined lyricism. As "The Palace of Art" demonstrates, in opposition to its overt moral, poetry's marginalization meant that those wanting to write it could do little but "live in art."

Tennyson wrote a few poems that followed the Apostles' moral program, such as "Conrad! why call thy life monotonous?," which urges "Conrad" not to float down the "wave of Life" (8) but to "cleave this calm to living eddies" (13).[18] Since Tennyson probably derived the name "Conrad" from *The Corsair*, the poem can be seen to critique the Byronic hero's passivity by urging a more active approach to life's problems. Yet the poem is perfunctory, a reduction of *Sartor*'s message into the space of a sonnet. Tennyson also wrote a few grand Shelleyan declamations like "The Poet," which quickly collapse into foggy hyperbole. Ultimately, for Tennyson to become the elite poet that the Apostles wanted him to be, he could not versify their Shelleyan programs because the social position of poetry as refined lyricism would not sustain them. He had to find a different aesthetic.[19] Tennyson turned to his great predecessor in derivativeness, Keats. Keats better than Shelley represented the ideal of pure lyricism and of literary language. At his most extreme, Tennyson pushed Keatsian lyricism to the point of writing poems that were almost pure sound; the subtitle to "Claribel," one of the 1830 volume's best poems, was "A Melody." Yet Tennyson's lyrics were not just imitation Keats. He gentrified Keatsian derivativeness from the position of an elite university poet. Whereas Keats's "Cockney" style marked him as a lower middle-class writer striving for refinement, Tennyson had the education for which Keats longed; it gave him the confidence to be even more otherworldly than Keats himself. In Tennyson's hands, Keats's aggressive sensuality vanished into the eroticism of language so refined as to challenge signification.

Yet the melodiousness of lyrics like "Claribel" was a dead end, since it took pure sound as far as it could go. In Tennyson's more ambitious poems, he faced the challenge of reinventing poetic subjectivity to explore what poetic self might be available to so derivative a writer. Doing so meant confronting Byron, vulgar as his success may have seemed, because he offered the most distinctive contemporary model of poetic subjectivity. Much more than with other Victorian writers, Tennyson's relation to Byron seems to occur outside of overt cultural mediation. For most Victorians, works such as Moore's biography were even more important than Byron's poetry, because they described Byron's personality, where his true interest was supposed to lie. Tennyson, in contrast, depended far more closely on Byron's texts as they were available to him, as if he were responding directly to Byron's words themselves. The extensive marginalia in Tennyson's edition of Byron reveal how closely he read the poetry. He put a vertical line in the margin next to passages that struck him and sometimes underlined words that seemed problematic. In a passage from *The Siege of Corinth*, "All that of living or dead remain, / Hurled on high with the shivered fane, / In one wild roar expired!" (973–75), he underlined the words "dead" and "expired" and put a question mark next to the latter to note that what was already dead could not properly be said to expire.[20] Similarly, in the stanza in *Childe Harold's*

Pilgrimage ending with the famous solecism "There let him lay" (iv.180), he underlined "vile" and "howling," probably to object to them. Regarding the solecism, he proposed two alternatives to "lay": "stay" and "bray," the latter a playful slam at Byron's egotism.[21] For Tennyson, Byron's poetry was not simply a body of stereotypes, as it mostly was for Carlyle, but texts that he knew in detail.

This thoroughness, which characterized his relation to many earlier writers, allowed him to respond to them as if he were responding to their language alone and not to their larger cultural reception. Although this book has emphasized that literary influence cannot be understood in a historical vacuum, Tennyson seems to write in just such a vacuum. He invents the mirage that relations between authors occur in a purely literary world, so that the cultural mediation of influence reveals itself, paradoxically, through its studied absence. The absolute literariness of his work's relation to earlier writers may be his most seductive achievement, because analyzing his work in its own ahistorical terms is so tempting. The following section will examine how Tennyson's reaction against Byron allowed him to construct his "pure" poetry in three works, "The Lady of Shalott," "Ulysses," and "Tithon."

Like other Victorians, Tennyson sought to develop narratives of transition away from Byron. In poems such as the sonnet to "Conrad" and "The Palace of Art," he wrote the transition in moral terms as a rejection of Byronic solipsism. Yet his own position as an elite poet made him an odd spokesman for active engagement with the social world. He was more successful imagining this transition in poems with figures who began in the alienated or exhausted state in which Byron's heroes usually ended. If Tennyson had to have characters, he made them as worn out as possible as his alternative to the stereotypical Byronic hero's energy. As a result, Tennyson's poetic energy would come not from the vitality of the poet's personality expressed through his characters, but from his technical skill in manipulating language.

The 1832 "The Lady of Shalott" describes the birth of Tennysonian lyric from the Byronic romance's exhaustion. The particular romance most relevant to the poem is *The Prisoner of Chillon*, which Tennyson remembered his grandmother reading to him

as a boy.[22] Like Tennyson's poem, Byron's describes a prisoner
who becomes a figure for the enclosed mind. At the climax,
Bonnivard, having burst his chains, climbs to look out of the
window of his cell:

> I saw the white-wall'd distant town,
> And whiter sails go skimming down;
> And then there was a little isle,
> Which in my very face did smile,
>   The only one in view;
> A small green isle, it seem'd no more,
> Scarce broader than my dungeon floor,
> But in it there were three tall trees,
> And o'er it blew the mountain breeze.   (339–47)

Although the scene is ordinary, the language's mesmerized details
transform it into a magical spectacle. Bonnivard collapses in
response to it. He never looks out of his prison again, becomes
apathetic, and regains his freedom only "with a sigh" (392).
Although Byron does not explain this collapse, its source seems
to be the indifference of the world that Bonnivard sees, rather
than its inaccessibility. His vision reveals that "[t]ime, and
change, in effect, can undo but cannot recreate a man."[23] He
prefers a cell in which he is all-important to a world in which
he does not matter.

Bonnivard's "little isle" (341) near which sails go "skimming
down" (340) becomes the Lady of Shalott's prison:

> The little isle is all inrailed
> With a rose-fence, and overtrailed
> With roses: by the marge unhailed
> The shallop flitteth silkensailed
> Skimming down to Camelot.[24]

The analogues to Byron's scene in *The Prisoner of Chillon* are
striking.[25] Even more telling than linguistic echoes are prosodic
ones; Tennyson imitates Byron's meter and stanza closely,
although he chooses a more difficult rhyme scheme. Yet these
similarities only reveal how much Tennyson's poem is the mirror
image of Byron's. The Lady initially is imprisoned in a version
of the indifferent "other" world that Bonnivard saw outside of
his prison. Tennyson has transformed Bonnivard's "outside" into
the Lady's "inside."

By reversing the protagonist's gender, Tennyson naturalizes her marginality. Romance conventions make the Lady's solitary life seem less imposed than Bonnivard's incarceration. The supernatural forces of a curse imprison her rather than the effects of political oppression. Many have interpreted her as an embowered artist who should be criticized for her narcissistic isolation; Daniel Albright, for example, describes "the Lady of Shalott's narcissism, her involution in the refuge of art."[26] Such interpretations overlook that the Lady's embowerment results from a curse; she does not choose her art freely. The curse's presence diminishes Byronic narrative's chief source of tension, threats to the hero's autonomy. The curse from the start drains away the autonomy of will so much at issue in poems like *The Corsair* or *Manfred*.

Tennyson's plot reverses the movement of Byron's by leading the Lady not from sympathy to apathy, like Bonnivard, but from apathy to sympathy. The first hint of this reversal occurs when her voice interrupts the narrator:

> But in her web she still delights
> To weave the mirror's magic sights:
> For often thro' the silent nights
> A funeral, with plumes and lights
>   And music, came from Camelot.
> Or, when the moon was overhead,
> Came two young lovers, lately wed:
> "I am half sick of shadows," said
> The Lady of Shalott.[27]

The narrator maintains that the Lady "still delights" to weave her web, but her "I am half sick of shadows" momentarily stills his voice. Her unexpected interruption underscores how Tennyson inverts the model of *The Prisoner of Chillon*, which occurs entirely within its hero-narrator's voice. Tennyson effaces the Lady's consciousness almost entirely. Yet her few moments of speech are climactic precisely because they are so few. Tennyson limits the presentation of her consciousness only to rivet attention on it.

For both the Lady and Bonnivard, the vision of the outer world brings about a kind of death, either literal or spiritual. Byron's poem describes Bonnivard's collapse; once the Lady chooses to look down to Camelot, the curse "comes upon" her and she dies. Nevertheless, despite the similarity of their fates, the meanings of their deaths differ. Bonnivard seals himself in his cell and his unchallenged solipsism, like the Lady at the poem's beginning. While he loses the ability to communicate, she gains it, though in a peculiar form. Although realizing that a curse is being fulfilled is not traditionally a spur to self-development, for the Lady it is oddly liberating.

In leaving the tower, she creates records of herself for others to see, unlike the web she wove in her tower. Tennyson presents two such records. First, she arrays herself in white and then, "below the carven stern" of her boat, she writes her name, "THE LADY OF SHALOTT."[28] As reviewers suggested, nobody could possibly see the name below the boat's stern, and in the 1842 revision, the Lady writes her name more visibly around the prow.[29] Yet Tennyson's first version may not have been a mistake, although he corrected it as if it were. The Lady's name, written where it is not visible, contrasts tellingly with stereotypes of Byronic self-assertion. Byron supposedly wrote his name across all his poems, but the Lady does so only beneath the stern of her boat. Although she appears in public, she hides this first sign of her identity to all except those who know to look beneath the surface. The artist knows where her name is written, although the public may not.

Yet by the end of the poem she produces a more tangible record, a lyric poem:

> There lay a parchment on her breast,
> That puzzled more than all the rest,
> The wellfed wits at Camelot.
> *"The web was woven curiously*
> *The charm is broken utterly,*
> *Draw near and fear not—this is I,*
> *The Lady of Shalott."* [30]

The poem moves through Byron's genre, the narrative romance, to reach Tennyson's preferred genre, the lyric. The Lady's lyric revises her first effort at writing by creating a second self-presentation. Her web merely copied the outside world, but her lyric revises a prior text by the Lady herself. For a moment, the poem masks how much it derives from others with a fiction that lyric derives from reinventing a writer's own original text.

The message of the Lady's poem is that lyric can reveal everything or nothing about the author, depending on the audience. For the wits, it is puzzling. For those who know the Lady's story, the lyric hints at her view of a history hitherto available only from the narrator. It is strikingly silent about Lancelot: erotic dissatisfaction plays no role in her explanation. Instead, although her adverb "curiously," meaning both "skillfully" and "strangely," suggests some ambivalence about her weaving, her rhyme word "utterly" records her triumph over her curse. Her substitution of "charm" for "curse" makes the curse seem less curse-like, as if it could only be called a charm once it had been broken as a curse. Her final assurance to her readers not to be afraid underscores how she has thrown off in death the supernatural machinery that imprisoned her. When she writes, *"this is I, / The Lady of Shalott,"* she becomes more Byronic than Byron himself. He portrayed himself in his poems; she becomes her poem.

Yet communicating her triumph is futile. When Byron wrote about himself, all believed that they knew his heart's depths, but when Tennyson's Lady writes about herself, no one understands her.[31] But Tennyson's uncomprehending audience is an implicit invitation to the poem's readers. It asks them to believe that they can be a more sympathetic audience that understands both the Lady's triumph and her futility. The reviewers of the 1833 volume ignored the invitation. Although it contained several poems that would eventually become among his most famous, it received scathing notices on its first appearance. While these wounded Tennyson, they may have confirmed his position as a poet who, like the Lady, was too good for "wellfed wits" like the reviewers. His eventual success occurred only once the lyricism that seemed ridiculously effeminate on its first appearance had become the model for refined poetic language, a development fostered by the work of such poets as Hemans, Landon, and other contributors to early Victorian annuals.[32] In 1833 however, Tennyson's style was still too close to Keats's class-marked language for reviewers such as Croker to ignore.

In response to these attacks and to the loss of Hallam, Tennyson became a poet so elite that he published only the barest minimum of new work. Little appeared for ten years, and when he at last published his 1842 *Poems* in two volumes, the first volume consisted of revisions of the 1833 poems. He wanted nothing to do with the mass market of literature. As he wrote to a hostile critic, "I prefer vegetating in a very quiet garden where I neither see or hear anything of the great world of literature."[33] Around 1839 he wrote a poem that he never published, describing what he imagined his fate would be if he became popular:

> I today
> Lord of myself and of my ways, the next
> A popular property, nauseate, when my name
> Shot like a racketball from mouth to mouth
> And bandied in the barren lips of fools
> May yield my feeling organism pain
> Thrice keener than delight from duest praise.
>
> ("Wherefore in these dark ages of the Press," 9–15)

This poem suggests that Tennyson dreaded most having a Byronic relationship with his audience. He imagines losing control of his name as it becomes a "popular property" (11). Being violated by popularity leads to a sense of near-cannibalism; his name acquires a grotesque substantiality that lets it be placed "in the barren lips of fools" (13) to yield his "feeling organism pain" (14). The bizarre image of a racketball being shot from mouth to mouth, with its nuance of erotic dispersal, further emphasizes his sense of physical violation. Although Tennyson's poem does not name Byron explicitly, no other poet qualified so vividly to be the model of the "popular property" that Tennyson dreaded becoming.

The 1833 volume avoided such vulgarity by demonstrating how thoroughly Tennyson had assimilated and exaggerated standards of literary language. His later style did not need to foreground its literariness quite so obviously, since he had already demonstrated that he could match any other poet at imitation. Similarly, since he had mastered the lyric, he could experiment with other modes to address the relation of poet to poem that Byron's career had rendered so problematic. "The Lady of Shalott" had placed the relation of author to text at an allegorical distance from Tennyson; the Lady asserted that "this is I," but he did not. In dramatic monologues, he found another form in which he could present confessions that were not his. Two monologues, "Ulysses" and "Tithon" (the first version of "Tithonus"), echo Byron's language ultimately to present themselves as alternatives to his representations of subjectivity.

"Ulysses" is one of the few Tennyson poems that modern critics

have taken seriously as involving Byron's influence.[34] Tennyson
jokingly suggested that Byron was a presence in it when he
complained that critics would not admit his originality: " 'They
allow me nothing,' he once said to me. 'For instance, "The deep
moans round with many voices." "The deep," Byron; "moans,"
Horace; "many voices," Homer; and so on.' "[35] He made fun of
critics who reduced his poems to a mélange of echoes, and he
was right to be annoyed. Although he never lost his characteristic
derivativeness, he altered his style after the 1830 and 1833 volumes so that it did not foreground quite so boldly his debt to
earlier writers. "Ulysses" for the most part avoids direct verbal
echoes of the kind that Tennyson parodies. Nevertheless, his
comment also suggests that Byron was an influence on "Ulysses"
that he was eager to deny, even though, as critics have demonstrated, parallels with *Childe Harold's Pilgrimage* are numerous.

While Tennyson revised a Byronic narrative in "The Lady of
Shalott," in his dramatic monologues, he turned to the work in
which Byron was supposed to have revealed himself most directly,
the later cantos of *Childe Harold*. Their interest lay in the emergence of Byron the "real" man as a poetic character whose
reactions to the scenes around him could be admired and imitated. No other poem offered a more renowned example of an
author doing what Tennyson so disliked by becoming a "popular
property." By using *Childe Harold* in "Ulysses," Tennyson implicitly contrasted Byron's self-revelation with the imagined confession of a character who was not himself.

When Tennyson associated Byron with "the deep," he was
probably thinking of the end of canto iv, "Roll on, thou deep
and dark blue ocean—roll!" (iv.179). These lines were among
the most widely memorized and quoted in all Byron's poetry.
Tennyson's marginalia suggest that he did not admire them, and
Allingham's diary supports this impression:

T.—"The famous lines about the sea in *Childe Harold* are abominably
bad."
We examined them. I suggested—
Thy waters washèd them while they were free—
as possible, but T. truly thought "washèd" was not like Byron; he was
more likely to write "wasted," sense or no sense.[36]

Tennyson and Allingham here debate a textual crux. Numerous editions garbled the conclusion so that the line "Thy waters washed

them power while they were free" (IV.182) appeared as "Thy waters wasted them while they were free." A stormy controversy in *Notes and Queries* between 1851 and 1854 pointed out that the line made no sense and debated alternatives; Murray eventually printed the correct version.[37] Evidently, neither Tennyson nor Allingham knew that the controversy had been settled and that they were debating a corrupt text. Yet even if Tennyson had known, he might have preferred the wrong line. His insistence on " 'wasted,' sense or no sense" is characteristic of his association between Byron and exhaustion, as in his use of *The Prisoner of Chillon* in the 1832 "The Lady of Shalott." The closer his language comes to Byron's, the more exhausted his characters are. As "Ulysses" demonstrates, language that in Byron suggests relentless energy in Tennyson suggests the weariness of refusing "to yield."

When Ulysses cries out against stasis, his language recalls Byron's description of the aspirers to whom quiet is a hell, but who eventually collapse:

> How dull it is to pause, to make an end,
> To rust unburnished, not to shine in use!
> As though to breathe were life. Life piled on life
> Were all too little, and of one to me
> Little remains. ("Ulysses," 22–26)

> Their breath is agitation, and their life
> A storm whereon they ride, to sink at last,
> And yet so nurs'd and bigotted to strife,
> That should their days, surviving perils past,
> Melt to calm twilight, they feel overcast
> With sorrow and supineness, and so die;
> Even as a flame unfed, which runs to waste
> With its own flickering, or a sword laid by
> Which eats into itself, and rusts ingloriously.
> (*Childe Harold* III.44)

As Leggett notes, "Byron ... furnishes the Tennysonian context, the adventurer whose days have melted to 'calm twilight,' who feels 'overcast with sorrow and supineness' like 'a sword laid by, / Which eats into itself, and rusts ingloriously.' "[38]

While Leggett notes similarities, differences are more striking and they depend on different relations of authors to texts. Byron's rhetoric of sincerity expresses the feelings of a Byron who is supposed to be identical with the biographical author. Since

Tennyson writes a dramatic monologue, he is present in a different way, as the Tennyson who is the absent cause of Ulysses'
voice. If the fiction of Byron's poem is that Byron the man
expresses himself, the fiction of Tennyson's is that the real Tennyson lurks behind his character. Mistrusting Ulysses seems to be
the way to get to the poet behind the poem. In particular, since
for twentieth-century readers "Tennyson" has been so preemi-
nently the poet of elegiac melancholy, it becomes almost impossible to take Ulysses at his word.

On the face of it, Ulysses exaggerates Byronic restlessness. He
insists on not melting to the "calm twilight" (*Childe Harold* III.44)
that Byron's aspirers reach. Even the verbs he uses to describe
inaction, "pause," "make an end" (22), "store and hoard" (29),
have more vitality than the decay that Byron's image of twilight
suggests. Moreover, Ulysses' sword image avoids the element of
internal corrosion in Byron's description of the sword "which
eats into itself" (*Childe Harold* III.44). Ulysses fantasizes that his
decay is only external and that he merely rusts "unburnished"
(23), as if he only needed a little polish.

Ulysses denies not only internal decay, but also the possibility
of internal change. The end highlights most powerfully his resistance to development:

> Though much is taken, much abides; and though
> We are not now that strength which in old days
> Moved earth and heaven; that which we are, we are;
> One equal temper of heroic hearts,
> Made weak by time and fate, but strong in will,
> To strive, to seek, to find, and not to yield. (65–70)

Although Leggett and Ricks note as a source Byron's " 'Tis too
late! / Yet am I changed: though still enough the same / In
strength to bear what Time cannot abate" (*Childe Harold* III.7),
I would point to a different passage:

> Thus far have I proceeded in a theme
> Renewed with no kind auspices:—to feel
> We are not what we have been, and to deem
> We are not what we should be,—and to steel
> The heart against itself. (*Childe Harold* III.111)

Byron here recognizes that he needs the stoicism that his
reviewers often recommended to him.

Unlike Byron, Ulysses believes he needs to seek a newer world instead of a newer self. While he recognizes his present limits, he denies any inner lack, so that he becomes a hero with no need for heroism. Instead, he insists that the sheer power of his will is inexhaustible. Yet, as readers have often noted, the vehemence of Ulysses' assertions undercuts them because he protests too much. Rather than seeming unconquerable, Ulysses seems exhausted.

Yet this ironic reading depends on more than Ulysses' character alone. What makes Ulysses' exhaustion credible is less what Ulysses himself says than the knowledge that the poem was written by Tennyson, the preeminent Victorian poet of exhaustion. When Owen Schur notes that Ulysses uses a "language of elegiac self-consciousness, a language of melancholy, which stems from his recognition that he is now only capable of looking back retrospectively at the self that was a mythic figure," he blurs the character's words with his sense of the poet.[39] Ulysses never recognizes that he is capable only of looking back. The melancholy that Schur finds in the monologue depends not on Ulysses but on Tennyson.

Schur reveals how the irony that critics are accustomed to find in Tennyson's dramatic monologues is a version of the Byronic fiction that Byron was his heroes. An ironic interpretation of Tennyson's poem depends on a sense of the "real" elegiac Tennyson who can be glimpsed underneath the "fictional" masks of Ulysses. Yet this "real" Tennyson is as much a romantic fiction as the "Byron" supposedly revealing himself in works like *Childe Harold*. In avoiding Byronic confessionalism, Tennyson developed as powerful a device as Byron had for seeming to express himself through his work. If Byron's fiction was that he was his heroes, Tennyson's was that he was not. He creates the mirage that the "real" Tennyson was accessible by reading underneath his characters.

"Tithon," the companion poem to "Ulysses," draws on *Childe Harold* iv as "Ulysses" draws on *Childe Harold* iii. Just as "Ulysses" saps the energy from Byronic aspiration, so "Tithon" drains the passion of Byronic eroticism, especially as described in *Childe Harold* iv. The Apostles thought that in *Childe Harold* iv, Byron had misinterpreted European art by finding passion where it did not belong. Hallam in 1827 wrote to Gladstone about Byron's description of the

Venus de Medici, "Surely Byron in his stanzas, *Childe Harold*, canto
IV, has mistaken the character of the statue; there is every trace of
divinity, but none of voluptuousness about her: contrasted with the
Titian Venuses in the same room, she seems like the 'icicle on Dian's
brow.' "[40] Trench similarly commented, in 1829, "Lord Byron has
singularly misunderstood it [the statue], and in it all sculpture, when
he talks of the gazer being dazzled and drunk with beauty."[41] *Childe
Harold* had become a tourist guide to Europe's great sites, so that in
arguing with Byron, the Apostles were rejecting his authority as a
cultural interpreter. They demonstrated their supposedly superior
discrimination by countering Byron's raptures with more composed
reactions.

Byron's passion comes from his fantasy that gazing at the
Venus de Medici breaks the boundaries between mortals and
immortals:

> And gazing in thy face as toward a star,
> Laid on thy lap, his eyes to thee upturn,
> Feeding on thy sweet cheek! while thy lips are
> With lava kisses melting while they burn,
> Showered on his eyelids, brow, and mouth, as from an urn!
>
> Glowing, and circumfused in speechless love,
> Their full divinity inadequate
> That feeling to express, or to improve,
> The gods become as mortals, and man's fate
> Has moments like their brightest; but the weight
> Of earth recoils upon us;—let it go!   (*Childe Harold* IV.51–52)

The Apostles accused Byron of mistakenly mixing human and
divine: he projected onto the statue of a divine figure a human
eroticism that it did not possess. In "Tithon," Tennyson reinter-
prets this moment by describing another failed union of mortal
and immortal:

> Ay me! ay me! with what another heart,
> By thy divine embraces circumfused,
> Thy black curls burning into sunny rings,
> With thy change changed, I felt this wondrous glow
> That, gradually blooming, flushes all
> Thy pale fair limbs: what time my mortal frame
> Molten in thine immortal, I lay wooed,
> Lips, forehead, eyelids, growing dewy-warm
> With kisses balmier than the opening buds.   (41–49)

The echoes of Byron's "circumfused in speechless love" (*Childe Harold* IV.52) in Tennyson's "by thine divine embraces circumfused" (42); Byron's "eyelids, brow, and mouth" (*Childe Harold* IV.51) in Tennyson's "lips, forehead, eyelids" (48); and the images of glowing and melting in love suggest that Tennyson has adapted Byron's language to a context recalling the dream vision in Shelley's *Alastor*.

As in "Ulysses," Tennyson's speaker intensifies the emotions of a Byronic subtext only to undercut them. Tithon's speech replaces Byron's supposedly mistaken voluptuousness with more authentically palpable eroticism. Tithon is "circumfused" not by abstract "speechless love" (*Childe Harold* IV.52) but by concrete "divine embraces" (42). Although for Byron's narrator, the "weight of earth" (*Childe Harold* IV.52) destroys his vision of a union of mortal and immortal, Tithon is closest to the divine when he is closest to a glowing version of the weight of earth, the nature represented by Aurora. He remembers divine sex not as statuesque silence but "growing dewy-warm" (48), "blooming" (45), and being kissed "with kisses balmier than the opening buds" (49).

Yet Tennyson creates this voluptuousness only to distance it from Tithon. Since Tithon's union with Aurora is ultimately a failure, he renounces his love:

> Release me: let me go: take back thy gift:
> Why should a man desire in any shape
> To vary from his kind, or beat the roads
> Of life, beyond the goal of ordinance
> Where all should pause, as is most meet for all?
> Or let me call thy ministers, the hours,
> To take me up, to wind me in their arms,
> To shoot the sunny interval of day,
> And lap me deep within the lonely west.   (19–27)

Tithon's disappointment at his union transforms the Apostle's critique of *Childe Harold* IV. The human and divine cannot mix as Byron imagined that they might. When the intensity of Byron's vision fades, he commands himself to "let it go!" because he can "recall such visions" (*Childe Harold* IV.52). Tennyson reverses Byron's "let it go!" in Tithon's imperative "let me go." While Byron's command suggested that memory might forever reconstruct the union of mortal and immortal, Tithon's suggests the union's hopelessness.

If passion remains for Tithon, it has less to do with Aurora than with death. Lines 24–27, which Tennyson later cut, bring an influx of erotic energy: the hours "take" him up, "wind" him, "shoot the sunny interval of day," and "lap" him in the lonely West. Death allows him to recreate in imagination the transcendent yet natural sexuality that he enjoyed with Aurora. Like the Lady of Shalott, Tithon treats death as a path toward heroism freed from any taint of fulfillment. From the standpoint of "Tithon," Byron's eroticism in *Childe Harold* IV was a sham in its blending of human and divine; "Tithon" posits a more genuine eroticism located in Tithon's narcissistic visions of death.

"Tithon" and "Ulysses" developed Tennyson's distinctive version of the Victorian transition away from Byron. Most Victorian authors wrote versions of works like "Locksley Hall," in which the hero leaves behind his Byronic melancholy to commence a supposedly more mature and socially meaningful life. In Tennyson's greater poems, his transition has less to do with moral programs than with generic ones. His dramatic monologues isolate characteristics of Byron's self-representation and rewrite them through the voice of mythic characters. In so doing, the poems open up a gap between character and author that undercuts the Byronic language. Although the dramatic monologue is sometimes treated as Tennyson's flight from Romantic self-representation, it is better treated as a more intricate form of such representation. The fiction of Tennyson as an authorial presence emerges once his characters are treated as dramatic representations. Raising suspicion about them makes room for Tennyson as their absent cause. The self-representation that he seems to exile from his work acquires a shadowy presence through the gaps and ironies in his characters' words.

The versions of "The Lady of Shalott" and "Tithon" familiar today do not have most of the material that indicates Tennyson's revision of Byron. As his career continued and he gained more of an identity in the literary world, the pressure to transform Byronic self-representation grew less immediate, just as the importance of foregrounding his knowledge of earlier authors faded after he published his first volumes. Yet even by the 1842 revision of "The Lady of Shalott," Tennyson omitted entirely the lyric with which the Lady ends the poem. He did so partly because Mill's review condemned it as a "lame and impotent conclusion."[42] Yet by 1842 he had also developed other forms of self-representation through his dramatic monologues that made the Lady's "this is I" a less momentous confession than it had been in 1833. Similarly, when "Tithon" became "Tithonus" in 1860, he cut almost all its Byronic language, because in 1860 Byron no longer mattered to Tennyson as he had in the early 1830s.[43]

After the 1842 volume's publication, Tennyson secured his status as an elite poet who had moved poetry away from Byron. R. H. Horne noted approvingly in 1845 that only readers of the finest sensibility appreciated Tennyson: "Choice and limited is the audience . . . to whom this favoured son of Apollo pours forth his melodious song."[44] He also praised Tennyson because he did not parade "any of his private personal feelings . . . before the public . . . after the fashion of Lord Byron"; instead, he withdrew "from every identification."[45] Such notices demonstrated that Tennyson successfully defined himself against Byron's audience, his "vulgar" popularity, and his perceived self-representation.

Only after attaining recognition as an un-Byronic poet did Tennyson publish a confessional poem, *In Memoriam*. Although in terms of chronology some of its lyrics were written near the same time as the dramatic monologues, they were published only after Tennyson gained a reputation as a respectably elite author. If in 1833 the Lady of Shalott announced that "this is I," by 1850 Tennyson had earned the right to do the same without seeming to succumb to Byronic vulgarity. In addition, he had chastened his derivativeness so that his language was less obviously a compendium of earlier writers. As a result, while *In Memoriam*'s style is still indebted to Wordsworth and Keats, among many others, it could be perceived as the product of an individual genius rather than as a compilation of previous styles.

In Memoriam was no straightforward confession, despite T. S. Eliot's famous description of it as "the concentrated diary of a man confessing himself."[46] As usual, Tennyson himself insisted most vehemently that he could be equated with the poem's "I": "It must be remembered . . . that this is a poem, *not* an actual biography."[47] Martin counters Tennyson by noting the poem's many references to autobiographical fact.[48] Yet after a career such as Byron's, an autobiographical poem was no longer one that merely included facts about the author's life. Byron's poetry and career had disseminated a confessional rhetoric that sexualized the deepest secrets of the inner self.

In Memoriam avoided the Byronic rhetoric of the inner self. Byron's confessionalism always implied that he was holding darkly erotic secrets in reserve. What is so striking about the eroticism of *In Memoriam* is how overt it is. Critics who get beneath the poem by revealing its secret as Tennyson's homoerotic love for Hallam are translating it into Byronic terms; they want to make it confess. Yet the poem never treats the eroticism of the speaker's love for "Arthur" as a secret to be uncovered. On the contrary, the openness with which it discusses love between men is the greatest barrier to reading it as Tennyson's confession, since so little sense of secrecy is involved. The homosexual element of *In Memoriam* may lie more in the felt inaccessibility of the "real" Tennyson than in any expressions of his love for Hallam. Whereas the "real" Byron seemed to his readers always to be dominant, the "real" Tennyson is always in the closet. The finished beauty of his language expresses everything but the personality of Alfred Tennyson.

Although *In Memoriam*'s homoeroticism troubled several Victorian readers, the poem made Tennyson's career by internalizing moral, religious, scientific, and social concerns as an individual lyricist's personal expression. Its sole Byronic aspect was its enormous success, which brought the laureateship with it. Almost overnight, Tennyson's position in the literary world altered. He was no longer an elite poet living in the quiet garden of aestheticism.

As such, he became Byron's heir regardless of the content of his poetry, simply because he was so popular. He spoke revealingly with William Allingham about his troubling sense of kinship with Byron:

A.—"[Byron] was a Lord, and talked about, and he wrote vulgarly, therefore he was popular."

T.—"Why am I popular? I don't write very vulgarly."

A.—"I have often wondered that you are, and Browning wonders."

T.—"I believe it's because I'm Poet-Laureate. It's something like being a lord."[49]

Whereas his earlier career had been the antithesis of Byron's, his popularity now brought him all too close to Byron's supposed vulgarity. His comment to Allingham suggests vividly how Byron's cultural reception made him a haunting presence even for a poet whose work was as different as possible from Byron's.

A burden of popularity was that Tennyson's critics urged him to treat contemporary social issues, much as the Apostles had done. While he liked to pretend to be unaffected by critics, he read their suggestions carefully and often followed them. In the early 1850s he published short political poems in newspapers, either anonymously or under a pseudonym. He had also published at the end of 1847 an ambitious poem, *The Princess*, about a contemporary issue, female education. Yet these did not answer the demand to produce a major work in his own name that would engage national issues. In particular, the events surrounding the Crimean War, the major crisis in British foreign policy in the 1850s and a signal moment for Britain's sense of itself as an international power, cried out for treatment by a poet who was supposed to be Britain's voice. Yet doing so seemed to demand that Tennyson popularize his poetry in a way that he had always avoided.

Maud and its attendant response to Byronism was his response. In an outstanding analysis of *Maud*'s relation to literary antecedents, Leslie Brisman begins by contrasting Tennyson's aggressive rewriting of Byron with his more responsive relation to Keats, but concludes by suggesting that these relations are actually the opposite of what they seem.[50] In arguing this thesis, some of Brisman's most suggestive moments occur when he ponders Byron's status in his argument, as when he questions "how much of what Tennyson opposes in *Maud* he opposes *because* it is Byron's."[51] One answer would be that it depends upon what is understood to be "Byron's." By the mid-1850s, opposing Byron should have been a dead issue for Tennyson. After two decades in which he and many other major writers had narrated transitions away from Byron, there ought to have been no need to dredge up old quarrels.

Yet by the 1850s, Byron's influence was closely associated with the Spasmodics, a popular school of poets whose fame challenged all that Tennyson represented. In the spectrum of mid-century Victorian poets, they fall between Tennyson, the elite, anti-Byronic laureate, and working-class poets like Thomas Cooper, the Chartist. Their use of Byron helped to define their position somewhere in the middle. As I argued in chapter 2, Byron's reception involved a time-lag. The further down the sociopolitical scale the writers were, the more likely they were to imitate Byron after more elite writers had rejected him. In addition, they were also more likely to associate him with political radicalism. By the 1840s, he had been disseminated widely enough that he had become an icon for the Chartist movement. Thomas Cooper, for example, invoked Byron as a hero in *The Purgatory of Suicides* (1845), a long poem that he wrote while in prison.[52]

Writers usually associated with the Spasmodic school, Philip James Bailey, Sidney Dobell, and Alexander Smith, came from differing social backgrounds, but their work had certain features in common.[53] Their long, diffuse closet dramas challenged the generic dominance of the lyric. In so doing, they also challenged poetry's elitism as established by writers such as Tennyson. Instead of privileging highly refined literary language, their works attempted to delineate the "modern" condition by synthesizing the age's most pressing questions. Like Carlyle in *Sartor Resartus*, they sought to demonstrate their seriousness by striving for philosophical profundity, although without Carlyle's irony; their work sustained instead a version of the Apostles' Shelleyan program. Their dramas featured heroes who were alienated, deeply self-conscious, and questing for answers to spiritual and political problems. Philosophical reflections become the vehicle through which the hero's personal dissatisfactions were seen to be synecdochic of larger social ills. These poems are interesting because they represent an attempt on the part of poets in the Victorian age to claim that poetry had immediate relevance to the same contemporary issues that novelists and essayists were addressing.

Stylistically, Spasmodic poems depended heavily on the language of the second-generation Romantics, especially Keats and Shelley. Whereas imitating these writers had marked Tennyson as an elite poet in the early 1830s, they had gained enough stature that by the mid-1850s they were the models to which "serious" poets thought they should aspire. Even more clichéd were the stereotypical Byronic heroes at the center of their dramas. Since these heroes were often poets, they invited the readers to make the Byronic connection between author and character. The heroes' characters more than anything else led mid-Victorian critics to associate the Spasmodics with Byron.[54]

The popularity of Spasmodic poems did not depend on originality. Rather, it arose from what looked like an exciting union between dominant poetic styles and the social and philosophical concerns of the mid-Victorian novel and essay.

Tennyson's earlier writing was not immune to these concerns. "Locksley Hall" was a miniature Spasmodic poem, and it eventually became one of his most popular. *The Princess* was his version of a narrative poem that engaged contemporary social issues, although it did so only through the vehicle of a romance fable. Even *In Memoriam* was hardly art for art's sake: the lyrics addressed a range of contemporary concerns. Nevertheless, to contemporary critics such as George Gilfillan and Arthur Clough, the turgid philosophizing of the Spasmodics far more than the refined lyricism of Tennyson summed up the concerns of the age.

Alexander Smith's *A Life-Drama*, the literary sensation of 1853, was the Spasmodic poem that Tennyson knew best.[55] Smith and his poem embodied all that threatened Tennyson as a poetic standard. As a Glasgow artisan with no formal schooling, Smith had a background as unlike Tennyson's as possible. His work attracted no attention until Gilfillan admired some of his lyrics; he urged Smith to write a longer poem that would represent his genius. Under pressure from Gilfillan, Smith used the conveniently loose structure of the Spasmodic poem to stitch together lyrics that he had already written. Gilfillan reviewed *A Life-Drama* enthusiastically, and his recommendation guaranteed large sales.

The most obvious influence on Smith's lyrics was Keats, and Smith's imitations were a good measure of Keats's growing reputation. Before Smith met Gilfillan, his lyrics would have posed no threat to Tennyson at all. Only after he united them into a closet drama, put a tormented hero at the center, and added passages of "philosophical" speculation did his work distinguish itself markedly from Tennyson's, and it did so because it looked closer to Byron than to Keats. Walter, Smith's hero, pays tribute to Byron's influence: "Beside that well I read the mighty Bard / Who clad himself with beauty, genius, wealth, / Then flung himself on his own passion-pyre / And was consumed."[56] Smith's poem revealed that tormented subjectivity was no longer the exclusive possession of aristocrats like Byron, but had descended to working-class imitators of Byron, like Smith. This descent bolstered the myth that true genius did not depend on high rank, a myth that paradoxically highlighted class origins of particular writers even while maintaining that they had been transcended.

Like most Spasmodic heroes, Walter goes through his share of trials, and like most Victorian revisions of the Byronic hero, he eventually abandons his solipsism and commits himself to communal good. While most of the poem concentrates on his personal troubles, it also contains occasional bouts of fiery social discontent:

God! our souls are aproned waiters! God! our souls are hired slaves:
Let us hide from Life, my Brothers! let us hide us in our graves.
Oh! why stain our holy childhoods? Why sell all for drinks and meats?
Why degrade, like those old mansions, standing in our pauper streets,
Lodgings *once* of kings and nobles, silken stirs and trumpet's din,
Now, where crouch 'mong rags and fever, shapes of squalor and of
    sin?[57]

Although *A Life-Drama* is not all rant, such passages marked the poem as one deeply concerned with the state of Britain. Its success revealed that poetry could no longer divorce itself from the difficult issues that novels were addressing. The pressure of contemporary social problems loomed as a prerequisite for much poetry that would be taken seriously in the early 1850s. As a result, by the 1850s the Spasmodics had created a strong link between Byronism and socially concerned poetry.

Smith sent a copy of his poem's second edition to Tennyson, who noted a passage of stereotypically Byronic despair: "How beautiful the yesterday that stood / Over me like a rainbow. I am alone. / The past is past. I see the future stretch / All dark and barren as a rainy sea."[58] Yet he may also have been struck by the passage quoted above whose furious octameters imitate "Locksley Hall." In reading Smith, Tennyson would have seen his poem rewritten and given a radical twist quite unlike the progressivist optimism with which Tennyson's hero concludes. Smith's poem was an implicit challenge to Tennyson: if he did not follow through on "Locksley Hall" 's political strain, others would. Moreover, those "others" would adopt the Byronic confessionalism against which he had positioned himself for so long.

Arthur Clough's review of Smith, which explicitly praised his social realism, may have heightened Tennyson's sense of being challenged by a more Byronic and more socially concerned poetry. Clough asserts that the novel has done a better job than poetry of holding contemporary audiences because it represents real life. In his eyes, Smith is valuable because he comes closer to the novel than most modern poetry:

These poems were not written among books and busts . . . There is a charm, for example, in finding, as we do, continual images drawn from the busy seats of industry; it seems to satisfy a want that we have long been conscious of, when we see the black streams that welter out of factories, the dreary lengths of urban and suburban dustiness,

> The squares and streets,
> And the faces that one meets,

irradiated with a gleam of divine purity.[59]

The snatch of poetry comes from a short lyric, "O, that 'twere possible," which Tennyson wrote when he was mourning the death of Hallam. It appeared in an album in 1837, but was not included in *In Memoriam*. The quotation plays an odd role in Clough's review, which is actually not about Tennyson at all. For the most part, it compares Matthew Arnold negatively with Smith. Nevertheless, the charges of otherworldliness that Clough levels at Arnold resemble the complaints that other critics had made about Tennyson. Gilfillan, for example, in a review written three years before, had maintained that "Tennyson's exquisite genius is neutralized, whether by fastidiousness of taste or by morbidity of temperament."[60]

Yet in the passage quoted, Clough implies that Tennyson is a poet of social realism. His poetry seems, in Clough's eyes, to be more like Smith's in its depiction of urban blight. Although nothing in "O, that 'twere possible" justifies Clough's association of it with "the black streams that welter out of factories," the message that Clough seems to be sending to Tennyson by quoting him is that his poetry *ought* to be more concerned with such matters. Just as Smith rewrites "Locksley Hall" in *A Life-Drama* to make Tennyson more socially conscious, so Clough recalls "O, that 'twere possible" as if it were poetry of social realism. In both cases, writers reshaped Tennyson's work into a more direct engagement with the condition of England and with the Spasmodic tradition.

Whether or not Tennyson actually recognized Smith's imitation of "Locksley Hall" or knew Clough's review, these writings

represent the challenges to his position as an elite lyricist that
Maud addressed. He even put "O, that 'twere possible" at the
poem's center, as if to respond to Clough's misappropriation. In
terms of his authorial position, Tennyson's popularity brought
him nearer to Byron than ever before, if only because he was at
the center of attention. In terms of the topics that his audience
wanted him to explore, he was being pushed toward poetry that
reflected the concerns of modern England, which the Spasmodics
had given a history of associations with Byronic archetypes,
particularly the rebellious Byronic hero. The popularity of *A
Life-Drama*, the critique of Tennyson's elitism, and the demand
for socially relevant poetry seemed to demand that Tennyson
abandon lyricism for the Spasmodics' Byronism.

Tennyson's response was unexpected. In *Maud*, he seemed to
give his audience what it wanted: the poem's plot was melodramatic and novelistic, the hero a stereotypically Byronic ranter,
and the content packed with observations about mid-Victorian
England. But rather than repeating the Spasmodics' success,
Maud was one of Tennyson's most controversial works. While it
adopted Byronic motifs, it turned them into the vehicle for a
poem so daringly experimental that it was incomprehensible to
its first readers. As Antony Harrison suggests, "*Maud* . . . sets
out to subvert Spasmodicism and to reaffirm the (post-Romantic)
originality of Tennyson's own work."[61] Harrison describes this
subversion in terms of Tennyson's refusal to endorse a clear
ideological position, unlike the Spasmodics. Yet *Maud's* most
distinctive aspect and the one most often noted by Victorians
was not its ironic distance from ideology, but its virtuosity.
Maud was above all the most sheerly virtuosic poem written by
Tennyson, an explosion of bravura after the hushed quatrains of
In Memoriam. While *Maud's* technical brilliance has received much
praise, I want to analyze how the poem's technique complicated
the web of pressures that the Spasmodics' Byronism raised for
Tennyson.

Just as Carlyle in *Sartor Resartus* had collapsed Moore's Byron
from inside, so Tennyson collapsed the politicized Byron of the
Spasmodics. What initially looks like a Byronic concentration on
the representation of tortured subjectivity becomes inseparable
from Tennyson's virtuosity. The interior of the hero's mind tends
to be less interesting than the precision with which the poem

manipulates rhyme, prosody, and sound symbolism to infuse an almost hysterical energy into its lyricism. In the process, Tennyson "rescues" Byronic art from its own excesses and creates a work so unusual for 1855 as to be avant-garde.

Although the Spasmodics forced Tennyson's relation to Byron to be far more mediated than in his earlier poetry, his language retains its characteristically close engagement with Byron's language. From close echoes to general parallels, his language is often nearer to Byron's than that of the Spasmodics:

That the smooth-faced, snubnosed rogue would leap from his counter
and till   (*Maud* 1.51)

Cold-blooded, smooth-faced, placid miscreant!
                                                    (*Don Juan* Dedic.12)

Seeing his gewgaw castle shine   (*Maud* 1.347)

Of Glory's gewgaws shining in the van
                                                    (*Childe Harold* iv.109)

I have not made the world, and He that made it will guide
                                                         (*Maud* 1.149)

I have not loved the World, nor the World me
                                                    (*Childe Harold* iii.113)

So dark a mind within me dwells   (*Maud* 1.527)

The wandering outlaw of his own dark mind
                                                    (*Childe Harold* iii.3)

Queen rose of the rosebud garden of girls
                                                         (*Maud* 1.902)

His queen, the garden queen, his Rose   (*The Giaour* 26)

"The fault was mine, the fault was mine"   (*Maud* ii.1)

"The fault, if fault there be, was mine"
                                              (*The Bride of Abydos* 1.55)

Tennyson is even more Byronic than the Byronists. His relation to Byron is more literal than theirs, since he echoes Byron's language, while they merely draw on Byronic stereotypes.

Tennyson's tendency to out-Byron the Byronists is evident in the plot as well. Instead of a loosely structured plot like Smith's, Tennyson portrays vivid, melodramatic events. Most sources that have traditionally been suggested for *Maud* are novels, such as Scott's *Bride of Lammermoor* (1819) or Bulwer Lytton's *Falkland* (1826).[62] Yet these continue a trend that I discussed in chapter 4, the translation of Byronic romance into the novel. Byron's Turkish Tales are the closest poetic source for *Maud*, even closer than "Locksley Hall." For example, *The Bride of Abydos* contains, like *Maud*, lovers raised in a brother–sister relationship, a hero's father destroyed by the heroine's father, a heroine nearly forced to wed an unworthy man, a violent confrontation between the lover and the heroine's relatives, and the death of the heroine from grief. Although Byron's orientalism is far from the insistent Englishness of *Maud*, Tennyson relocates the violence of Byron's Turkish Tales on English soil. When Maud and the hero nickname her brother "the Sultan," for example, they figure their experience in terms like those of Byron's fictions: Maud's brother resembles the repressive Giaffir of *The Bride of Abydos* or Seyd of *The Corsair*. In *Maud*, Byron's orientalism becomes what it may always have been, an elaborate metaphor through which to describe the violence of English domestic life.

By 1855, the sheer repetition of such romance motifs in novels and poems had become clichéd. Tennyson returned to a Byron who had been worn threadbare, as George Brimley suggested when he noted that many critics viewed the plot as "a melodramatic story of suicide, murder, and madness, dished up for popular applause."[63] Yet Tennyson's turn to the popular is more apparent than real. *Maud*'s plot matters little to its overall effect. In the poem as it was first published, the plot is presented so elliptically that it is impossible to follow.[64] Few narrative poems owe so little to the suspense of what happens next. Byron had written a poem of fragments as well in *The Giaour*, but whereas *The Giaour* offered vivid glimpses of present-tense action, *Maud* reserves action for the spaces between its divisions. Such gaps allow Tennyson to have a Byronic plot without really having it. The more melodramatic it becomes, the more it seems to be merely a device that he is employing for other ends.

In particular, it allows Tennyson to portray a tremendous variety of emotional and psychological states, and the poem's fragmentary structure allows each to be captured at high intensity. Like "Locksley Hall," *Maud* largely dispenses with the philosophical speculations of which the Spasmodics were fond. But the weaknesses of "Locksley Hall" become *Maud's* strengths. By writing in fragments, Tennyson solves the earlier poem's problem of lacking any transition between public and private concerns. He incorporates into his work's formal structure the fragmentation that his hero thinks characterizes Britain. Part of the poem's point is that no philosophical system exists to explain or to redress the chaotic jumble of modern life.

The fragments also foreground the importance of the speaker's subjectivity. Although the plot may derive from the Turkish Tales, the obsessive concentration on the hero's voice more closely resembles *Manfred*. As I suggested in chapter 1, *Manfred* transformed Byron's relation to his audience because his separation provided an extrapoetic event that grounded the play's obsession with incest. The presence of incest as the poem's "secret" encouraged readers to take it as Byron's direct confession. Ralph Rader's analysis of *Maud's* genesis in Tennyson's disappointment with Rosa Baring has encouraged Tennyson scholars to read it as a confessional poem like *Manfred*.[65] Parallels certainly exist between Tennyson's hero and Tennyson, who underwent his share of brooding melancholia and erotic frustration. I want to question, however, whether Tennyson's mental life ought therefore to be treated as the genesis of work.

As in the case of *In Memoriam*, the greatest barrier to treating the hero as Tennyson is that the poem has so little to hide. While Manfred was supposed to be Byron because he possessed a consciousness whose mysteries were never fully revealed, *Maud's* hero has no mystery about him at all. From the beginning he insists upon graphic, proto-Freudian accounts of his trauma. His subjectivity realizes itself completely in language: he never claims to be unable to represent his interior state. Tennyson replaces the mystery of Byron's heroes with a stridency that denies the possibility of unplumbed depths. To make this observation is not to accuse him of poor characterization. Rather, he externalizes his hero's mental states because, unlike Byron, he is not interested in having his audience identify him with his heroes.

Tennyson avoids Byronic subjectivity most strikingly by having the hero's voice evaporate into lyric at moments of greatest urgency. In his narratives, Byron used lyrics as interludes, as

did Tennyson in *The Princess.* In *Maud,* the lyrics are not interludes
but part of the action itself, so that they attain an urgency
quite unlike the languor of the songs in *The Princess.* The hero's
subjectivity cannot quite sustain itself without the prop of Tennyson's lyricism. His desperation is most eloquently expressed in
the elaborate artificiality of a lyric such as "Come into the
garden, Maud." The hero may border on hysteria, but Tennyson
the artist is in full command. As a result, he realizes *Maud's*
speaker in terms less of psychological verisimilitude than of poetic
opportunities.

The poem's plot embodies how aesthetic forms unify a consciousness otherwise verging on stereotypes of Spasmodicism.
Maud herself is first of such forms. In the famous section beginning "I have led her home, my love, my only friend," the hero,
after viewing the indifferent stars, maintains that Maud allows
him to triumph over their coldness:

> But now shine on, and what care I,
> Who in this stormy gulf have found a pearl
> The countercharm of space and hollow sky,
> And do accept my madness, and would die
> To save from some slight shame one simple girl. (1.639–43)

Although for Byron's heroes, the Byronic heroine was a destabiliz-
ing challenge to the psyche's uniqueness, for Tennyson's hero,
Maud is valuable precisely because she has no interiority. The
distance between the "countercharm of space and hollow sky"
and "one simple girl" measures the hero's own awareness of the
process by which he turns Maud into a "pearl" rescuing him
from chaos. Through her, the world becomes more beautiful and
more purely artificial: "A livelier emerald twinkles in the grass, /
A purer sapphire melts into the sea" (1.649–50).

A. Dwight Culler suggests that the hero and Maud have
reached erotic consummation at this point, but nothing so merely
natural as physical sex intrudes upon the delicacy of the hero's
pastoral.[66] Tennyson instead indicates a deeper consummation in
the line "I . . . do accept my madness." Aestheticizing Maud
gives the hero no access to her consciousness, but clarifies his
own. Potential union with Maud creates an actual union within
himself. Seeing in Maud a "countercharm of space and hollow
sky" offers the sole glimmer of possibility for redeeming his

madness. As "one simple girl," she anchors his imagination by giving it a stable center.

Maud, like all such erotic ideals, exists largely so that she can be lost and mourned. Yet, unlike Byron's heroes, Tennyson's finds substitutes for her countercharm. On the beach in Brittany, he views a beautiful shell on which he obsesses strangely:

> See what a lovely shell,
> Small and pure as a pearl,
> Lying close to my foot,
> Frail, but a work divine,
> Made so fairily well. (II.49–53)

With a few changes of wording, he might be describing Maud. Like her, the shell has just enough exteriority to let him unify his psyche around his reaction to it. A hint of violence ("Slight, to be crush'd with a tap / Of my finger-nail" [II.69–70]) underlines the fragility less of the shell than of his own consciousness. When he marvels that the mind "by being so overwrought, / [Should] suddenly strike on a sharper sense" (II.110–11), the shell's countercharm briefly gives him an aesthetic distance from history's sordidness.

Tennyson heightens the value of aesthetic distance by portraying madness as its reverse. In the madhouse, the hero experiences a nightmare of Byronic confessionalism:

> For I never whisper'd a private affair
> Within the hearing of cat or mouse,
> No, not to myself in the closet alone,
> But I heard it shouted at once from the top of the house. (II.285–88)

As Tucker notes, "The maddening thing about the dead men's chatter, from the hero's standpoint, is its violation of the Victorian decorum that segregates public from private spheres."[67] The madmen resemble parodic versions of Byronic heroes who pour out their souls in "nothing but idiot gabble!" (II.279) to an audience grown indifferent or annoyed. The hero suffers Tennyson's agony of having his name become a "public property," as Byron's had, so that his private life becomes chatter. His frustration suggests how commonplace his torture has become: the world is filled with others all equally eager to rant.

The poem rescues the hero through yet one more version of

the stereotypical Victorian narrative of transition away from Byron. If Victorian authors did not kill off their Byronic characters, they had them abandon their solipsism to rejoin history, as in *Sartor Resartus*, and Tennyson notoriously packs his hero off to the Crimea. This action has no parallel in the careers of Byron's heroes but an obvious one in Byron's life, especially as biographers and elegists mythologized his involvement in Greece as a turn from self-indulgence to fighting for a noble cause. Although his actual death at Missolonghi was wretched, the goals behind his participation in Greek politics seemed noble enough to represent for some his conversion to improved spirituality.

Tennyson similarly exploits the move to war as a device to bring about a conclusion that could not have been more commonplace in 1855. Yet its shock is how little of a conversion in the hero has occurred. The hero's treatment of the war is remarkably close to his treatment of Maud. The intense critical embarrassment that this ending has occasioned may stem less from its jingoism than from the half-lunatic, half-magnificent integrity with which the poem sustains its aestheticism. For example, the hero's desire that "the cobweb woven across the cannon's throat / Shall shake its threaded tears in the wind no more" (III.27–28) reveals that the poem is not so wrapped up in patriotic fervor that it cannot introduce a lyrical reminder of elegiac beauty. Such lyricism creates an aesthetic distance between the hero and the masses whom he seems to have joined. Despite his claim "I am one with my kind," it seems truer that he is one with his madness. The peculiar wording of such lines as "[I] mix'd my breath / With a loyal people shouting a battle cry" (III.34–35) is revealing: he seems to say that he shouted with the "loyal people," but he only mixes his breath with them, not with their shout. The synecdoche allows him to maintain separation; mixing breath sounds less fervent than shouting a battle cry. The war matters less as an actuality than as an ideal whose "blood-red blossom" (III.53) exists on an aesthetic continuum with Maud.

The hero's need for aestheticized objects that rescue him from history's embarrassments has its counterpart in Tennyson's use of his poetic technique to distance him from the vulgarities of Byronism. The 1855 poem concluded with an image of war that dissolved the specifics of the Crimea into an alliterative turn on the poem's obsessive flower imagery. While in dramatic mono-

logues irony supposedly revealed the poet behind the poem, in
Maud Tennyson is present in his sensed control over prosody,
tempo, alliteration, stanza, and other formal matters.[68] While
such control is evident in all Tennyson's poetry, few other poems
so foreground what Christopher Caudwell refers to as
"*skill-fetishism*."[69]

More than anything about its content, *Maud*'s difficult form
guaranteed that it would not appeal to readers pleased either by
In Memoriam's accessibility or by Spasmodic profundities. Like
Emily Brontë in *Wuthering Heights*, Tennyson transformed Byronism's commonplaces into a shocking work. Whether or not he
actually intended it to be unpopular, he enjoyed treating *Maud*
as his misunderstood work of genius. He did so despite that fact
that it sold well since, as a misunderstood work, it established
his artistic power far more effectively than another best-seller
like *In Memoriam*.[70] *Maud* was a difficult work requiring detailed
explication, rather than a sentimental narrative for undiscriminating readers.

Shortly after the appearance of *Maud*, Robert Mann defended
it in *Maud Vindicated*. Mann insisted that the poem was too good
to be popular: "Mr. Tennyson cannot be a *popular poet* in the
ordinary and familiar sense of the term. The people does not
yet comprehend precision of language. Nine-tenths of the words
it employs, it actually does not know the *precise* meaning of."[71]
Tennyson approved highly, and his son Hallam included an
excerpt from it in the "official" Eversley edition of Tennyson's
works. Others agreed with Mann that *Maud*'s formal artistry
prevented its easy success. Hepworth Dixon in *The Athenaeum*
commented, " 'Maud' is a mystery—a parable—an allegory. But
the mystery resides in the form of the poem, rather than in the
meaning."[72] Emily Tennyson wrote revealingly about the British
public, "It will take, I think, some time before they understand
either the metres or the thoughts."[73] She put the "metres" before
the thoughts, as if the poem's formal character were the principal
stumbling-block.

If Tennyson hoped that *Maud*'s virtuosity would prevent it
from becoming an icon of sentimental bourgeois taste, he
reckoned without Victorian consumer culture's ingenuity. Many
of *Maud*'s most ardent admirers simply ignored its most troubling
aspects. Characteristically, late Victorian commentators reduced

it to lyric effusions: "Over all this wondrous combination is cast a magic fascinating light, while every line has a haunting rhythm, instinct with unborn melody."[74] In the case of "Come into the garden, Maud," the poem's most accessible lyric, numerous composers supplied the "unborn melody," such as John Blockley, Otto Dresel, and Michael Balfe. In W. G. Cusins's collection of songs with lyrics by Tennyson, published in 1880, the most famous composers, Saint-Saëns, Liszt, and Massenet, set lyrics from *Maud*.[75] The poem's plot faded before the supposedly superior interest of its lyrics.

Tennyson's public readings of *Maud* countered this commercialization, which too much resembled that of Byron. His readings should be understood less as his endorsement of the poem's politics than as opportunities for him to demonstrate his technical mastery as a reader. They reminded his auditors that he alone held the key to the true experience of the poem because he alone could read it.[76] He enjoyed boasting about his reading; he told Allingham, "That was very hard to read; could you have read it? I don't think so."[77] Gladstone and Van Dyke publicly retracted their dislike of *Maud* after having heard Tennyson, as if the poem revealed itself only from the author's mouth.[78] Tennyson's readings prevented *Maud* from ever fully becoming a market commodity, unlike Byron's work, because the "true" experience could not be detached from Tennyson's physical voice. Though individuals may have bought the poem or products based on it, they missed the deepest meanings so long as they could not hear Tennyson. Only the relatively few privileged to hear him could experience *Maud* in its genuine form as a work of high art.

Maud marked Tennyson as a poet who would not become a second Byron because he did not express himself through his poem; he expressed himself as his poem, like the Lady of Shalott. *Maud* was for connoisseurs who could appreciate a true artist rather than for the many who wanted mere sentimentality. After having proven his independence from his public's good will by composing *Maud*, Tennyson could turn to the more accessible *Idylls of the King*, although the readers who admired *Maud* were generally the first to condemn the *Idylls* as a sentimental indulgence. *Maud*, however, remained his eccentric rebellion against the literary market after Byron.

Yet any rebellion may share aspects of the trends against

which it rebels. Looking at literature alone masks how the ideal of formal mastery was not solely artistic in Victorian Britain. In other Victorian discourses, it acquired an almost visionary aura. Andrew Ure, for example, in 1835 defined a factory as "a vast automaton, composed of various mechanical and intellectual organs, acting in uninterrupted concert for the production of a common object, all of them being subordinated to a self-regulated moving force."[79] Samuel Smiles's fantasy of Victorian military discipline reads as if Foucault ought to have quoted it in *Discipline and Punish*: "These soldiers . . . were once tailors, shoemakers, mechanics, weavers and ploughmen; with mouths gaping, shoulders stooping, feet straggling, arms and hands like great fins hanging by their sides; but now their gait is firm and martial, their figures are erect, and they march along to the sound of music, with a tread that makes the earth shake."[80] The army transforms the working classes from crude, ugly shapes into beautifully disciplined machines. As with Ure, this quotation has little to do with actual conditions: the Crimean War proved that the army had no such disciplinary power. Nevertheless, as indications of a Victorian fantasy, such quotations provide a telling forecast to Walter Benjamin's famous conclusion that fascism is "the consummation of '*l'art pour l'art*.' "[81] For Ure and Smiles, admiration for the aesthetics of discipline, either industrial or military, momentarily overwhelms a sense of the ends that it might serve.

The formalism of the factory or army had a practical application: it was supposed to increase speed and efficiency. Tennyson's poetic virtuosity, in contrast, was not so constrained, so that it could be admired "in itself." His work realized the utopian possibility of mastering a physical medium for its own sake.[82] At the hero's most hysterical moments in *Maud*, the language verges on an almost mechanical privileging of form over content, as in the notorious "Go not, happy day": "Blush from West to East, / Blush from East to West, / Till the West is East, / Blush it thro' the West" (1.591–94). The formal properties of language override all others as the poetry becomes almost self-generating. Tennyson's recording of the last stanza of "Come into the garden, Maud" subordinates the individual words and their meanings to a larger musical phrase, in which his voice begins at one pitch, rises as the stanza progresses, and then falls dramatically for the final lines. The semantic content of the words is less important than their physical properties as sounds in a carefully controlled vocal arrangement. Tennyson has trained his voice to become an instrument that he can manipulate. His reading almost alienates words from their content to make them phonic markers for his vocal discipline.

Maintaining that *Maud*'s technique more perfectly fulfills the visionary formalisms of writers such as Ure and Smiles should not flatten it to a reflection of prior history, as if the pounding lines of "Go not, happy day" ought to be heard as the clatter of assembly lines. Instead, I want to explain why *Maud*, which has so often been read as a *cri de cœur*, seems to me Tennyson's most steely triumph of poetic calculation. Its formal control is double-edged. It loudly separated Tennyson from the sprawl of the Spasmodics by reasserting the primacy of poetic technique. The favorite poem in the 1855 volume was "The Brook," a comfortably sentimental narrative.[83] If Tennyson had continued to write such poetry, he would have been more beloved by nineteenth-century readers and more scorned by twentieth-century ones. Yet the aspects of *Maud* that make it go against so many trends of the 1850s also register most accurately its historical place in an increasingly technological society. Only in Tennyson's art could formal discipline liberate itself from the ends of profit or efficiency and come into its own as pure technique.

If the Victorians sentimentalized *Maud*, the poets of high modernism recovered the full ambivalence of its rebellion and conformity. T. S. Eliot in particular was a careful student; in "The Love Song of J. Alfred Prufrock," for example, he echoes the same lines in *Maud* that Clough quotes: "There will be time, there will be time / To prepare a face to meet the faces that you meet."[84] At one level, Prufrock's obsession with his appearance is a metaphoric commentary on Eliot's own exacting concern with his poetry's formal aspects. In his essay on Tennyson, Eliot veiled as a snub a remarkable insight into himself and Tennyson when he maintained that "Tennyson's surface . . . is intimate with his depths."[85] Consciously or not, he was revising and expanding Tennyson's comment on Byron: "Byron's merits are on the surface."[86] Tennyson's faint praise hides his engagement with Byron as much as Eliot's hides his with Tennyson. Their comments suggest a mini-genealogy for modernism as a movement from the hidden depths of Romanticism's rebellious heroes to the oblique self-revelations of modernism's avant-garde technique. Tennyson's engagement with Byron demonstrated for modernism how to secure the artist's presence in the text without making the act of writing equivalent to transparent self-confession.

CHAPTER 6

The shady side of the sword
Bulwer Lytton, Disraeli, Wilde, and Byron's homosexuality

Eve Kosofsky Sedgwick has argued that "issues of modern homo/heterosexual definition are structured, not by the supersession of one model and the consequent withering away of another, but instead by the relations enabled by the unrationalized coexistence of different models during the times they do coexist."[1] This chapter will use Byron's reception to explore models of homosexuality that have been overlooked in work on sexual definitions in Victorian Britain. Some, following the lead of Foucault, have focused on the discursive construction of homosexuality in the disciplines of medicine and law.[2] Others, making more essentialist assumptions, have examined the writings of authors who were attracted to other men.[3] In either case, the object of investigation is recognizable as homosexual experience, either in terms of Victorian legal and medical definitions or in terms of a more transhistorical notion of homosexuality.

This chapter questions this recognizability by describing circumstances in which cultivating the appearance of sexual deviance could function as a means of self-advancement. The key is "cultivating an appearance," because for Edward Bulwer Lytton and Benjamin Disraeli, the authors on whom I will concentrate first, appearance was all. While whether or not they were "really" homosexuals is an alluring question, it is unanswerable because of the impossibility of defining a "real" homosexual in this period. What is clear is that both men imitated potentially scandalous aspects of Byron's behavior, as they understood it, to achieve social prominence. By almost transgressing codes of respectable behavior, they represented themselves as ersatz Byrons, whom they knew as the great celebrity and as one who committed the most unspeakable sexual crimes. "Performing" Byron was respectable and scandalous at once. The relation between celebrity and homosexuality allowed homosexual performance, far from behavior to be hidden or closeted, to be a risky ticket to success.

Foucault is a necessary but problematic influence on my analysis. His treatment of how "the nineteenth-century homosexual became a personage, a past, a case history, and a childhood, in addition to being a type of life, a life form, and a morphology, with an indiscreet anatomy and possibly a mysterious physiology," has become indispensable.[4] Yet Foucault disturbingly obscures relations between the body and agency: "The problem is that Foucault . . . operates without a developed notion of desire or its equivalent; thus Foucault's body is only the prey of *reactive* forces — normalising and individuating forces, and Foucault's genealogy remains incomplete."[5] While Foucault insists that discourse producing homosexuality allowed for resistance as well as normalization, the challenge is to describe not merely the production and deployment of the category of the homosexual, but also the uses to which possessing a homosexual body might be put.

I want to address this challenge by appropriating Pierre Bourdieu's category of "symbolic capital" in the way that Toril Moi has appropriated the term for feminist purposes.[6] Moi describes how a Bourdieuean perspective "assumes that gender is always a socially *variable* entity, one which carries different amounts of symbolic capital in different contexts."[7] She suggests that in analyzing a woman's career, gender cannot be assumed to be automatically disadvantageous in all contexts, at least not always to the same extent. While gender and sexuality are not commensurate as analytical categories, I would suggest that the category of symbolic capital is useful in Moi's terms for analyzing homosexuality in Victorian Britain. I will argue in particular that despite harsh legal penalties for buggery, contexts arose in which *being perceived* as homosexual could function as positive symbolic capital. These contexts depended on Byron's career as the most famous poet of his day and the one with the most scandalous sexual history. Byron's fame invited others to imitate him, but Victorians could react with considerable tension to which aspects of Byron young men were choosing to imitate.

Bulwer Lytton and Disraeli, as "imitation" Byrons, amassed symbolic capital by performing Byron's behavior. This imitation underscores the impossibility of understanding their behavior in terms of whether or not they were "really" homosexuals. Treating performance as symbolic capital undermines any explanation pointing to an "innate" sexuality as an originary cause. A Byronic role was such a central aspect of both men's careers, from such an early age, that it is pointless to ask if they imitated Byron because they actually were homosexuals or if they acted like homosexuals because they imitated Byron. Judith Butler's description of gender provides a more useful way of conceptualizing their relation to sexuality: "Consider gender . . . as *a corporeal style*, an 'act,' as it were, which is both intentional and performative, where *'performative'* suggests a dramatic and contingent construction of meaning."[8] Rather than adjudicating priority, I am more interested in how both men gained symbolic capital by performing with such skill that, rather than being forced to flee the country like Byron, they landed themselves in Parliament.

How did Byron's homosexuality become part of his popular legend? The first issue to face is that of definition, since, as Louis Crompton has noted, *"homosexual* and *gay* are both words that would have puzzled Byron's contemporaries."[9] Of the many models for male-male sexuality that Byron might have inherited from eighteenth-century discourses, the most prominent was what Randolph Trumbach describes as the "effeminate sodomite," who had sex exclusively with males and took on feminine characteristics, including the possibility of a passive role in sex.[10] As described in the eighteenth century, this role associated a tendency toward sexual action, intercourse with other males, with gendered behavior, effeminacy, which was seen as morally degenerate. As Ed Cohen notes about an eighteenth-century description of sodomites, " 'sodomy' . . . is merely the theoretical designation for an extreme form of social dissolution predicated on the negation of the 'manly' ideal."[11]

Although effeminacy negated a social ideal, it was not illegal; anal penetration and emission (known as buggery) were. Blackstone's *Commentaries*, which Byron read, outlawed "that sodomitical, detestable, and abominable Sin called Buggery, (not to be named among Christians)."[12] A man might commit buggery and not be effeminate, as one writer discovered to his surprise in 1813 when he learned that "males who prostituted themselves were often not effeminate men, but coalmerchants, police runners, drummers, waiters, servants, and a grocer."[13] By the same token, a man might be effeminate and not guilty of buggery. The discursive association of effeminacy with buggery created room for interpretive ambiguity in the face of effeminate behavior. Such behavior was not an *infallible* sign that a man practiced buggery, but it allowed conjecture that he *might*.[14] The association between a personality type (the effeminate) and particular sexual action (buggery) created a potential for ambiguity that Byron's career made available to Bulwer Lytton and Disraeli as a source of symbolic capital.

As Jerome Christensen has argued, ambiguity was at the center of conflicts surrounding Byron's sexuality.[15] While no one has invented a model to account for a sexuality as omnivorous as his, contemporaries often noted a strongly effeminate side to his character. Lady Blessington found his "voice and accent . . . effeminate," while Thomas Moore saw "a feminine cast of character" in "his caprices, fits of weeping, sudden affections and dislikes."[16] Byron's contemporaries often associated this effeminacy with his dandyism. Isaac Disraeli wrote about him: "I once met Lord Byron before he was known, before he travelled. Such a fantastic and effeminate thing I never saw. It was all rings and curls and lace. I was ashamed to speak to him; he looked more like a girl than a boy. I remember his shirt collar was all thrown over from his neck, and I observed him, while he spoke to some one, fence with a light cane in a very affected manner."[17] Scrope Davies said that he caught Byron once with his hair *en papillote*, at which Byron said, "I am as vain of my curls as a girl of sixteen."[18] While it would be misleading to argue that effeminacy was the sole or even dominant trait in Byron's character, it was marked enough to be noticed by a wide variety of observers. Although no contemporary accounts explicitly link suspicions about Byron's sexual relations with other males to his effeminacy, rumors about his being a sodomite that appeared after his separation from Lady Byron were probably made more credible because of his often-noticed effeminacy.[19]

To describe the contemporary response to Byron's sexuality, I borrow D. A. Miller's term, the "open secret."[20] An open secret is scandalous information that most in a particular group know, but none discusses. The aristocrats in Regency society reinforced their class solidarity by tolerating behavior that flouted norms associated with Victorian "bourgeois morality" as set out in the work of writers such as Hannah More, Maria Edgeworth, and Jane Taylor. As Alison Adburgham has argued, a married aristocrat, far from being an angel in the house, "could indulge in delicate *amitiés amoureuses*—always provided she conducted them with discretion. The one unpardonable sin was indiscretion."[21] The lines between acceptable and unacceptable behavior were sharply drawn: Lady Holland, who had been divorced, was accepted into society only after many years, while Lady Blessington, who had been a kept woman, was never considered respectable. As Virginia Woolf noted of Regency society, "the shadow of a sword" fell across women's lives. On one side all was "correct, definite, orderly"; on the other, all was confusion in which "[t]he brilliant fade; the great mysteriously disappear; the diamonds turn to cinders."[22] On one side of the sword, Byron's sodomy was secret; on the other, it was "open."

Sodomy, which I will equate with buggery at the risk of some historical oversimplification, was the most charged of open secrets because it was a capital offense. Notes accompanying *Don Leon*, a poem written in the 1830s describing Byron's life in terms of homosexual encounters, list members of the upper classes arrested on charges of sodomy; these arrests may be taken as evidence of more widespread tendencies. The arrest of William Bankes, a man whom Byron knew at Cambridge, provides a good example of the lengths to which the upper classes would go to protect an open secret. In 1833, after Bankes, MP for Dorsetshire, was caught "with his breeches and braces unbuttoned at ten at night" in the company of a "soldier named Flower," aristocrats, professors, and clergymen attested that he "was never yet known to be guilty of any expression bordering on licentiousness or profaneness."[23] The jury acquitted Bankes despite incriminating evidence because so many attested that his character was not that associated with sodomites. The acquittal sustained the pretense that Bankes was not guilty; his sexuality could remain an open secret, rather than an open scandal.

Byron never faced anything so public as a sodomy trial. The crisis in his career occurred during his separation from his wife. The most widely publicized reason for it, the rumored affair with the actress Mrs. Mardyn, was largely a sop for the general public. The fashionable world speculated about more refined vices, sodomy and incest prominent among them. In the Renaissance, these were perceived as related, and sodomy and incest still appeared side by side in language about Byron's separation, as if they were equivalent, unmanly forms of "depravity."[24] For example, Byron's best friend, John Cam Hobhouse, hoping to intervene for Byron's benefit, drew up a memorandum in which Lady Byron was to disavow "cruelty, systematic unremitted neglect, gross & repeated infidelities—incest & —."[25] Sodomy, as the less speakable of the two, had to be simultaneously acknowledged and hidden; Hobhouse forced it into secrecy even as he gestured to it as "—."

Vivid traces of the mentality of the open secret occur in a letter by Amelia Opie; she reproaches Lady Byron: "She was excused—every one knew the character of Lord Byron. Why then did she, as if in self-justification, make every one in her circle acquainted with his most secret depravity? I never can excuse Lady Byron's conduct, though I can make allowances for her as a spoiled child, and a flattered woman, who never knew contradiction till she became a wife."[26] Opie reproaches Lady Byron not because Byron's secrets are too shocking to be described, but because they are not secrets. Since "every one knew the character of Lord Byron," Lady Byron is to be blamed for forcing upon society the unwanted acknowledgment of a previously open secret. For her part, Opie restores Byron's secret by leaving his "depravity" unspecified.

Yet even as she does so, she writes herself into the special circle that knows "details" about Byron, as opposed to those who simply know that he and his wife had separated. In blaming Lady Byron, Opie positions herself as someone who is in the know, but who is more refined than Lady Byron because she recognizes proprieties about what should not be described. The letter contributes to reproducing an inner circle by reifying a "world," to which Opie belongs, that knows Byron's character and therefore does not need Lady Byron's insinuations.

After Byron's death, his sexuality continued to occasion gestures such as Opie's through which high society could construct itself as an elite. To be in the know about Byron in the late 1820s and 1830s stamped one as belonging to an inner circle, whether one wanted the distinction or not, as William Macready's diary for August 11, 1835 indicates:

At dinner the conversation led to the alleged cause of Lord Byron's parting with Lady Byron, and some observations were made which occasioned me disagreeable sensations; being evidently perceived, it made me quite embarrassed, and I did not in consequence recover the tone of my mind all day, uncomfortable as to the impression my want of self-possession might have caused, for which there was no actual reason. In the same way I always became embarrassed and confused before I had children, when the want of them was alluded to. I am very weak in this respect.[27]

Macready's embarrassment signals, among other things, the discomfort of a man not yet at ease with knowing the secrets belonging to his social circle. He is less explicit than Opie about causes of his embarrassment; he attributes it merely to having heard "some observations." Yet Macready's ability to hear "observations" and to be disturbed by them marks him, like Opie, as someone in the know about Byron. And like Opie, Macready preserves the secret by giving no details. Sodomy could not be named even in personal writing. Keeping it out of writing also kept Byron's secret out of circulation beyond the small circle to which Macready and Opie belonged.

Leonore Davidoff and Catherine Hall have traced the construction of a normative masculinity during this period, which they describe as being organized around "a man's determination and skill in manipulating the economic environment, always within an abiding belief in a world shaped by religious forces."[28] Since Byron had flouted this norm's economic and religious aspects, his fame was useful in early Victorian society; it contained masculine deviance by isolating it in the figure of a glamorous author. It is difficult to create a population study of young men who imitated "Byron" during the 1820s and 1830s, but writers of the period frequently noted his effect on masculine behavior, as I noted in chapter 2. Imitating Byron in fashionable society carried a special charge because of its possession of Byron's open secret. Byronic modes of behavior carried a faint aura of scandal: a man *might* be a sodomite, as Byron supposedly had been, but one could never be sure. An upper-class imitator of Byron could leave his peers guessing just how far his imitation extended.

For young men aspiring to enter the fashionable world, performing Byronic effeminacy was a dangerous but certain way to attract attention. It operated as a form of symbolic capital that might compensate for the lack of more conventional forms of social capital, such as family connections. While not all Byron's imitators chose to reproduce the ambiguity of his sexuality, Bulwer Lytton and Disraeli did so quite effectively. They used an aura of sexual deviance to catapult themselves to prominent positions in London's fashionable world. As I will argue, the sexual secrets to which their public appearances seemed to point served as seductive covers for more banal but more damaging secrets that they needed to hide.

The fashionable world was politically powerful as well as socially and culturally exclusive because several of its members were actual or potential legislators: "Literature, politics, and fashion were inextricably mingled in the shifting strata of society after the Napoleonic Wars."[29] The social capital that Bulwer Lytton and Disraeli acquired through their imitations of Byron, which consisted chiefly of powerful connections, turned them not merely into local celebrities but also into potential politicians. Their novels, particularly Bulwer Lytton's *Pelham* and Disraeli's *Venetia*, narrate transitions from characters associated with Byron's sexual and political precedents (dandies) to ones that manifest a more "mature" sexual and political state (Members of Parliament). Partly on the strength of these novels' political stances, Bulwer Lytton and Disraeli became politicians. It was a canny move for young men wanting to break into the hetero-social world of fashionable London to look like homosexuals, although they had to reform themselves into respectable hetero-sexuals to gain access to the homosocial House of Commons. These sexual and social contortions were made possible through skilled reconstructions of Byron's homosexual role.

No documents that I have seen about Bulwer Lytton and Disraeli indicate that they knew that Byron had sexual relations with other men. My reasons for believing that they knew are, first, that their personal writings and novels frequently mention admiration for Byron and their interest in his scandal, and second, that these men became part of a society that constituted itself as an elite partly through its knowledge of Byron's open secret.[30] They were also closely acquainted with each other and with several of those whom I quoted for their descriptions of Byron's effeminacy. If there were secrets to be known about Byron, they were in a position to know them.

Shortly after Byron's death in 1824, Bulwer Lytton had an affair with Lady Caroline Lamb.[31] As he confessed in his autobiographical fragment, having an affair with Lamb was the next best thing to having an affair with Byron himself:

> She interested me chiefly ... by her recollections and graphic descriptions of Byron, with whom her intimacy had lasted during the three most brilliant years of his life in England ... At the time I now speak of, there was no bitterness in her talk of him, and whatever faults she found in his character, she fired up in his defence if any one else abused him. Of the hideous calumnies concerning himself and Mrs. Leigh (indeed, of all calumnies involving the charge of crime) she certainly acquitted him.[32]

Written during Bulwer Lytton's conservative middle age, this reminiscence whitewashes himself, Byron, and Lamb. Lamb had been a major source of the "hideous calumnies" that were spread about Byron during the separation scandal, particularly the charges of incest and sodomy.[33] Bulwer Lytton's account is more convincing in its suggestion that Lamb interested him because of her ability to pronounce upon those "calumnies" than in its claim that she acquitted Byron of the charges. Although Lamb "certainly acquitted" Byron of all "calumnies involving the charge of crime," it sounds as if she were more incriminating about calumnies involving lesser charges.

The affair with Lamb is a vivid example of how Bulwer Lytton performed his life as an echo of Byron's. More important, this echo included his imitations of Byron's effeminacy in terms of dandyism. Charles Sumner, for example, noted, "Bulwer was here a few moments ago in his flash *falsetto* dress, with high-heel boots, a white great coat, and a flaming blue cravat."[34] For Sumner, Bulwer's attention-getting falsetto dress was his most salient characteristic; Bulwer Lytton's effeminacy succeeded in catching the eye, if not in gaining approval. In 1830, H. F. Chorley described how Bulwer Lytton had impressed him as they left one of Lady Blessington's gatherings: "I had guessed pretty much of what I did see — an egotism, a vanity — all thrown up to the surface. He is a thoroughly satin character, but then it is the richest satin. There was something inconceivably strange to me in his dwelling, with a sort of hankering tone, on D'Orsay's physical advantages."³⁵ Chorley goes further than Sumner in associating Bulwer Lytton's effeminacy with male-male desire. The bafflement at Bulwer Lytton's "inconceivably strange" behavior is another example of the open secret at work. Although Chorley does not connect Bulwer Lytton's action with Byron or Byronism, Bulwer Lytton was imitating Byron who, seven years earlier, had also hankered over D'Orsay. After meeting him, Byron wrote to Thomas Moore that Lady Blessington had "a very handsome companion . . . who has all the air of a *Cupidon déchaîné* " (*LJ*, x: 136). Bulwer Lytton's Byronic hankering allowed him to perform himself as the puzzling object for the gaze of those such as Chorley.

An 1839 cartoon drew Bulwer Lytton and Disraeli as dandy doubles of one another: their close friendship encouraged their contemporaries to view them as a pair.³⁶ Bulwer Lytton's Byronically dandyish behavior characterized Disraeli as well. Commenting on Isaac Disraeli's description of Byron as "all rings and curls and lace," Disraeli's biographer notes that "such a description could have fitted [Isaac's] own affected son" during Disraeli's Wycombe campaign.³⁷ The young Disraeli modeled his appearance after Byron's, with his dark curls, pale skin, and dandyish clothes, and he attracted comments similar to those made about Bulwer Lytton. William Bates, for example, called him "the perfumed boy-exquisite who forced his way into the salons of peeresses," and N. P. Willis noted that his hair was "parted and put away with the smooth carefulness of a girl's."³⁸ He fashioned his behavior in relation to women and instructed himself to "talk to women as much as you can. This is the best school."³⁹ Disraeli's clothes attracted attention: he appeared in society dressed "in a black velvet suit, lined with white satin, gorgeously embroidered waistcoats, his breast a medley of gold chains, rings on his fingers, and, attached to his wrist by a tasselled cord, one of the canes that had astounded Gibraltar."⁴⁰

Regenia Gagnier has detailed how dandies simultaneously reinforced and challenged normative masculinity. Her suggestion that the dandy "infiltrates society with minimal repression, for, after all, he is 'only posing' " explains why neither Bulwer Lytton nor Disraeli ever faced a Wildean débâcle.⁴¹ Dandyism, like maintaining Byron's open secret, reinforced the boundary between an elite class and the rest of society. While dandyism did not involve open sanction of sodomy, it did encourage "poses" that were titillating precisely because, if they were "real," they could bring down the full fury of Victorian law, as happened in the case of William Bankes. In imitating Byron's dandyism, Bulwer Lytton and Disraeli were at once playing with fire and playing it safe: the more open they were, the less the members of fashionable society needed to concern themselves with a secret. Byronism provided them with a repertoire of poses for impersonating the success vital to the fashionable world that had so much power over literary and political careers in the 1820s and 1830s.

In emphasizing homosexual performativity, I am not denying that the two men may have had erotic attractions to other men. On the contrary, I am convinced they did, although the evidence is slender. Bulwer Lytton's marriage, like Byron's, ended in a separation that became one of the scandals of Victorian society. In 1856 when his wife Rosina made public his mistreatment of her, she called herself a "pauper of those Sodom and Gomorrah sinks of iniquity, the Park Lane and Knebworth *Unions*."[42] Even admitting her flair for the histrionic, I find her Sodom and Gomorrah reference is telling because it associates Bulwer Lytton with traditional images of sodomy. Later, she suggested that Bulwer Lytton acknowledged the parallel between Byron and himself: "[O]ne day at a dinner at our house, when some vituperative humbug was going on about poor Lord Byron, and someone said, 'No woman could have lived with such a man,' my Lord Lytton pointed to me, and said, 'There is one that could, for she has lived with me.' "[43] As for Disraeli, his biographer notes that the "homosexual element in Disraeli's friendships with younger men . . . cannot be ignored . . . even if the relationship was almost certainly not physical."[44] My point, however, is that such a "homosexual element" cannot be used to explain why either Bulwer Lytton or Disraeli imitated Byron in the way that he did. Imitating Byron and being a homosexual had no necessary connection. These men performed themselves as ersatz Byrons not because of what they were, but because of what they wanted to become.

Why would they imitate Byron if he were so risky a precedent? The answer involves the advantages and disadvantages surrounding secrecy. While imitating Byron may have been thoroughly commonplace in the circles in which Bulwer Lytton and Disraeli moved, it had the potential to raise suspicions about possible deviance. For both men, such suspicions functioned as a cover, only not for their "true" sexuality. Rather, reproducing the open secret of Byronism allowed them to keep in the closet not fascinating sexual secrets but the more banal ones of their social positions. Although Bulwer Lytton had the advantage of an established family, he was poor. When his mother, outraged by his marriage, cut off his allowance, he was driven to adopt the ungentlemanly career of novelist: "A great part of every night was occupied with earning money to spend the following day. But always expenditure exceeded income, and the debts began to pile."[45] Bulwer Lytton's elegant Byronism masked harsh realities: better . to be suspected of sexual deviance than of fiscal insolvency. Playing a dandyish Childe Harold/Don Juan masked the laborious grind of being a literary hack.

Disraeli's Byronism was more brazen than Bulwer Lytton's because he faced greater barriers to success. As a Jew, Disraeli had no access to the schools where Byron and Bulwer Lytton formed social connections. Moreover, he faced an entrenched tradition of British anti-Semitism that would have coded him as sexually deviant. His father's literary career had given him some connections in the literary world, and his first novel *Vivian Grey* (1826) was a *succès de scandale* because it seemed to have been written by a member of the fashionable world who was fictionalizing real people. Actually, Disraeli had little firsthand experience of the life he portrayed, and *Blackwood's Magazine* quickly unmasked him as "an obscure person for whom nobody cares a straw."[46] Undaunted, he decided to become "a literary prostitute" for "Tempting Mother Colburn," the leading publisher of silver-fork novels.[47] He accordingly wrote *The Young Duke*, which he subtitled "A Moral Tale, Though Gay" after Byron's *Don Juan*, and sent it to Bulwer Lytton for his comments and advice. As a result, the two became fast friends, to the point of even visiting brothels together: in one of his letters, Bulwer Lytton makes an appointment to meet Disraeli at the "Naughty House."[48] Bulwer Lytton's friendship was a valuable means of entrance for Disraeli into a world that might otherwise have been shut to him. Disraeli's own effeminacy might be seen as his imitation of Bulwer Lytton's imitation of Byron. For both, performing Byron provided a role by which to create themselves as social successes.

Although I have thus far described them as if their Byron imitations were solely an aspect of their public behavior in high society, their novelistic careers complicated their relation to Byron and homosexual performativity. More than anything else, these novels guaranteed that their perilous balance between Byronic fame and Byronic scandal remained safe. They could be outrageous in society because their novels, written for a far wider audience, took so critical a stance toward Byron. The plots put characters modeled on Byron in close emotional relations with other men, but ultimately retreat to more normative heterosexual ties. Whether or not their plots entirely silenced the suspicions of contemporaries, they effectively countered those who might accuse Bulwer Lytton and Disraeli of copying Byron too closely, in any sphere.

The novels also provided a way for both to present themselves to readers not belonging to London's social elite and whose codes of masculinity therefore may have been closer to those described by Davidoff and Hall. Both authors followed the familiar pattern of a narrative of transition, using the model of the *Bildungsroman* to construct narratives about growing beyond Byron into what they represented as Victorian norms. While this pattern occurred in several of their works, the stigmatization of Byron was most vivid in novels with characters explicitly modeled on him, *Pelham* and *Venetia*. In these novels, they created a respectable role for themselves by positioning it against a more suspect representation of Byronic sexuality. Bulwer Lytton and Disraeli developed myths of historical succession in which the sexual, literary, and political shortcomings of Romanticism were corrected by what these novels represented as a compromise between "bourgeois" and "aristocratic" systems of value. Although the Byron figures fall in love with women, the heterosexual relations are incorporated into a triangulated pattern of homosocial desire, which Sedgwick has described as one in which a female character mediates desire between two male ones.[49] I use her categories because I want to demonstrate how patterns that she has shown to operate transhistorically acquired local political uses in the early Victorian period.

Such narratives of compromise had political benefits: Bulwer

Lytton entered Parliament three years after the publication of *Pelham*, and Disraeli entered the year *Venetia* appeared. Their movement from literature to politics was not unusual for the London elite, because in the 1830s cultural and political hegemony went hand in hand.[50] Byron's political career in England as a Radical Whig had been brief and unsuccessful. Bulwer Lytton and Disraeli faced the challenge of defining themselves against it. Their novels associated Romanticism with Byron, homosocial desire, poetic romance, and failed political radicalism; the Victorian era, with characters who stood for themselves, heterosexual marriage, novelistic realism, and successful political platforms. Differences in circumstances led them to endorse opposite political platforms, but both appropriated the movement from homosocial to heterosexual as a paradigm for the movement from the Romantic to the Victorian legislator.

Pelham and *Venetia* are silver-fork novels, a genre almost entirely ignored by the contemporary academic canon of Victorian novels.[51] Given the upsurge of interest in how novels shaped Victorian subjectivities, class relations, and gender roles, it seems that these novels would be a significant focus of interest, but they remain known only to the most dedicated specialists. Bulwer Lytton's and Disraeli's lasting literary reputations come from novels that they wrote in other genres, such as Bulwer Lytton's historical romance *The Last Days of Pompeii* and Disraeli's industrial novel *Sybil*.

The marginalization of the fashionable novel may comment on the academy's own fears of fashion. It also points to how these novels marginalize their own subject-matter. As Bonnie Anderson notes, they treat fashion as "repetitious, boring, and false," even while they revel in it.[52] The goal of all the heroes and heroines is to leave the fashionable world for a happy home. Hence the silver-fork novels initiated the trend leading to their own supersession by the socially committed novels of the 1840s. Even as writers exploited the fashionable world's allure, they insisted on the greater depth of life beyond it. This generic self-destructiveness provided the perfect background for Bulwer Lytton's and Disraeli's narratives of transition away from Byron. They could align Byronic characters with the silver-fork world that needed, at last, to be replaced by a home more in line with

new religious, literary, and legal norms. Characters who could
be understood to stand for themselves, in contrast, reached heterosexual happiness and, at the same time, membership in
Parliament.

Bulwer Lytton's *Pelham*, which is best known as the object of
Carlyle's satire in *Sartor Resartus*, responded to Disraeli's *Vivian
Grey*. Vivian, a dandy, was taken to embody the satirical Byron;
the novel had been puffed as "a sort of Don Juan in prose."[53]
Pelham starts out as another Vivian, imitating in prose the satiric
insouciance of *Don Juan*: "For a coxcomb there is no mercy—for
a coquet no pardon. They are, as it were, the dissenters of
society—no crime is too bad to be imputed to them; they do
not believe the religion of others—they set up a deity of their
own vanity—all the orthodox vanities of others are offended.
Then comes the bigotry—the stake—the *auto-da-fé* of scandal.
What, alas! is so implacable as the rage of vanity?" (p. 84).[54]
Pelham, an idealized Bulwer Lytton, here recognizes similarities
between Promethean Byronic hero and Byronic coxcomb: both
rebel against society. He mimics Byronic rebelliousness so well
that he becomes impatient with Byronism itself. Instead of imitating Byronic fashions, he decides not to curl his hair and to
dress entirely in black. Contemporary readers quickly translated
Pelham's dandyish iconoclasm into a fad for all-black outfits.[55]

If Pelham's character derives from the satiric Byron, his friend
Reginald de Glanville conforms to the clichés of the Byronic
hero. As Bulwer Lytton noted in his 1840 Preface, "Sir Reginald
Glanville was drawn purposely of the would-be Byron School as
a foil to Pelham" (p. 452). He is "a man of even vast powers—
of deep thought—of luxuriant, though dark imagination . . . subject, at times, to a gloom and despondency, which seemed almost
like aberration of intellect" (p. 189). Like Byron, Glanville is a
handsome aristocrat and a best-selling poet who captures the
imagination of women and whose first speech in Parliament
makes a great impression. Bulwer Lytton emphasizes that Glanville is no mere imitation Byron but the genuine article: "Nothing
like the dramatic brown studies, and quick starts, which young
gentlemen, in love with Lara and Lord Byron, are apt to practice.
There never, indeed, was a character that possessed less cant of
any description" (p. 190). Since Byron himself was famous for
his detestation of cant, Lord Glanville appears as the "real"

Byron, as opposed to mere imitators like the "young gentlemen."

The plot depends on the intense affection between Pelham and Glanville. Pelham repeatedly avows his admiration for Glanville: "I had never seen so perfect a specimen of masculine beauty, at once physical and intellectual" (p. 184). When Glanville is suspected of murder, Pelham initially believes him to be guilty. To his relief, however, Glanville explains his part in the melodramatic events that cast unjust suspicion upon him. As a result, Pelham dedicates himself to Glanville more fervently than ever: "Let me accompany you abroad; I will go with you to whatever corner of the world you may select. We will plan together every possible method of concealing our retreat ... I will tend upon you, watch over you, bear with you, with more than the love and tenderness of a brother. You shall see me only when you wish it" (p. 380). Although Glanville refuses this offer, Pelham sets out to clear his name. He risks his life to discover witnesses to Glanville's innocence; through his efforts, all charges against Glanville are dropped, but Glanville, exhausted by his trials, dies. In the course of his efforts, Pelham (unlike Vivian Grey) outgrows his superficial dandyism to espouse solid values of self-improvement. As he tells Glanville, "If the past is gloomy, I do not see the necessity of dwelling upon it. If the mind can make one vigorous exertion, it can another: the same energy you put forth in acquiring knowledge, would also enable you to baffle misfortune" (p. 222).

As J. W. Oakley has argued, *Pelham* is not about the abdication of the aristocracy, but about the construction of the reformed gentleman who "could be adequate to the increasing ambiguity of social boundaries."[56] Bulwer Lytton hoped that Pelham, as a reformed gentleman, would replace Byron as a heroic ideal for readers of popular literature. In his 1840 preface, he boasted that the work

contributed to put an end to the Satanic mania, — to turn the thoughts and ambition of young gentlemen without neckcloths, and young clerks who were sallow, from playing the Corsair, and boasting that they were villains. If, mistaking the irony of Pelham, they went to the extreme of emulating the foibles which that hero attributes to himself, those were foibles at least more harmless, and even more manly and noble, than the conceit of a general detestation of mankind. (p. 452)

Whether or not clerks actually played the Corsair, *Pelham* directed

them to close their Byron and open their Bulwer Lytton. When
one character wonders if any poet will ever be as popular as
Byron, another replies that a "thorough revolution in taste" is
necessary, which will "build itself a temple out of the ruins of
the old worship" (p. 473). Bulwer Lytton attempted to create
such a revolution by replacing Glanville's "Satanic mania" with
Pelham's "manly and noble" style.

Pelham's moral growth has an erotic component: the novel
rewards him with Glanville's sister, Ellen. Bulwer Lytton's treatment of her is a good example of what Sedgwick calls "the
novelistic tradition in which the routing through women of male
homosocial desire had the most perfunctory presence."[57] Glanville
conveniently expires in Pelham's arms immediately after Pelham's
wedding to Ellen; at the moment of his death, Pelham feels that
his "whole frame shuddered from limb to limb" (p. 475). The
eroticism of his relation with Glanville remains far greater than
that of his relation to Ellen, whom he does not even mention in
the final chapter describing his married life. Nevertheless, Ellen's
perfunctory presence is vital to establishing Pelham's credentials
as a model heterosexual hero.

The novel connects the overthrow of Byronism to Pelham's
growth as a politician. Although Glanville is a skilled orator,
Pelham becomes the model Radical. He breaks with his friend
Lord Vincent because Vincent's allies are too oligarchic and
describes one as a "Whig, who says in the Upper House, that
whatever may be the distresses of the people, they shall not be
gratified at the cost of one of the despotic privileges of the
aristocracy. Go to!—I will have none of him" (p. 216). Even
after the leader of his party does not give him a promised political
office, Pelham stays loyal because he wishes to remain above
personal considerations: "[I]t has ever been the object of my
maturer consideration to direct my particular attention to that
side of the question which such undue partizans are the least
likely to espouse" (p. 344). Pelham the dedicated reformer
replaces Pelham the scheming dandy. Whereas Glanville, like
Byron himself, contributes only a few speeches, Pelham sticks to
his party to become a powerful legislator. He ends by describing
himself as deep in study to become an even more effective
politician. The implication is that Pelham, as a figure for Bulwer
Lytton, has outgrown Byronic sexuality and dandyism and,

having married, is ready for Parliament. The novel imagines a moment of historical transition with Bulwer Lytton, the reformed dandy, in the vanguard.

Pelham's spectacular success alone did not make Bulwer Lytton a politician. The novel did, however, bring him considerable fame in the literary and fashionable world, and reviewers commented upon its political sympathies. For example, the *Examiner* noted that "its piquant exposures . . . will lead persons to reflect who would resist any more laboured and direct assaults of reason."[58] *Pelham* was an important start because it transformed the rumors about Byron's relations with men into an allegory about the growth of a new breed of aristocrat responsive to a range of concerns wider than that of the Byronic Glanville. It made Bulwer Lytton known to those outside the small circle of London's fashionable elite. The radical sentiments of *Pelham* and his other novels "so impressed his personality on the minds of reformist leaders that all through the summer of 1830 . . . invitations and suggestions to contest this constituency or that poured in upon him."[59] He had succeeded when in 1831 he was returned as the member for St. Ives. By then, *Fraser's Magazine* had begun the brutal attacks on his works that continued throughout the 1830s and made him all the more visible as a political Radical. Responding to Byron was not enough for his political success, but it gave him a start that could not be ignored.

Before turning to Disraeli, I must note how Thomas Moore's biography of Byron, which I discussed in chapter 2, altered early Victorian discourse about Byron's sexuality. Moore described in greater detail than any other biographer Byron's relations with other men, although he employed the anxious vocabulary of "romantic friendships."[60] His biography mystified Byron's sexuality enough that it earned Byron posthumous admiration as a paragon of masculine devotion. *Blackwood's Magazine* rhapsodized, "His longings for the love of brotherhood were intense and incessant; and, till they were satisfied by a return of affection, he knew no happiness."[61] John Wilson's effusiveness here sustains Byron's open secret by assimilating it to the norm of "brotherhood."

Not everyone was as gullible as Wilson. The author of *Don Leon*, the poem outing Byron as a sodomite, learned much from

Moore; the footnotes to the poem frequently refer to the biography for corroboration of Byron's passions. William Beckford's marginalia in his copy of Moore reveal his suspicions about Byron's sexuality:

When we combine together the various characteristic anecdotes contained in this compilation, instead of a wreath of laurel or a chaplet of roses we are presented with a garland of rue and vervaine, worthy of the boudoir of Proserpine. — If that most curious piece of autobiography said to have been committed to the flames, exhibited an ampler bouquet of the more fatal flowers, poisonous indeed must it have been, but for raking up bits and scraps — no matter how deteriorating — or publishing letters — no matter how confiding or confidential — no Enemy can match a friend — especially a literary one, well paid for the job in the bargain.

More records of attachments *à la Grecque*, a bit out of the common way it must needs be confessed, but perfectly pure and no doubt platonic if we take that excellent judge and pattern of purity, Mr. T. Moore's word for it.

Tell truth and shame the Devil — This old saw might be interpreted to mean that Ld. Byron's piratical amusements in the Levant — unknown to Hobhouse — were of a character to make Satan himself blush infernal sanguine red — Hell's proper hue.[62]

Beckford's comments about what he calls the "not always so mild, so *brotherly* Byron" suggest that he read behind Moore's elaborately euphemisms. While for readers such as Wilson, Moore's idealization of male friendship hid Byron's involvement in other relations, for those such as William Beckford, the biography all but shouted Byron's homosexuality. In general, the appearance of Moore's biography made Byron's relations with men at once more safe and more risky: the topic seemed acceptable, but had a lurking potential to be turned to scandal.

Moore's book had an immediate effect on the ways that the novels of Bulwer Lytton and Disraeli represented Byronic dandyism. If Bulwer Lytton had written *Pelham* after the publication of Moore's book, I suspect that he would have toned down the intensity of some of Pelham's professions for Glanville. He did make some telling alterations, such as changing Pelham's description of Glanville's "pale, but more than beautiful countenance" (p. 64) to "pale and remarkable countenance" (p. 461). When in 1830 he read the manuscript of Disraeli's *The Young Duke*, he advised Disraeli to "lop off" its "ornate and showy effeminacy," confessed that he found the "blonde edgings" of the Duke's dress "too bold," and added that "these are things ... that make enemies and scarcely make friends."[63] By 1837, when Disraeli wrote *Venetia*, he had taken Bulwer Lytton's advice and toned down the "effeminacy" of his earlier novels. Yet his strategy in writing *Venetia* was similar to Bulwer Lytton's in *Pelham*: he presented himself as the moral, political, and literary successor to Byron by manipulating the representation of Byron's sexuality. Although his book is a Tory *riposte* to Bulwer Lytton's Radical appropriation of Byron, Disraeli represents Byron's relations with other men with far greater distance than Bulwer Lytton.[64]

Emotional coolness does not make *Venetia* more conventional than *Pelham*; on the contrary, it is so odd that it can best be described as kooky. It has occasioned enormous confusion because its central characters have such peculiar relations to their historical originals. According to one critic, "the Byron of *Venetia*" is Plantagenet Cadurcis, while "Shelley is the prototype" of Marmion Herbert.[65] According to another, "Byron ... appears as Herbert, and Shelley, as Cadurcis."[66] A contemporary reviewer confessed to "extreme bewilderment" over the identities of the characters: "The characters, the fortunes, the lives, for example, of Byron and Shelley are traceable in these pages— yet no two events scarcely, in the life of either, are connected, or represented as they occurred."[67] The confusion, as Richard Garnett noted in 1887, arose because Disraeli "cuts Byron's relations with Lady Byron and Ada ... off from the character of Cadurcis, and superimposes them upon Herbert, leaving the rest unaltered ... The situation is Byronic, but the character is Shelleyan."[68]

Although Shelley had been the target of considerable abuse, he was never, so far as I know, subjected to rumors about sodomy resembling those that had spread about Byron. Disraeli in *Venetia* rewrote history as if the separation between Byron and Lady Byron were a separation between Shelley (Marmion Herbert) and Lady Byron (Lady Annabel), thereby deflecting from Byron the major scandal of his career.[69] The Byron character (Plantagenet Cadurcis) is young enough to fall in love with Venetia, the daughter of the marriage between Shelley and Lady Byron. This odd rearrangement of biographies allows Disraeli to keep Byron as a perpetual adolescent because his behavior is set against that of the more mature Shelley.

The novel's first part concerns the childhood friendship between Cadurcis and Venetia, which eventually leads to his requesting her hand in marriage; Disraeli's plot isolates the young Cadurcis from close relations with any other men except his tutor. Yet a different bond thwarts Cadurcis's love for Venetia, her loyalty to the father, Marmion Herbert, whom she has never seen. When Cadurcis denounces Herbert as a man who "is, at the same time, a traitor to his king and an apostate from his God!", Venetia scorns him (p. 201).[70] Immediately, in reaction to his disappointment, Cadurcis becomes Disraeli's version of the misanthropic but ambitious young Byron, who determines to make a name for himself in the world since he has been disappointed in love. He accordingly turns into a famous poet, much admired by women. Disraeli's portrayal closely resembles Moore's Byron before the separation scandal. The novel reproduces the interpretation of Byron that gained the most respectability among Disraeli's contemporaries.

After rejecting Cadurcis, Venetia becomes more obsessed with her father, and longs for a reunion with him. The novel's climax seems to come when she at last meets him in Italy and her passionate entreaties effect a surprisingly easy reconciliation between her parents. Yet the unexpected meeting in Italy of Herbert and Cadurcis quickly supplants this climactic reestablishment of a father–daughter bond. The intense attachment that develops between them overshadows the plot involving Venetia. She fades into one more female figure mediating the workings of homosocial desire. Like Bulwer Lytton in *Pelham*, Disraeli uses this "friendship" to define himself against the shortcomings of Romanticism.

We soon find Herbert thinking that Cadurcis was "by far the most hearty and amusing person he had ever known" (p. 411), and he confesses, "Cadurcis! It is very strange how often I have mused over that name. A year ago it was one of my few wishes to know him" (p. 413). For the most part, the dialogue that Disraeli gives them is fairly wooden, as when he flattens one of Shelley's most ringing statements: " 'Well, we will not compliment each other,' said Cadurcis; 'for, after all, it is a miserable craft. What is poetry but a lie, and what are poets but liars?' 'You are wrong, Cadurcis,' said Herbert, 'poets are the unacknowledged legislators of the world' " (p. 438). Nevertheless, at moments, the presentation acquires more erotic overtones, as when Herbert tells Cadurcis, "I can assure you, Lord Cadurcis, you have not a more sincere admirer of your genius. I am happy in your society" (p. 418), and Cadurcis, "putting his arm affectionately in Herbert's as they walked along," responds, "Dear friend! . . . all the happiness and all the sorrow of my life alike flow from your roof!" (p. 418).

Unlike Bulwer Lytton in *Pelham*, Disraeli does not represent the movement from Romantic to Victorian in a single character's life. Instead, the attachment of Herbert and Cadurcis underscores the extent to which they are both outdated as literary and political figures, despite their age difference. By allowing Herbert to reach an age that Shelley never attained, Disraeli can fantasize about Shelley's later development. He decides, unsurprisingly, that Shelley became disillusioned with some aspects of his idealism; Herbert tells Cadurcis, "Mine were but crude dreams. I wished to see man noble and happy; but if he will persist in being vile and miserable, I must even be content. I can struggle for him no more" (p. 415). Through the character of Cadurcis, Disraeli suggests that Byron's radicalism was only a pose to hide his more fundamental skepticism. Cadurcis says, "As for philosophy and freedom, and all that, they tell devilish well in a stanza; but men have always been fools and slaves, and fools and slaves they always will be" (p. 415). When Disraeli brings both men into contact, he replaces their republicanism with a weary pessimism that contrasts with the energy of his own Tory platform.

The novel strikes a similar note about literature; both Cadurcis and Herbert condemn themselves for their literary flaws:

"I have written like a boy," said Cadurcis. "I found the public bite, and so I baited on with tainted meat. I have never written for fame, only for notoriety; but I am satiated; I am going to turn over a new leaf."

"For myself," said Herbert, "if I ever had the power to impress my creations on my fellow-men, the inclination is gone, and perhaps the faculty is extinct . . . I am not altogether void of the creative faculty, but mine is a fragmentary mind; I produce no whole. Unless you do this, you cannot last; at least, you cannot materially affect your species." (p. 438)

In Disraeli's rewriting of history, Byron and Shelley reach maturity by deciding to conform to the images of them developed by the periodical reviews. Byron vows to abandon his instability and chart a new and more morally sound course. Shelley recognizes faults usually pointed out by reviewers and decides to stop writing. These artistic deaths prefigure their literal deaths: soon after this conversation, Cadurcis and Herbert both drown in a boating accident.

Disraeli narrates the transition away from Byron by replacing Herbert and Cadurcis with Venetia and George, Cadurcis's cousin. After Herbert and Cadurcis drown, George remains to inherit Cadurcis's title and become the ideal Tory hero. He returns Venetia and Lady Annabel to their ancestral home, Cherbury.[71] At Venetia's urging, George takes his seat in the House of Lords, and finally, in front of Cherbury, "the ancient pile lately renovated under [her] studious care" (p. 482), he proposes to her. His role is an idealization of Disraeli's as the outsider who can emerge as the true representative of Tory landed interests. In *Venetia*, those born to rank, Herbert and Cadurcis, fail it by falling into radicalism. Only George who, like Disraeli, grew up "without a single advantage save those that nature had conferred upon him" (p. 337), is left to become the aristocracy's savior. As in *Pelham*, Disraeli's novel associates political effectiveness with the movement from Byronic homosociality to normative heterosexuality.

Bulwer Lytton used Byron to support Radical positions while Disraeli used him to support Tory ones. When Bulwer Lytton wrote *Pelham*, Disraeli himself was a Radical, but in the early 1830s, he repeatedly failed as a Radical candidate. Tories were far more willing to welcome an outsider such as Disraeli; moreover, as *Venetia* reveals, Tory ideology offered him greater political capital because he could play the role of the outsider rescuing aristocratic privilege. Yet if the platforms of Bulwer Lytton and Disraeli differed, the vehicles through which they expressed them were similar. Just as the periodical press had been instrumental in disseminating Bulwer Lytton's views, so journals such as *Fraser's Magazine* spread knowledge of Disraeli's politics by responding to his novels' political views. *Fraser's* review of *Venetia* recognized Disraeli as an alternative to Bulwer Lytton's "frippery" and "foppery," and looked forward to his political career: "[W]e are convinced that, morally and political speaking, the Conservatives have received, and are likely to continue to receive, good service from the younger Disraeli."[72] As with Bulwer Lytton, the representation of sexuality in novels alone was not enough to make Disraeli's political fortune, yet a novel such as *Venetia* allowed his politics to reach more widely than they otherwise would have done. Although he had made several attempts to enter Parliament, he was not successful until 1837, the year *Venetia* was published.

Disraeli's dedication of *Venetia* to his patron, Lord Lyndhurst, provides a telling comment on the distinction between Disraeli the novelist and Disraeli the politician. He met Lyndhurst by sharing Lady Sykes, his mistress, with him. As Disraeli's private secretary later wrote, "The allegation, at the time, was that D. had introduced her to Lord L. and made use of the influence she acquired over Lord L., to forward his own advancement."[73] The contrast between the thinly veiled homoerotic machinations of history and the serenely heterosexual conclusion of *Venetia* can stand for the uses to which both Bulwer Lytton and Disraeli put their representations of Byron. Their novels' conclusions should not be taken to mean that they entirely rejected the "cover" of the homosexual role that had served them well during their climb to success. But once they had achieved literary and political recognition, they could, paradoxically, afford to be more closeted because they no longer needed the fashionable world's adulation. Whatever Shelley thought about poets and the law, Bulwer Lytton and Disraeli demonstrated that skillful responses to Byron's homosexuality allowed novelists to become the acknowledged legislators of Britain.

This chapter's second part examines Oscar Wilde's career, which engaged the most important aspects of Byron's reception in the later part of the Victorian era. One such aspect was a growing knowledge about Byron's homosexuality. Whereas for earlier writers, the question of whether or not they were "really" homosexuals was necessarily vexed, the case is different for Wilde, whose career was an originary moment in defining what a homosexual "really" was. Nevertheless, my hypothesis that homosexual performativity could function as symbolic capital does not become irrelevant simply because Wilde was a "real" homosexual practically by definition. He also used his sexuality as a daring pose through which to compensate for weaknesses in his social position.

Yet Wilde pushed his pose to an extreme. Although I have described the posing of Bulwer Lytton and Disraeli as their mode of protecting themselves, Wilde's more outrageous posing led to his downfall. The card left by the Marquess of Queensberry that started the chain of events leading to Wilde's trials read, "To Oscar Wilde posing Somdomite [*sic*]," which during the trials became "posing as a Sodomite."[74] Queensberry's accusation, at least initially, was not that Wilde really was a sodomite, but that he posed as one. His accusation was made more believable because Wilde, unlike Bulwer Lytton and Disraeli, did not use his writing to tame his scandalous performances. If Byron's poetry offered the reading public a commodified subjectivity, *The Picture of Dorian Gray* offered a commodified sexuality that was worth commodifying because it represented itself as deviant. Bulwer Lytton and Disraeli wrote themselves into a position of such respectability that they entered Parliament. Wilde's novel, in contrast, challenged codes of respectability even as its plot seemed to reinforce them.

Although Wilde's biography makes it tempting to treat his sexuality as the primary ground for any interpretation of him, I want to look at Byron's reception to suggest how Wilde's writing intertwined homosexuality with other developments in the later nineteenth century, especially the increasing split between "high" and "low" representations of literary value. Byron appeared both in the high, monumentalizing criticism of Matthew Arnold and in the low, enormously popular sensation novels of Mary Elizabeth Braddon and Louise de la Ramée (known as Ouida). Wilde's novel draws on late Victorian stereotypes about Byron's life and work to situate itself in an anomalous position between high and low forms. By so doing it indicates its simultaneous debt to and distance from the institutions enabling both forms: the academy and the book trade.

If questions remained in the first half of the century about Byron's enduring fame, events of the 1870s and 1880s resolved them. Uniform admiration did not suddenly replace older controversies, since squabbles between Browning and Alfred Austin and between Swinburne and Arnold attested to continuing disagreement about him.[75] What mattered more was Byron's inclusion in the endeavor to assimilate competing strands of British culture into what was polemically named "English" culture through projects such as the *Oxford English Dictionary* and the Early English Text Society. With regard to literature, one of the most important of such efforts was the English Men of Letters series, in which Byron received a full treatment by John Nichol in 1880. Similar signs of Byron's inclusion in English culture were discussions of him in Margaret Oliphant's *Literary History of England in the End of the 18th Century and Beginning of the 19th Century* (1882), George Saintsbury's *A Short History of English Literature* (1882), John Dennis's *Heroes of Literature: English Poets, a Book for Young Readers* (1883), and Leslie Stephen's *Dictionary of National Biography* (1886). Such projects determined that Byron became part of the English canon while a writer such as Felicia Hemans did not, although her popularity earlier in the century had nearly equaled his.[76]

Wilde's early writing participated in the canonization of Byron. In his Newdigate prize poem "Ravenna," Byron appears as a Great English Author: "And England, too, shall glory in her son, / Her warrior-poet, first in song and fight" (*WW*, IX: 8). Similarly, "The Tomb of Keats" (1877) praises Byron, along with Spenser, Shakespeare, Shelley, and Elizabeth Barrett Browning, as belonging to "the great procession of the sweet singers of England."[77] As a national and cultural outsider, Wilde used his poetry and essays to appropriate English culture as his own.[78]

After establishing his familiarity with English literature, he was free in his later work to range beyond the English canon. Doing so suggested his cosmopolitan knowledge of contemporary literature and the parochialism of those without it. In later Wilde, Byron appears as much a member of the French canon as the English one. "Byron, Shelley, Browning, Victor Hugo, Baudelaire" are independently wealthy great authors in "The Soul of Man Under Socialism"; "The Critic as Artist" praises "Cicero and Balzac, Flaubert and Berlioz, Byron and Madame de Sévigné" as great writers of letters.[79] Such lists make a small stab at the British reading public for not knowing how to appreciate Byron as well as French readers. Wilde goes his audience one better not only by knowing French literature but by knowing that Byron's reception was warmer in France than in Britain.

For Wilde, demonstrating his assimilation of English and French culture involved responding not only to Byron but also to Byron's reception. Wilde's letters and essays suggest that for

him the most important critical writing on Byron was Matthew
Arnold's essay, first published in 1881 and reprinted in 1888 in
Essays in Criticism, Second Series.[80] Arnold emphasizes that his
placement of Byron in the second rank of poets, a little below
Wordsworth but above Leopardi, is meant to be *the* estimate of
Byron: "The time has come for him . . . when he must take his
real and permanent place, no longer depending upon the vogue
of his own day and upon the enthusiasm of his contemporaries."[81]
Arnold finds this "permanent" place by draining Byron's exciting
qualities from him and reducing him to a pathetic figure: "[T]his
passionate and dauntless soldier of a forlorn hope, who . . . waged
against the conservation of the old impossible world so fiery
battle."[82] His praise becomes enthusiastic only when he imagines
Byron as an earlier version of himself, so that he admires Byron's
hatred of "the prejudices and habits of the British Philistine" as
if *Don Juan* were a precursor of *Culture and Anarchy*.[83] Arnold's
Byron is a safe rebel whose heterodoxy never goes further than
Arnold's.

Wilde's most sustained commentary on Byron demonstrates
his familiarity with Arnold's essay: "Byron's personality, for
instance, was terribly wasted in its battle with the stupidity, and
hypocrisy, and Philistinism of the English. Such battles do not
always intensify strength: they often exaggerate weakness. Byron
was never able to give us what he might have given us."[84] Like
Arnold, Wilde admires Byron for fighting Philistines, but also
maintains, like Arnold, that his "personality" never reached full
maturity. Although Wilde was no uncritical admirer of Arnold,
by appropriating Arnold's opinions, he reinforced his credentials
to participate in elite English culture even as he simultaneously
challenged it. His essays absorbed the high, predominantly male
Victorian authority that established the English canon.

But this tradition was not the only facet of English culture
shaping Wilde's response to Byron. Arnold's and Wilde's elitism
arose in a tense relation to more popular forms of culture,
including the Byronic sensation novel, whose origins reached
back to Caroline Lamb's *Glenarvon* (1816). Charles Knight recognized the connection between Byron and sensation novels when
he wrote in the 1870s, "What we now call 'sensation' dramas
and 'sensation' novels are the lineal descendants of the verse
romances in which . . . Byron was pouring forth his own feel-

ings."[85] While several male writers were associated with sensationalism, many of its most famous representatives were women. If Arnold's culture was elite, "disinterested," essayistic, and masculine, the culture of Braddon and Ouida was popular, profitable, novelistic, and feminine, although male publishers retained considerable control over the novels.[86]

The most sensational of the sensational writings about Byron was Harriet Beecher Stowe's *Lady Byron Vindicated* (1870). It created a furore by revealing incest as the secret behind Byron's separation. Several critics have explored the repercussions of the Stowe scandal, so I will highlight only a few aspects of it.[87] Stowe placed a secret about illicit sexuality at the center of Byron's career and made it the key to understanding him. In doing so, she wrecked the bland Byron of respectable culture, and much of the canonizing energy around Byron in the 1880s worked to repair the damage to Byron's reputation. Most responses to Stowe defended Byron, but she revived the scandal surrounding his name that had largely, though never entirely, faded by mid-century.

While Stowe was reviled for associating Byron with sexual secrets, sensation novelists such as Braddon and Ouida, both tremendous admirers of Byron, made huge profits by doing the same thing in novels. Uwe Böker has detailed Braddon's debt to Byron, particularly as it was mediated through her mentor Bulwer Lytton.[88] In novels like *Eugene Aram* (1832), Bulwer Lytton had turned the tormented heroes of Byron's verse narratives into a novelistic motif: the man with a secret. Braddon modified this motif by giving secrets to her heroines and centering them on sexual transgression. In *Aurora Floyd* (1863), for example, the secret is Aurora's unintentional bigamy. The novel guarantees the association of this secret with Byronic stereotypes through passages such as those describing the villain Conyers, who looks like "Lara returned to his own domains," or Aurora herself, characterized by the fact that "a certain gloomy shade would sometimes steal over her countenance . . . a darkly reflective expression quite foreign to her face."[89] George Bernard Shaw noted the transgendering of the Byronic hero when he maintained that in the second half of the nineteenth century "Don Juan had changed his sex and become Doña Juana."[90] Don Juan for Shaw was not Byron's Don Juan but a character closer to the Byronic

hero as rebel against God and society. Shaw's comment acknowledges that characters embodying stereotypically Byronic characteristics in late Victorian literature were female, not male.

Although no article similar to Böker's has traced Ouida's
Byronism, references to him in her critical essays and letters
make clear that she was as great an admirer as Braddon.[91] Her
novels make fewer direct references to him, but she, even more
than Braddon, draws upon the clichés that Bulwer Lytton had
associated with Byron earlier in the century: dark, brooding
heroes, florid descriptions, and settings in high society. The hero
of her novel *Folle-Farine* (1871), for example, is weary "of passion,
of pleasure, of pain; of the kisses that burn, of the laughs that
ring hollow, of the honey that so soon turns to gall, of the sickly
fatigues and the tired cloyed hunger that are the portion of men
upon earth."[92] (Bulwer Lytton was a great admirer of this novel,
and wrote Ouida a long letter praising it.) Like Braddon, she
places sexuality at the center of the characters' secrets; Folle-
Farine secretly prostitutes herself to protect the artist whom she
loves, but who refuses her overt help. From Bulwer Lytton to
Braddon to Ouida, fetishizing secrecy was the popular Byronic
romance's hallmark.

Wilde could be scathing about female novelists' appropriation
of Byron. He demolished one novel by noting, "When we add
that there is a stanza from Byron on the title-page . . . we have
possessed the discerning reader of all necessary information both
as to the matter and the manner of Mrs. Cameron's performance"
(*WW*, xiii: 56). For a critic trying to write himself into the
company of Arnold, Pater, and Ruskin, the novels of Mrs.
Cameron represented the degeneration of high culture into Philistinism. Later in life, Wilde mocked English women "with their
'fatal gift of duty,' " adapting Byron's description of the "fatal
gift of beauty" (*Childe Harold* iv.42).[93] He used Byron's words to
make a joke about women, as if to turn Byron's poetry against
those like Cameron who had misappropriated it. With such jokes,
he attempted to place himself above their supposedly derivative
culture.

Yet Wilde was not as far above Cameron as his reviews
implied that he was. Having neither independent income nor
academic post meant that he wrote for a living, especially after
he married and had children.[94] He belonged not to elite academic

institutions but to the same trade governing the writing of authors like Braddon and Ouida. Such women were vital to his success, because he conquered London society in the 1880s partly through his performances at their salons, as he admitted when he wrote of Ouida in 1887, "We have no *lionne* now but Ouida."[95] Lady Knightley glimpsed his typical appearance at such salons; she had seen him in 1883 at "an amusing party at Mrs. Tennant's": "Oscar Wilde was amusing to contemplate with his curling locks, black stock, turned-back cuffs, and bunch of seals . . . I met him again at Mrs. Jeune's afterwards."[96] The parties of such literary ladies gave Wilde his stage.

Wilde's own mother, who ran one of these salons, was another admirer of Byron.[97] She discussed Byron extensively in her essays, and Wilde's opinions about Byron derive from his mother as much as from Arnold. In an essay on Wordsworth, she noted, "Byron was the poet of this transition state [from doubt to faith]—the incarnation of his own era. The corroding wretchedness, the unsatisfied aspirations, the infinite yearnings of the human heart found in him their complete utterance."[98] When Wilde commented in *De Profundis* that he "stood in symbolic relation to the art and culture" of his age, and that Byron also "was a symbolic figure, but his relations were to the passion of his age and its weariness of passion," his letter echoed his mother's opinion of Byron as "the incarnation of his own era."[99] Much as Wilde may have wanted his critical opinions on Byron to have descended from Arnold's Olympian heights, they also arose from a more familiar and domestic context.

Even more important for the Byron-Wilde relation than salons or Lady Wilde, Wilde in November 1887 became editor of *Woman's World*, a journal devoted to women's issues. During his years as editor, he requested contributions from the most prominent women writers in England, including Ouida. Wilde himself wrote reviews for it, so this popular institution of female culture became the vehicle for his elite literary criticism, despite his allegiance to academic writers such as Arnold and Pater. He could not simply scorn the admiration for Byron that characterized this female literary culture. Although *Woman's World* carried no essays exclusively on Byron, miscellaneous references to him dotted its pages.[100] The journal assumed that readers would recognize the most casual references to his career.[101]

Dorian Gray originated in 1890 as a novel written for the July issue of *Lippincott's Monthly Magazine*. Although it is sometimes treated as a novelistic translation of aestheticism, its status as magazine fiction put Wilde closer to the popular book trade than to the exalted pronouncements of sages such as Pater. Examining his 1889 review of Ouida's *Guilderoy* demonstrates how much Ouida's writing was a model for *Dorian Gray*. Although Wilde does not mention Byron, he connects Ouida directly to the Byronic novel tradition: "Ouida is the last of the romantics. She belongs to the school of Bulwer Lytton" (*WW*, XIII: 494). What is so striking about his review is how close he makes Ouida sound to himself. Like *Dorian Gray*, *Guilderoy* is "an elaborate psychological study" and a "resplendent picture of our aristocracy" (XIII: 495). Wilde particularly admires the titular hero, who sounds like a cruder version of Dorian: "He is thoroughly weak, thoroughly worthless, and the most fascinating person in the whole story" (XIII: 496). Like Dorian, Guilderoy imagines that he falls in love with a woman, only to discover that she is completely unsuited to him. When Wilde quotes from the novel, it reads like a preview of Dorian's decadent fantasies: "Busts of dusky yellow marble, weird bronzes stretching out gaunt arms into the darkness, ivories brown with age, worn brocades with gold threads gleaming in them, and tapestries with strange and pallid figures of dead gods, were all half revealed and half obscured in the twilight" (XIII: 498). Most strikingly, Wilde excerpts sixteen of Ouida's aphorisms, which read like less clever versions of his own. No wonder that *Dorian Gray*'s first reviewers compared it to Ouida's work.[102] Wilde even sent a copy of *Dorian Gray* to her, and she commented that she "*did* understand it."[103]

By 1890, when Wilde wrote *Dorian Gray*'s first version, the sensation novel's vogue had passed. Male romancers had emerged, including H. Rider Haggard and Robert Louis Stevenson, whose aggressively masculine adventure stories differed markedly from the domestic intrigues of the female novelists. Wilde did not ignore these new writers; as critics have often noted, *Dorian Gray*'s plot is indebted to Stevenson's *Dr. Jekyll and Mr. Hyde*. Yet Wilde translates elements of Stevenson's plot into Ouida's idiom because he could surround the latter with a nostalgic evocation of decadent grandeur. By imitating Ouida in *Dorian Gray*, he implicitly distanced himself from current novelistic trends to recall older ones, whose claptrap, vulgar as it may have been in its day, acquired retrospective nobility.

Wilde's novel also participated in a less publicized aspect of Byron's reception, the growing association between him and homosexuality.[104] To a degree, treating this aspect of Byronism in isolation is misleading, since Stowe's revelations about Byron's incest, for example, could be read as encoding even more damaging information. Yet the Victorian history of knowledge about Byron's homosexuality was distinctive enough to deserve separate treatment. Evidence for Wilde's association of Byron with homosexuality is abundant. As early as "Ravenna," his reference to "Slander's venomed spite" having crawled "like a snake across his [Byron's] perfect name" (*WW*, IX: 9) reveals his knowledge of the rumors spread about Byron. By the 1890s, Wilde hypothesized that the friendship between Byron and Shelley ended "when Byron attempted to make love to Shelley and Shelley broke off the relationship."[105] He is the only nineteenth-century writer I have read who made such an inspired guess about the possibility of homoerotic tension in the friendship between Byron and Shelley.

After Wilde's trial, his perceived relation to Byron's homosexuality grew stronger. His comparison of himself to Byron in *De Profundis*, cited above, is hardly coincidental: both were hounded from British society because of sexual misconduct, although Byron at least avoided the spectacle of Wilde's trials. A later letter by Wilde reinforces this comparison when, discussing an appropriate French translation for the word "outcast" in *The Ballad of Reading Gaol*, he notes almost casually, "Lord Byron était un *outcast*."[106] Such a comment assimilates Byron's career to Wilde's even more than it deserves, since Wilde had his status as outcast thrust on him in a way that Byron did not.

In terms of Wilde's published writing before *Dorian Gray*, his most revealing document about responding to Byron's sexuality is his 1886 review of Roden Noel's *Essays on Poetry and Poets*. Noel, himself a homosexual, wrote a long, positive essay about Byron that included one of the most explicit Victorian discussions of Byron's relations with other men.[107] Intriguingly, Wilde's review trounced Noel's book for a Wildean fault: the book "tells us far more about his [Noel's] own personal feelings than it does about the qualities of the various works of art that are criticised"

(*WW*, XIII: 117). He points out the lack of taste that leads Noel to claim that Byron has "the splendid imperfection of an Aeschylus"; that " 'Sardanapalus' is perhaps hardly equal to 'Sheridan' "; that "Edgar Allan Poe, Disraeli and Mr. Alfred Austin are artists of note whom we may affiliate on Byron"; and that *Cain* is "one of the finest poems in the English language" (XIII: 118). Wilde damns Noel for his inability to distinguish greatness from mediocrity.

Wilde's most severe criticism is less that Noel's tastes are poor than that he is so shameless about revealing them. The book "is simply a record of the moods of a man of letters," which Noel displays without subtlety or nuance: "So facile is his style that it constantly betrays him into crude and extravagant statements" (XIII: 119, 117). According to Wilde, Noel's effusions rob him and the poets whom he discusses of mystery. If Noel pointed admiringly to Byron's passions for other men, he also cheapened Byron into a figure so dull as to be hardly worth admiring. *Dorian Gray* responded implicitly to Noel by rejecting his bland Byron. Instead, Wilde suggested how Byronic precedent, far from being comfortably assimilated to Victorian sexual mores, could challenge them and the representations of subjectivity on which they were based.

Dorian Gray was the most ambitious work that Wilde had yet put before the Victorian public. In writing it, he moved from his reviews and lectures to a popular, profitable genre. His novel assimilated the high, male academic discourse of canonicity to the popular, profitable, female genre of the sensation novel through the figure of the homosexual. From the start, the novel is overtly concerned with defining the origins of the secret that defines homosexual identity. To do so, it brilliantly conflates Wilde's sexual and professional origins: his narrative transforms the conflict between high and low literary modes that shaped his authorial career into a personal drama about the origins of homosexuality. The first half of the novel provides Dorian with a father and a mother. Dorian's spiritual father is Lord Henry, with his Paterian seductions. His biological mother is Margaret Devereux, whose fatal beauty Dorian inherits. Between them they embody two sides of the stereotypical late Victorian Byron: Byron the witty and rebellious dandy and the feminized Byron of the sensation novel. For Wilde, these two characters and the sides of Byron that they represent had institutional affiliations. Lord Henry is a Byronic dandy voicing the language of Victorian aesthetes. Margaret Devereux, the passionate heroine, derives from the work of Braddon and Ouida, and her melodramatic story is a miniature sensation novel. The narrative recodes Wilde's public, institutional division between gendered literary cultures as a more private split between possible origins for Dorian.

"Influence" is the novel's name for the effect of Lord Henry on Dorian. If homosexuality for Bulwer Lytton and Disraeli was inseparable from their imitations of Byron, *Dorian Gray* describes the influence of a Byronic figure as metaphorical homosexuality. Specifically, Lord Henry understands "the exercise of influence" as the ability "to convey one's temperament into another as though it were a subtle fluid" (p. 44).[108] He makes sex seem dull compared to the passionate excitement of influencing another man. Much of this excitement comes from the thrill of domination, since conveying subtle fluids is an act of invasion rather than of sharing. As Lord Henry admits, "All influence is immoral—immoral from the scientific point of view" (p. 24). Wilde's text underscores a sense that male-male "influence" is even more fraught with the pleasures and tensions produced by hierarchical power relations than heterosexual sex.

Yet Lord Henry's seductive comments on the dangers of influence mask how normative "influential" relations between men are. Wilde's novel dramatizes the imperceptible distinction between the subtle fluid of influence and the mundane homosociality through which men enforce cultural conformity. Although Lord Henry's aestheticism is an outrageous pose that no one except Dorian takes seriously, no character except Basil questions his right to dominate Dorian, even his wife. Basil reproaches Lord Henry for having a bad influence on Dorian because he is jealous: he too wants to dominate Dorian. In the relations between Lord Henry and Dorian, the novel embodies the banal but coercive institutional pressure of late Victorian aestheticism as the seductive lures of a belated Byronic dandy.[109]

If Lord Henry's influence, simultaneously deviant and normative, forms one explanation for Dorian's origins, Margaret Devereux's story offers another. She descends from the Byronic

heroines of Ouida and Braddon, as Lord Henry's summation of
her story as "a strange, almost modern romance" (p. 43) suggests.
She is a beautiful woman who, in "risking everything for a mad
passion," experiences "a few weeks of happiness cut short by a
hideous, treacherous crime" (p. 43) when her father has her
husband murdered. Her story suggests fierce Byronic passion
latent in Dorian's nature that needs only Lord Henry's prodding
to awaken it.

Ultimately, Wilde does not give priority to the Byronism of
either Lord Henry or Margaret Devereux in describing Dorian's
origins. Indeed, his imagery assimilates them to each other. Wilde
describes Lord Henry's philosophy as a female figure who, in "her
wine-stained robe and wreath of ivy, danced like a Bacchante over
the hills of life, and mocked the slow Silenus for being sober"
(p. 50). Here, the Bacchante image stands for the wildness of
Lord Henry's ideas, through which male influence's subtle fluid
penetrates Dorian. Later, the Bacchante image recurs to describe
instead Dorian's female origins. When he looks at his mother's
picture, the narrator notes, "She laughed at him in her loose
Bacchante dress. There were vine leaves in her hair. The purple
spilled from the cup she was holding"; Dorian had received from
her "his beauty, and his passion for the beauty of others"
(p. 160). Through the Bacchante image, Wilde parallels the
Byronic dandyism of Lord Henry and the Byronic romanticism
of Margaret Devereux. The effect is to assimilate what looked
like two different influences so as to avoid giving precedence to
either as the source of Dorian's character.

While the novel does not resolve this doubleness, Dorian's
picture absorbs and redirects it by drawing on the central motif
of the Byronic sensation novel: the secret. Dorian shifts from being
shaped by forces outside of himself, Lord Henry's philosophy or
his mother's body, to responding entirely to ones inside him, as
represented by the picture. Although the picture portrays these
inner forces as outer ones, Dorian controls them more directly
than he does the kinds of influence represented by Lord Henry
or his mother. Once the picture begins to alter after Sibyl's
death, its influence, rather than that of Lord Henry or his mother,
dominates him because he wants to hide it as his secret.

As Ed Cohen has argued, the picture locates " 'the problem'
of male homoerotic desire on the terrain of representation

itself."[110] The Byronic inner self was mysterious because it could never fully be revealed. Dorian's picture, in contrast, is an embarrassingly visible answer to Byron's rhetorical question, "[W]ho hath seen, or e'er shall see / Man as himself—the secret spirit free?" (*The Corsair* 1.247–48). Nevertheless, confusion about what it represents characterizes it from the start. At its most basic, this confusion consists in a blurring of soul and body. At times, the novel equates the two, as when Lord Henry says to Dorian about his youth, "Some day, when you are old and wrinkled and ugly, when thought has seared your forehead with its lines, and passion branded your lips with its hideous fires, you will feel it . . . terribly" (p. 29). Lord Henry's speech almost wishfully conflates the effects of thought and passion with the effects of physical aging. Although lines appear on foreheads quite apart from the searing effects of thought, Lord Henry's speech suggests an allegorical logic in which physical appearance encodes character. Commonplace though such logic may have been elsewhere in Victorian culture, it has peculiar effects in Wilde's novel.

The painting's significance does not remain solely allegorical. Dorian's wish is that he will remain young while the painting grows old: "If it were I who was to be always young, and the picture that was to grow old!" (p. 33). But the plot seems to demand Lord Henry's allegorical sense of representation in which physical ugliness equals moral decay. After Sibyl's death, the painting reappears with "a touch of cruelty in the mouth" (p. 103), registering not Dorian's physical aging, but his moral deterioration; it is "a visible symbol of the degradation of sin" (p. 109). The narrator notes that Dorian "had uttered a mad wish that he himself might remain young, and the portrait grow old; that his own beauty might be untarnished, and the face on the canvas bear the burden of his passions and his sins" (p. 103). Although Wilde places the second clause in apposition with the first as if it were restating it, the first involves biological aging, while the second figures moral experience as if it were physical.

In such episodes, Wilde treats the picture's blurring of body and soul as a given. In others, however, he separates the two. When Dorian considers hiding the portrait, he hopes that he might improve morally so that "the cruel look would have passed away from the scarlet sensitive mouth" (p. 137). At such a moment, Dorian acts as if he had direct power over the picture's appearance. But his thoughts promptly shift: "It might escape the hideousness of sin, but the hideousness of age was in store for it . . . there would be the wrinkled throat, the cold, blue-veined hands, the twisted body" (p. 137). Here, the picture's alteration is a matter of necessity rather than free will: Dorian inevitably grows old. So distinct does Wilde make the effects of moral and physical decay that Dorian soon becomes expert in distinguishing the two. He takes "a monstrous and terrible delight" in "wondering sometimes which were the more horrible, the signs of sin or the signs of age" (p. 143). His wonder depends upon recognizing differences between them, yet it is impossible to tell what represents the body's decay and what represents the soul's, since both appear as physical ugliness. Although the picture's significance should be immediately apparent, the descriptions obscure its supposed clarity by juggling the physical and spiritual.

The picture's doubleness internalizes the split between Byronic influences: Dorian's moral decay is associated with male influence, particularly Lord Henry's philosophical dandyism; his physical decay with female influence, the body that he was given by his mother. Yet the particulars of this doubleness are less important than its effects. The secrets that Dorian wishes to hide are multiple: his soul's sins and his body's decay. This doubleness itself suggests a larger unrepresentability in Dorian's crimes because they are too excessive to define precisely. The novel makes it impossible to answer what exactly about himself Dorian hides when he hides his picture.

This excess of secrecy, far more than actual relations between men, distinguishes homosexual character in *Dorian Gray*. It invents the homosexual as a man with too many secrets. In doing so, it draws on Byron's precedent as the figure who would have defined the association between homosexuality and a plethora of secrets. The secret behind Byron's separation was supposed to have been everything from adultery to sodomy. The many possible explanations arose because contemporaries treated him as one of his heroes; since Byron's heroes lacked any clearly defined origins for their alienation, multiple explanations could be entertained.

Byron's relevance to *Dorian Gray* is most vivid once Dorian has begun to earn the plurality of secrets in his picture. Suddenly, he resembles Byron, especially when Wilde puts him "at his great house in Nottinghamshire, entertaining the fashionable young men of his own rank who were his chief companions, and astounding the county by the wanton luxury and gorgeous splendour of his mode of life" (p. 157). The use of Nottingham-shire, the location of Byron's Newstead Abbey, looks like a direct bow to Byron as portrayed in Victorian biographies, especially Moore's. Moore, like Wilde, described his hero entertaining fashionable men of his own rank at his country house in Notting-hamshire and astonishing the county by his wanton life; Byron was "gaily dispensing the hospitalities of Newstead to a party of young college friends" (*M*, 1: 171–72). To avoid having to say too much about their activities, Moore includes a letter from one of Byron's friends, who describes the daytime festivities and adds, "The evening diversions may be easily conceived" (*M*, 1: 174). As Beckford's marginalia cited earlier suggest, he was right: knowing readers had little trouble in conceiving the nature of Byron's "evening diversions."

In portraying Dorian, Wilde conflates this early period of Byron's life with the separation scandal. Moore writes that the public had "an ample supply of reasons for the breach [between Lord and Lady Byron],—all ... representing him ... as a finished monster of cruelty and depravity" (*M*, 1: 652); Roden Noel described the same episode by suggesting that "the darkest rumours gathered about the husband, bursting anon over his head in a tempest of most virtuous execration."[111] The Victorian reception of Byron's sexuality gave Wilde a model for moments in which "men would whisper to each other in corners, or pass him with a sneer, or look at [Dorian] with cold searching eyes, as though they were determined to discover his secret" (pp. 157–58). As with Byron, the scandals about Dorian "increased, in the eyes of many, his strange and dangerous charm" (p. 158). Wilde's novel transforms Moore's "ample supply of reasons" for scandal into the excess of secrets that defines Dorian as a homosexual.

Dorian's mystery, like Byron's, is part of his charm. Yet Wilde's novel does not merely write an echo of Byron's career into Dorian's character. It takes the secrecy surrounding the homosex-ual one step further by suggesting the impossibility of ever revealing the "truth." Dorian's mysteriousness may be a strategy to avoid the possibility that any secret, such as sodomy, might be singled out as the "real" one. Yet the result is that Dorian's psyche becomes inaccessible because no one ever knows what is being hidden. This inaccessibility adds a more sinister edge to the novel: Dorian is the first homosexual in fiction precisely because his secret cannot be revealed.

For other characters, who lack Dorian's excess of secrets, revealing secrets uniformly produces catastrophe. Basil confesses to Lord Henry his fascination with Dorian, and Lord Henry promptly steals Dorian for himself. Sibyl confesses to Dorian the depth of her love, and he scorns her. Basil confesses his love to Dorian, and Dorian calls it "a very disappointing confession" (p. 130). When Dorian reveals his picture to Basil, Basil's reaction is almost as inadequate as Dorian's: "Let us kneel down and try if we cannot remember a prayer" (p. 175). To the extent that a speaker as ironic as Lord Henry can confess, he does so when he tells Dorian, "I have sorrows, Dorian, of my own, that even you know nothing of. The tragedy of old age is not that one is old, but that one is young. I am amazed sometimes at my own sincerity" (p. 239); Dorian, characteristically, is too self-obsessed to care. Most disastrously, Dorian tries to confess to himself when he identifies his picture as his conscience and imagines that by stabbing it, he will erase his moral sins. He ends up merely destroying his physical body.

Characters are uniformly more misunderstood after they come out than before, so that confessing secrets produces greater alienation, not greater intimacy. Such alienation is not entirely bad, since, as Byron's precedent revealed, it can have considerable pleasures. In particular, it preserves for Dorian, if not for the others, the autonomous subjectivity of Byron's heroes. Although his portrait may rule his life, at least it allows his own narcissism to control him rather than the male or female forms of influence detailed in the novel's first half. Nevertheless, the novel pitilessly develops the consequences of appropriating the Byronic gesture of turning the self into a repository of secrets that cannot be revealed. While for Bulwer Lytton and Disraeli, the closet could be easily discarded, at least in their writing, Wilde constructs in *Dorian Gray* the image of the permanent closet. The carefully contrived shallowness of the novel, the puppet-like nature of his characters, works like a metaphor for the impossibility of fully revealing the inner self.

Byron's characters appeared extraordinarily real to his audiences because their passions were so vivid that no writer could have just imagined them. He eroticized the representation of subjectivity so that sexual secrets seemed the darkest and most authentic self-revelations possible. *Dorian Gray* empties the power of this eroticized subjectivity as the psyche's ultimate representation. Instead, subjectivity is only a picture whose grotesque shallowness evokes nostalgia for a Byronic moment when the inner self had substance. Dorian's picture removes to a location outside the self all that Byronism put inside it. This removal traps an archaic, allegorical logic of representation inside a narrative that otherwise follows the conventions of late Victorian realism. The disparity between them results in the striking emptiness of the novel's representation of subjectivity, as if the characters' "real" identities are always just beyond what Wilde describes. The formal structure of the closet outlasts the possibility that it contains anything communicable.

The novel's first critics recognized its evacuation of the Byronic inner self. Like the works discussed in other chapters, *Dorian Gray* had a stormy reception; responding to Byronism proved once again to be simultaneously the most clichéd and the most radical mode for a Victorian writer. While controversies over *Dorian Gray* manifested some outrage at its suggestions of homosexuality, they concentrated more on what *The Theatre* called its "absence of human interest."[112] Similarly, the *St. James's Gazette* objected to it not because it was "dangerous and corrupt" but because it was "incurably silly"; others commented on its "theatrical cynicism."[113] Wilde's reviewers were troubled by the same phenomenon that T. S. Eliot identified in Tennyson: his surfaces were intimate with his depths. In choosing to focus on the novel's shallowness, these critics were in some ways more perceptive about the effects of Wilde's representation of homosexuality than modern critics who bypass the more disturbing implications of Wilde's novel. They implied that the superficiality of Wilde's novel had turned upon subjectivity itself in ways that unsettled the assumptions that Byron's reception had done so much to create.

Sedgwick distinguishes two possibilities for reading *Dorian Gray*, an "empty," modernist one in which the novel's secrets are understood as vacant signifiers, and a "full," homosexual one, in which the novel's secrets point to the secret of homosexuality.[114] The contemporary reviewers, however, suggest that Wilde responds most directly to the Byronic tradition of the secret when he reveals that these are not as different as they might seem. The fullness of the homosexual secret might as well be an empty one given what the novel represents as the absolute impossibility of communicating it. Wilde's turn on the Victorian response to Byron produces the most striking aspect of *Dorian Gray*'s representation of homosexuality: the necessary permanence of the closet.

Afterword

While visiting Paris in 1824, Anne Lister, a lesbian of good family and a native of Halifax, discussed in her diary the prospect of exchanging gifts with Maria Barlow, a widow whom she wanted to seduce: "I foolishly told her I meant to give her Lord Byron's works. She mentioned Galignani's edition, which I knew not of, & I must give it."[1] Later in her trip she bought a seven-volume edition of Byron for herself, which she presumably bought more cheaply in Paris than in England.[2] Lister had always been an admirer of Byron and used his poetry to mediate lesbian relationships. In 1818, for example, she wrote of a woman who had struck her fancy: "I have thought of her all the way home, of writing to her anonymously and (as she said, when I asked her if she liked Lord Byron's poetry, 'Yes, perhaps too well') of sending her a Cornelian heart with a copy of his lines on the subject. I could soon be in love with the girl."[3] She imagined appropriating Byron's lines to further her potential romance.

Although nowhere in the diaries that have as yet been published does Lister explicitly connect Byron with male–male desire, her use of him repeatedly suggests that she appropriates his expressions of desire between men for desire between women. Byron had originally written the poem on the Cornelian heart to express his love for John Edlestone, so Lister imagines using a lyric that Byron wrote for male–male desire as a code for female–female desire. While well-bred young women frequently copied Byron's "On a Cornelian Heart Which Was Broken" in their commonplace books, Lister finds undertones in it not available to most.[4] Byron's popularity with his female readers depended as much on identification as on difference, and Lister takes this identification one step further. It probably helped that Byron was an aristocrat, for Lister's own sexual identity was

247

shaped not only by her lesbianism but also by her status as a member of the gentry: "My manners are certainly peculiar, not all masculine but rather softly gentleman-like."[5] Even more, her class allowed her to claim some family interest in Byron's career, since, in a part of the diary that has not yet been published, she mentions that her father had been "attached" to "a Miss Millbank, Lady Byron's aunt."[6]

When Lister visited Sarah Ponsonby, one of the Ladies of Llangollen, she spoke with her about a group of authors whose works all represented male same-sex desire or cross-dressing: Virgil, Tasso, and Byron. Ponsonby said that "[s]he was almost afraid of reading *Cain*, tho' Lord Byron had been very good in sending them several of his works. I asked if she had read *Don Juan*. She was ashamed to say she had read the 1st canto."[7] Although other visitors doubted if Ponsonby and Lady Eleanor Butler were lesbians, Lister did not: "I cannot help thinking that surely [their relationship] was not platonic. Heaven forgive me, but I look within myself & doubt."[8] In his youth Byron had had similar opinions; he boasted that his love for Edlestone would "put *Lady E. Butler* & Miss *Ponsonby* to the Blush" (*LJ*, 1: 125).[9] His sending "several of his works" to them suggests that he may have seen their sexuality as a model for his. In turn, Byron became a code author for Lister and Ponsonby in what looks like a miniature lesbian subculture.

In many ways, Lister's relation to Byron is typical of women of her education and class. She took a copy of *Childe Harold's Pilgrimage* from her local library and copied stanzas from it, would not admit in company that she had read cantos I and II of *Don Juan*, and lamented Byron as the "greatest poet of the age!" when he died.[10] Byron for her as for others shaped at the abstract level their participation in culture and at a concrete one their relations to other people, particularly in terms of sexuality. Lister's lesbian use of Byron can be seen as an extension of the role of identification in female attraction to Byron that I discussed in chapter 2.[11] At the same time, Lister is unique. Her diaries subvert many paradigms for understanding lesbian history by providing evidence of what looks like a conscious and "modern" understanding of sexual identity. At the more local level, her relationship to Byron, though it bears some resemblance to that of other women, is also unlike them because of the ways in which

Lister uses Byron's same-sex male representations to mediate her same-sex female ones.

I place Lister in my conclusion to draw attention to her account of her lesbianism and to the role that Byron played in it. More generally, her diaries are one of the most vivid examples to me of how the sheer variety of Byron's reception forestalls any totalizing description of it. The specificity of Lister's situation as a lesbian cannot be explained away or fitted neatly into a scheme that would include all of nineteenth-century Britain. For every writer I discuss, there are others whose relationships to Byron were every bit as interesting, including canonical authors like Arnold or Swinburne, semi-canonical ones like Elizabeth Barrett Browning or Felicia Hemans, and entirely non-canonical ones like Catherine Gore. Furthermore, there are many like Lister who were not professional writers whose relations to Byron deserve equal attention. Yet a "complete" discussion of Byron and the Victorians would eventually be indistinguishable from a history of Victorian literature and culture themselves.

If conclusions invite sweeping generalizations, my most useful conclusion may be that Byron's reception frustrates any such generalizations. A common thread in my discussion has been the master narrative of the Victorian authorial career, which often took the form not of a flat rejection of Byron but of a painful and sometimes gradual transition away from him. An array of interrelated possibilities fastened to the progress of these narratives of transition: Romanticism to Victorianism, youth to maturity, homosociality to heterosexuality, failure to success, individual to community, alienation to integration. The specifics are less interesting than the frequency with which Victorian authors created themselves in relation to a past associated with Byron. The master narrative of the transition from Byron became an all-purpose device through which Victorian authors defined their "original" voice.

Yet these narratives are not a "key" to understanding Byron and the Victorians. Instead, I want to suggest the complexity of Byron's influence, which has usually been treated as a relatively straightforward phenomenon because of the supposed obviousness of the Byronic hero. If this book disrupts the ease with which literary critics use the term "Byronic hero," it might clear away some of the clichés surrounding how the nineteenth century appears to the twentieth. Historicizing influence may ultimately be a way to reveal as far more multiple and far less coherent the very histories that it has knit together.

Notes

INTRODUCTION: ON INFLUENCE

1 For a recent overview of Bloom's work, see Louis A. Renza, "Influence," in *Critical Terms for Literary Study*, ed. Frank Lentricchia and Thomas McLaughlin (University of Chicago Press, 1990), pp. 186–202.
2 Kristeva, "Word, Dialogue and Novel," *The Kristeva Reader*, ed. Toril Moi (New York: Columbia University Press, 1986), p. 39.
3 See John Mowitt, *Text: The Genealogy of an Antidisciplinary Object* (Durham and London: Duke University Press, 1992), pp. 104–16.
4 Clayton and Rothstein, "Figures in the Corpus: Theories of Influence and Intertextuality," *Influence and Intertextuality in Literary History*, eds. Jay Clayton and Eric Rothstein (Madison: University of Wisconsin Press, 1991), pp. 3–36.
5 Culler, *The Pursuit of Signs: Semiotics, Literature, Deconstruction* (Ithaca: Cornell University Press, 1981), p. 109.
6 Mowitt, *Text*, pp. 111–16.
7 Clayton and Rothstein, "Figures in the Corpus," p. 4.
8 See D. A. Miller's *Bringing Out Roland Barthes* (Berkeley: University of California Press, 1992).
9 Ford, *Keats and the Victorians: A Study of His Influence and Rise to Fame, 1821–1895* (New Haven: Yale University Press, 1944).
10 Mitchell, "Influence, Autobiography, and Literary History: Rousseau's *Confessions* and Wordsworth's *The Prelude*," *ELH* 57 (1990): 643–64; 661.
11 Williams, *Marxism and Literature* (Oxford University Press, 1977), p. 115.
12 *The Foucault Reader*, ed. Paul Rabinow (New York: Pantheon, 1984), pp. 101–20.
13 Nancy Armstrong and Leonard Tennenhouse, *The Imaginary Puritan: Literature, Intellectual Labor, and the Origins of Personal Life* (Berkeley: University of California Press, 1992), p. 209.
14 Jauss, "Literary History as a Challenge to Literary Theory," *Toward an Aesthetic of Reception*, trans. T. Bahti (Minneapolis: University of Minnesota Press, 1982), p. 22.

15 Ibid., p. 39.
16 See Manon Brunet, "Pour une ésthetique de la production de la récep-
   tion," *Etudes françaises* 19.3 (1984): 65–82; Marilyn Butler, "Against
   Tradition: The Case for a Particularized Historical Method," *Historical Studies and Literary Criticism*, ed. Jerome J. McGann (Madison: University of Wisconsin Press, 1985), pp. 25–47.
17 Radway, *Reading the Romance: Women, Patriarchy, and Popular Literature*
   (Chapel Hill: University of North Carolina Press, 1984).
18 Bourdieu, *The Field of Cultural Production: Essays on Art and Literature*,
   ed. Randal Johnson (New York: Columbia University Press, 1993),
   p. 60.
19 Three books that offer different but interesting approaches to
   historicizing influence are Richard Brodhead, *The School of Hawthorne*
   (New York: Oxford University Press, 1986); Antony Harrison,
   Victorian Poets and Romantic Poems: Intertextuality and Ideology
   (Charlottesville: University of Virginia Press, 1990); and John Allen
   Watkins, *The Specter of Dido: Spenser and Virgilian Epic* (New Haven:
   Yale University Press, 1995).
20 John Edmund Reade, *Cain the Wanderer . . . and Other Poems* (London:
   Whittaker, Treacher, and Co., 1829), pp. 3–4.
21 For one of the most sustained such investigations, see Donald Stone,
   The Romantic Impulse in Victorian Fiction (Cambridge, MA: Harvard
   University Press, 1980).

I BYRON AND THE SECRET SELF

1 Scott, "*Childe Harold's Pilgrimage. Canto IV. By Lord Byron*," *Quarterly
   Review* 19 (1818): 215–32; 217–18.
2 *The Letters of Sir Walter Scott*, ed. H. J. C. Grierson, 12 vols. (London:
   Constable, 1932–37), III: 98–99.
3 I am particularly indebted to McGann, *Fiery Dust: Byron's Poetic Devel-
   opment* (University of Chicago Press, 1968) and *"Don Juan" In Context*
   (University of Chicago Press, 1976); Robert F. Gleckner, *Byron and the
   Ruins of Paradise* (Baltimore: Johns Hopkins University Press, 1967);
   Michael G. Cooke, *The Blind Man Traces the Circle: On the Patterns and
   Philosophy of Byron's Poetry* (Princeton University Press, 1969); Peter J.
   Manning, *Byron and His Fictions* (Detroit: Wayne State University
   Press, 1978); Frederick Garber, *Self, Text, and Romantic Irony: The
   Example of Byron* (Princeton University Press, 1988); Jerome Chris-
   tensen, *Lord Byron's Strength: Romantic Writing and Commercial Society*
   (Baltimore: Johns Hopkins University Press, 1993); Susan J. Wolfson,
   " 'Their She Condition': Cross-Dressing and The Politics of Gender
   in *Don Juan*," *ELH* 54 (1987): 585–617, and " 'A Problem Few Dare
   Imitate': *Sardanapalus* and 'Effeminate Character,' " *ELH* 58 (1991):
   867–902.

4 McGann, "Introduction" to *Byron,* Oxford Authors (Oxford University Press, 1986), p. xii.

5 Christensen, *Lord Byron's Strength,* p. 16.

6 Ibid., p. 147.

7 See Nancy Armstrong, *Desire and Domestic Fiction: A Political History of the Novel* (New York and Oxford: Oxford University Press, 1987).

8 Millbanke quoted in Mabell, Countess of Airlie, *In Whig Society, 1775–1818* (London: Hodder and Stoughton, 1921), pp. 162–63.

9 McGann, *Towards a Literature of Knowledge* (University of Chicago Press, 1989), pp. 38–39.

10 *The Complete Poetical Works of Sir Walter Scott,* ed. Horace E. Scudder (Boston: Houghton Mifflin, 1900), p. 11.

11 Hodgson, "*The Corsair,* a Tale. By Lord Byron," *Monthly Review* 73 (1814): 189–200; 194; for other examples of critics who cite this particular passage, see the reviews in the *New Review* 3 (1814): 339–43; 342, and the *Scots Magazine* 76 (1814): 124–27; 126.

12 See Sonia Hofkosh, "The Writer's Ravishment: Woman and the Romantic Author—The Example of Byron," *Romanticism and Feminism,* ed. Anne K. Mellor (Bloomington: University of Indiana Press, 1988), pp. 93–114.

13 Foucault, *The History of Sexuality—Volume I: An Introduction,* trans. Robert Hurley (New York: Random House, 1978), p. 59.

14 Foucault, *The Order of Things: An Archaeology of the Human Sciences* (New York: Random House, 1970), pp. 250–302.

15 For a general discussion, see Jean Hall's *A Mind That Feeds Upon Infinity: The Deep Self in English Romantic Poetry* (Rutherford, NJ: Fairleigh Dickinson University Press, 1991).

16 See Bertrand Evans, "Manfred's Remorse and the Dramatic Tradition," *PMLA* 62 (1947): 752–73.

17 Marshall, *The Surprising Effects of Sympathy: Marivaux, Diderot, Rousseau, and Mary Shelley* (Chicago and London: University of Chicago Press, 1988).

18 Wilson, "*Childe Harold's Pilgrimage.* Canto the Fourth. By Lord Byron," *Edinburgh Review* 30 (1818): 87–120; 88–89.

19 Franklin, *Byron's Heroines* (Oxford: Clarendon, 1992).

20 Hume, *A Treatise of Human Nature,* ed. L. A. Selby-Bigge, 2nd ed. (Oxford: Clarendon, 1978), p. 521.

21 These reflections were prompted by Eve Kosofsky Sedgwick's discussion of desire and identification, *Epistemology of the Closet* (Berkeley: University of California Press, 1990), pp. 157–63. For a different reading of incest, see Joanna E. Rapf, "The Byronic Heroine: Incest and the Creative Process," *Studies in English Literature, 1500–1900* 21 (1981): 637–45.

22 See Alan Richardson, "The Dangers of Sympathy: Sibling Incest

in English Romantic Poetry," *Studies in English Literature, 1500–1900* 25 (1985): 737–54.

23 Watkins, *Memoirs of the Life and Writings of the Right Honourable Lord Byron* (London: Henry Colburn, 1822), pp. 198–99. For more recent treatments, see Marina Vitale, "The Domesticated Heroine in Byron's *Corsair* and William Hone's Prose Adaptation," *Literature and History* 10 (1984): 72–94; Malcolm Kelsall, "Byron and the Romantic Heroine," *Byron: Augustan and Romantic,* ed. Andrew Rutherford (New York: St. Martin's, 1990), pp. 52–62; Franklin, *Byron's Heroines,* pp. 64–68; and Nigel Leask, *British Romantic Writers and the East: Anxieties of Empire* (Cambridge University Press, 1993), pp. 45–54.

24 [Anon.], "Original Criticism," *Universal Magazine* 21 (1814): 129–36; 135.

25 Franklin, *Byron's Heroines,* pp. 85–86.

26 Watkins, *Social Relations in Byron's Eastern Tales* (Rutherford, NJ: Fairleigh Dickinson University Press, 1987), p. 86.

27 See Frank D. McConnell, "Byron's Reductions: 'Much Too Poetical,' " *ELH* 37 (1970): 415–32.

28 Christensen, *Lord Byron's Strength,* pp. 16–17.

29 See Leslie A. Marchand, *Byron: A Biography,* 3 vols. (New York: Knopf, 1957), esp. vol. II, chs. 15 and 16, and Christensen, *Lord Byron's Strength,* pp. 78–87.

30 Guillory, "The English Common Place: Lineages of the Topographical Genre," *Critical Quarterly* 33 (1991): 3–27.

31 Ibid., p. 7.

32 Ibid., p. 12.

33 For a detailed treatment of Byron's relation to this style, see McGann, " 'My Brain is Feminine': Byron and the Poetry of Deception," *Byron: Augustan and Romantic,* ed. Rutherford, pp. 26–51.

34 St. Clair, "The Impact of Byron's Writings: An Evaluative Approach," *Byron: Augustan and Romantic,* ed. Rutherford, pp. 1–25; p. 11.

35 Manning, "Childe Harold in the Marketplace: From Romaunt to Handbook," *Modern Language Quarterly* 52 (1991): 170–90; 176–79.

36 McGann, *Fiery Dust,* p. 49.

37 See Buzard, "The Uses of Romanticism: Byron and the Victorian Continental Tour," *Victorian Studies* 35 (1991): 29–49, and Manning, "Childe Harold," pp. 187–88.

38 See Atara Stein, " 'I Loved Her and Destroyed Her': Love and Narcissism in Byron's *Manfred,*" *Philological Quarterly* 69 (1990): 189–215.

39 Richardson, "Romanticism and the Colonization of the Feminine," *Romanticism and Feminism,* ed. Mellor, p. 19.

40 Cooke, *Blind Man,* p. 65.

41 See Garber, *Self, Text, and Romantic Irony*, pp. 126–35.

42 See McGann's revision of his earlier position on the poem in *The Romantic Ideology: A Critical Investigation* (University of Chicago Press, 1983), pp. 137–45.

43 See Manning, "*Don Juan* and Byron's Imperceptiveness to the English Word," *Studies in Romanticism* 18 (1979): 207–33.

44 Wolfson, " 'Their She Condition,' " p. 611.

45 See Franklin, *Byron's Heroines*, pp. 99–127.

46 Jeffrey, "*Childe Harold's Pilgrimage*, Canto the Third. By Lord Byron," *Edinburgh Review* 27 (1816): 277–310; 280.

47 E. D. H. Johnson, "*Don Juan* in England," *ELH* 11 (1944): 135–53.

48 The best analysis remains Cooke, "Byron's *Don Juan*: The Obsession and Self-Discipline of Spontaneity," *Acts of Inclusion: Studies Bearing on an Elementary Theory of Romanticism* (New Haven: Yale University Press, 1979), pp. 218–41.

49 Wolfson, " 'Their She Condition,' " p. 590.

50 See Claude Rawson, "Byron, Shelley, and Heroic Discredit" in his *Satire and Sentiment, 1660–1830* (Cambridge University Press, 1993), pp. 98–132.

51 Lockhart quoted in *Byron: The Critical Heritage*, ed. Andrew Rutherford (New York: Barnes and Noble, 1970), p. 183.

52 T. S. Eliot, "Byron," rpt. in *English Romantic Poets: Modern Essays in Criticism*, ed. M. H. Abrams, 2nd ed. (London: Oxford University Press, 1975), pp. 261–74; p. 271.

2 THE CREATION OF BYRONISM

1 "What Is an Author?", reprinted in *The Foucault Reader*, ed. Paul Rabinow (New York: Pantheon, 1984), pp. 101–20; see also Nancy Armstrong and Leonard Tennenhouse, *The Imaginary Puritan: Literature, Intellectual Labor, and the Origins of Personal Life* (Berkeley: University of California Press, 1992), pp. 1–26.

2 Jerome Christensen, *Lord Byron's Strength: Romantic Writing and Commercial Society* (Baltimore: Johns Hopkins University Press, 1993), pp. 142–49.

3 Marx, *Capital: A Critique of Political Economy*, vol. 1, trans. Samuel Moore and Edward Eveling, ed. Frederick Engels (New York: International, 1967), p. 77.

4 Carlyle, *Past and Present*, ed. A. M. D. Hughes (Oxford: Clarendon, 1921), p. 139.

5 See E. P. Thompson, "Eighteenth-Century English Society: Class Struggle Without Class?" *Social History* 3 (1978): 133–65; Raymond Williams, *Keywords* (New York: Oxford University Press, 1985), pp. 60–69; and Stephen A. Resnick and Richard D. Wolff, *Knowledge and Class* (University of Chicago Press, 1987).

6 Baudrillard, *Selected Writings*, ed. Mark Poster (Stanford University Press, 1988), p. 19.

7 Neil McKendrick, John Brewer, and J. H. Plumb, *The Birth of a Consumer Society: The Commercialization of Eighteenth-Century England* (Bloomington: Indiana University Press, 1982); see also W. Hamish Fraser, *The Coming of the Mass Market, 1850–1914* (Hamden, CT: Archon, 1981) and Thomas Richards, *The Commodity Culture of Victorian England: Advertising and Spectacle, 1851–1914* (Stanford University Press, 1990).

8 Scott, "Review of *Childe Harold's Pilgrimage. Canto IV. By Lord Byron*," *Quarterly Review* 19 (1818): 215–32; 217.

9 For competing discussions of class emulation during this period, see Harold Perkin, *The Origins of Modern English Society, 1780–1880* (London: Routledge and Kegan Paul, 1969) and Colin Campbell's response to it in *The Romantic Ethic and the Spirit of Modern Consumerism* (Oxford: Blackwell, 1987), pp. 17–35.

10 See Andrew Rutherford's comments on the reception of the 1812 *Childe Harold* in *Byron the Best-Seller* (Nottingham: Byron Foundation Lecture, 1964).

11 Fabricant, "The Literature of Domestic Tourism and the Public Consumption of Private Property," *The New Eighteenth Century: Theory, Politics, English Literature*, eds. Felicity Nussbaum and Laura Brown (New York: Methuen, 1987), pp. 254–75.

12 For a classic account of this development, see Raymond Williams, *Culture and Society, 1780–1950* (1958; rpt. New York: Doubleday, 1960), pp. 35–40; see also Philip W. Martin, *Byron: A Poet Before his Public* (Cambridge University Press, 1982), pp. 30–44.

13 Richard D. Altick, *The English Common Reader: A Social History of the Mass Reading Public, 1800–1900* (University of Chicago Press, 1957), p. 386.

14 John Scott, "Living Authors, No. IV: Lord Byron," *London Magazine* 3 (1821): 50–61; 59.

15 Richard and Maria Edgeworth, *Memoirs of Richard Lovell Edgeworth Esq.*, 2 vols. (London: R. Hunter, 1821), II: 356.

16 Jon Klancher, *The Making of English Reading Audiences, 1790–1832* (Madison: University of Wisconsin Press, 1987), p. 69. See also Marilyn Butler, "Culture's Medium: The Role of the Review," *The Cambridge Companion to British Romanticism*, ed. Stuart Curran (Cambridge University Press, 1993), pp. 120–47.

17 Jeffrey, "Lord Byron's *Corsair* and *Bride of Abydos*," *Edinburgh Review* 23 (1814): 198–229; 208, 209, 214, 217.

18 *The Brownings' Correspondence*, ed. Philip Kelley and Ronald Hudson, 10 vols. to present (London: Wedgestone, 1984–), I: 45.

19 See, for example, *The Beauties of Byron, Consisting of Selections from His Works*, ed. Alfred Howard (London: T. Davison, 1835[?]).

20 William and Edward Finden, *Byron Beauties: Or, the Principal Female Characters in Lord Byron's Poems* (London: Charles Tilt, 1836).

21 I am drawing here on an unpublished paper by Emily B. Todd, "Byron, Beauty, and the Construction of Bourgeois Values" (University of Minnesota, 1993).

22 See Ian Jack, *The Poet and His Audience* (Cambridge University Press, 1984), pp. 61–89; Herman M. Ward, *Byron and the Magazines, 1806–1824* (University of Salzburg, 1973); and Keith Walker, *Byron's Readers: A Study of Attitudes Towards Byron, 1812–1832* (University of Salzburg, 1979).

23 [Anon.], "Review of Canto IV of *Childe Harold's Pilgrimage*," *Edinburgh Magazine*, quoted in Theodore Redpath, *The Young Romantics and Critical Opinion, 1807–1824: Poetry of Byron, Shelley, and Keats as Seen by Their Contemporary Critics* (London: Harrap, 1973), p. 228; John Wilson, "*Childe Harold*. Canto Fourth," *Edinburgh Review* 30 (1818): 87–120; 118.

24 Abrams, *The Mirror and the Lamp: Romantic Theory and the Critical Tradition* (1953; rpt. New York: Norton, 1958), esp. pp. 226–62.

25 Jeffrey, "Lord Byron's *Childe Harold*," *Edinburgh Review* 19 (1812): 466–77; 467.

26 [Anon.], "Lord Byron's *Childe Harold*, and *Prisoner of Chillon*," *British Critic*, 2nd ser. 6 (1816): 608–17; 609.

27 Roberts, "*Childe Harold's Pilgrimage*. Canto IV," *British Review* 12 (1818): 1–34; 23; Scott, "*Childe Harold*, Canto III — and Other Poems," *Quarterly Review* 16 (1816): 172–208; 208.

28 *The Spirit of the Age* in *The Complete Works of William Hazlitt*, ed. P. P. Howe, 21 vols. (London: Dent, 1930–34), XI: 70.

29 Edward John Trelawney, *Records of Shelley, Byron, and the Author*, 2 vols. (1878; rpt. New York: Benjamin Blom, 1968), I: 29.

30 See Peter J. Manning's discussion of this letter, "Childe Harold in the Marketplace: From Romaunt to Handbook," *Modern Language Quarterly* 52 (1991): 170–90; 188–90.

31 *Medwin's Conversations of Lord Byron*, ed. Ernest J. Lovell, Jr. (Princeton University Press, 1966), p. 206.

32 Gifford, "Mrs. Hemans's *Poems*," *Quarterly Review* 24 (1820): 130–39; 131.

33 [Anon.], "Review of New Publications: *Tales of the Hall*. By the Rev. George Crabbe, LL.B.," *Christian Observer* 18 (1819): 667–68; 667.

34 Mitford quoted in *The Library of Literary Criticism of English and American Authors*, ed. Charles Wells Moulton, 8 vols. (New York: Henry Malkan, 1910), IV: 736.

35 See Anne K. Mellor, *Romanticism and Gender* (New York and London: Routledge, 1993), pp. 1–11.

36 *Reynolds–Rathbone Diaries and Letters, 1753–1839*, ed. Mrs. Eustace Greg (privately published, 1905), p. 199.

37 Peacock, "Essay on Fashionable Literature," *Romantic Critical Essays*, ed. David Bromwich (Cambridge University Press, 1987), pp. 187–98; p. 188.
38 Gary Kelley, "Romantic Fiction," in *The Cambridge Companion to British Romanticism*, ed. Curran, pp. 196–215.
39 Hume, "Of the Study of History," *Essays Moral, Political, and Literary*, eds. T. H. Green and T. H. Grosse, 2 vols. (London: Longmans, 1889), II: 388.
40 Rousseau, *Emile, or On Education*, trans. Allan Bloom (New York: Basic Books, 1979), p. 387.
41 See A. D. Harvey, *English Poetry in a Changing Society, 1780–1825* (New York: St. Martin's, 1980), pp. 132–41.
42 Lamb, *Glenarvon*, 3 vols. (London: Henry Colburn, 1816), II: 51–52.
43 Hofkosh, "The Writer's Ravishment: Women and the Romantic Author – The Example of Byron," *Romanticism and Feminism*, ed. Anne K. Mellor (Bloomington: Indiana University Press, 1988), pp. 93–114.
44 *Memoirs and Correspondence of Susan Ferrier, 1782–1854*, ed. John A. Doyle (London: John Murray, 1898), p. 131. My generalizations about the reactions of this set of women to Byron are based on the information collected in the appendix of my dissertation, "Byron, Byronism, and the Victorians" (Ph. D. thesis, Yale 1992).
45 See David H. Richter, "The Reception of the Gothic Novel in the 1790s," *The Idea of the Novel in the Eighteenth Century*, ed. Robert W. Uphaus (East Lansing, MI: Colleagues Press, 1988), pp. 117–37; Patricia Meyer Spacks, "Splendid Falsehoods: English Accounts of Rome, 1760–1798," *Prose Studies* 3 (1980): 203–16.
46 See, for example, their argument over Fielding (James Boswell, *Life of Johnson*, ed. R. W. Chapman [Oxford University Press, 1970], p. 480).
47 Green, *Extracts from a Diary of a Lover of Literature* (Ipswich: John Raw, 1810), p. 188.
48 *Letters of Harriet Countess Granville, 1810–1845*, ed. the Hon. F. Leveson Gower (London: Longmans, 1894), p. 219.
49 *Lady Morgan's Memoirs: Autobiography, Diaries, and Correspondence*, 2 vols. (London: William H. Allen, 1862), II: 21.
50 Rogers quoted in *Byron: The Critical Heritage*, ed. Andrew Rutherford (London: Routledge and Kegan Paul, 1970), p. 35.
51 *Brownings' Correspondence*, eds. Kelley and Hudson, I: 67.
52 Leonore Davidoff and Catherine Hall, *Family Fortunes: Men and Women of the English Middle Class, 1780–1850* (University of Chicago Press, 1987), p. 159.
53 *The Letters of John Clare*, ed. Mark Storey (Oxford: Clarendon, 1985), p. 651.
54 Margaret Fox Schmidt, *Passion's Child: The Extraordinary Life of Jane Digby* (New York: Harper and Row, 1976), pp. 31, 33.

55 *Barclay Fox's Journal*, ed. R. L. Brett (Totowa, NJ: Rowman and Littlefield, 1979), p. 275.
56 *A Dear Memory: Pages from the Letters of Mary Jane Taylor*, ed. Elizabeth Mary Cadbury (Birmingham: Cornish Brothers, 1914), p. 84.
57 Radway, *Reading the Romance: Women, Patriarchy, and Popular Literature* (Chapel Hill: University of North Carolina Press, 1984), p. 212; see also Helen Taylor, *Scarlett's Women: "Gone With the Wind" and Its Female Fans* (New Brunswick: Rutgers University Press, 1989).
58 See David Piper, *The Image of the Poet: British Poets and Their Portraits* (Oxford: Clarendon, 1982), pp. 126–45.
59 Dickens, *The Old Curiosity Shop* (London: Oxford University Press, 1970), pp. 216–17.
60 Lockhart, *John Bull's Letter to Lord Byron*, ed. Alan Lang Strout (Norman: University of Oklahoma Press, 1947), pp. 80–81.
61 [Thomas Bailey?], "A Layman," *A Sermon on the Death of Lord Byron* (London: Longman, 1824), pp. 26–27.
62 Boott, MS. letter in Yale University's Beinecke Library; quoted with permission.
63 Godman, *The Fields of War: A Young Cavalryman's Crimea Campaign*, ed. Philip Warner (London: John Murray, 1977), pp. 57–58. Byron wrote, "There's not a sea the passenger e'er pukes in, / Turns up more dangerous breakers than the Euxine" (*Don Juan*, v.5).
64 *The Early Married Life of Maria Josepha, Lady Stanley*, ed. Jane H. Adeane (London: Longman, 1899), p. 394.
65 *Extracts of the Journals and Correspondence of Miss Berry from the Year 1783 to 1852*, ed. Lady Theresa Lewis, 3 vols. (London: Longman, 1866), III: 34.
66 Maria Edgeworth, *Letters from England, 1813–1844*, ed. Christina Colvin (Oxford: Clarendon, 1971), p. 339.
67 *The Letter-Bag of Lady Elizabeth Spencer-Stanhope . . . 1806–1873*, ed. A. M. W. Stirling, 2 vols. (London: John Lane, 1913), II: 74.
68 See also, however, the male admirers of Mr. Cypress in Thomas Peacock's *Nightmare Abbey* (1818).
69 Fuss, "Fashion and the Homospectatorial Look," *Critical Inquiry* 18 (1992): 713–37.
70 *The Early Married Life of Maria Josepha, Lady Stanley*, ed. Adeane, p. 345.
71 *Absolom Watkin: Extracts from his Journal, 1814–1856*, ed. A. E. Watkin (London: T. Fisher Unwin, 1920), p. 29.
72 Ellis Cornelia Knight quoted in *The Marlay Letters, 1778–1820*, ed. R. Warwick Bond (London: Constable, 1937), p. 305.
73 Eleanor Anne Franklin quoted in *The Friendships of Mary Russell Mitford as Recorded in Letters from her Literary Correspondents*, ed. the Rev. A. G. L'Estrange (New York: Harper and Brothers, 1882), p. 111.

74 *Memoir and Correspondence of Mrs. Grant of Laggan*, ed. J. P. Grant, 3 vols. (London: Longman, 1844), III: 58–59.
75 [Anon.], "Remarks on *Don Juan*," *Blackwood's Magazine* 5 (1819): 512–22; 517.
76 Grant, *Memoir and Correspondence*, ed. Grant, III: 58.
77 Opie quoted in *Three Generations of English Women: Memoirs and Correspondence of Susannah Taylor, Sarah Austin, and Lady Duff Gordon*, ed. Janet Ross (London: T. Fisher Unwin, 1893), pp. 58–59.
78 Alice Catherine Miles, *Every Girl's Duty: The Diary of a Victorian Debutante*, ed. Maggy Parsons (London: Andre Deutsch, 1992), pp. 134–35.
79 Quoted in N. John Hall, *Salmagundi: Byron, Allegra, and the Trollope Family* (Pittsburgh: Beta Phi Mu, 1975), p. 57.
80 For the classic account, see Samuel C. Chew, *Byron in England: His Fame and After-Fame* (London: John Murray, 1924); see also Clement Tyson Goode, "A Critical Review of Research" in Oscar José Santucho, ed., *George Gordon, Lord Byron: A Comprehensive Bibliography of Secondary Materials in English, 1807–1924* (Metuchen, NJ: Scarecrow, 1977).
81 Frederick Richard Chichester, Earl of Belfast, *Poets and Poetry of the Nineteenth Century* (London: Longman, 1852), p. 101.
82 I am indebted in the following discussion to the work of Chew, Doris Langley Moore in *The Late Lord Byron: Posthumous Dramas* (1961; rpt. New York: Harper and Row, 1977), and Leslie A. Marchand in *Prefaces to Byron* (Norwood, PA: Norwood Editions, 1978). I discuss only a few of the many biographies that appeared.
83 [Anon.], *Narrative of Lord Byron's Voyage to Corsica and Sardinia* (London: J. Limbird, 1824), pp. vii, 60–61, 76. It was widely accepted as accurate and was included in Iley's undiscriminating compilation until Leigh Hunt denounced it in his 1828 biography (Chew, *Byron in England*, p. 165).
84 Hunt, *Lord Byron and Some of His Contemporaries* (Philadelphia: Carey, Lea, and Carey, 1828), pp. 42–43.
85 *Miss Eden's Letters*, ed. Violet Dickinson (London: Macmillan, 1919), pp. 209–10.
86 I am indebted in this paragraph to David Rothstein's unpublished essay "Thomas Moore's *Life of Byron*: Story, History, and Their Uses for the Production of Culture" (University of Minnesota, 1993).
87 See Howell's superb book, *Byron Tonight: A Poet's Plays on the Nineteenth-Century Stage* (Windlesham, Surrey: Springwood, 1982).
88 Joseph Jekyll noted of this production, "Lord Byron ... has been sacrificed to processions and elephants of pasteboard" (*Correspondence of Mr. Joseph Jekyll with his Sister-In-Law Lady Gertrude Sloane Stanley, 1818–1838*, ed. the Hon. Algernon Bourke [London: John Murray, 1894], p. 70).
89 Buzard, *The Beaten Track: European Tourism, Literature, and the*

Ways to Culture, 1800–1918 (Oxford: Clarendon, 1993), pp. 114–30.
90 Louis Bonnerot, *Matthew Arnold, Poète: Essai de Biographie Psychologique* (Paris: Marcel Didier, 1947), p. 16.
91 Alexander Melville Bell, *The Principles of Elocution, with Exercises and Notations*, 6th ed. (London: Paul, Trench, Trübner, and Co., 1893), pp. 200, 204, 206, 207, 208, 214–15, 231, 232, 234.
92 See listings in Bryan N. S. Gooch and David S. Thatcher, *Musical Settings of British Romantic Literature: A Catalogue*, 2 vols. (New York: Garland, 1982), I: 481–600. Even their extensive listings are partial: during my research on this topic in Yale's Beinecke Library, I found several Byron settings not in their catalogue.
93 See Thomas L. Ashton, *Byron's Hebrew Melodies* (Austin: University of Texas Press, 1972.)
94 Piper, *Image of the Poet*, p. 133.
95 Henry G. Huntington, *Memories: Personages, People, Places* (London: Constable, 1911), pp. 241–42.
96 Richard D. Altick, *Paintings From Books: Art and Literature in Britain, 1760–1900* (Columbus: Ohio State University Press, 1985), pp. 436–43.
97 See Luke Herrmann, *Turner Prints: The Engraved Work of J. M. W. Turner* (Oxford: Phaidon, 1990), pp. 191–94.
98 Robert Copeland, "Ceramic View of Byron Country," *Country Life* (Nov. 4, 1976): 1296–97.
99 See, for example, "Oxoniensis" (pseud. of John Henry Todd), *A Remonstrance Addressed to John Murray, Respecting a Recent Publication* (London: F. C. & J. Rivington, 1822), pp. 18–19.
100 Cumming quoted in George Eliot, "Evangelical Teaching: Dr. Cumming," *Essays of George Eliot*, ed. Thomas Pinney (New York: Columbia University Press, 1963), p. 169.
101 Sumner Jones, "Ebenezer Jones: In Memoriam," *Studies of Sensation and Event: Poems of Ebenezer Jones* (London: George Redway, 1883), p. xxx.
102 Marx quoted by Philip Collins in *Thomas Cooper, the Chartist: Byron and the "Poets of the Poor"* (Nottingham: Nottingham Byron Lecture, 1969), p. 22.
103 Hone quoted in Peter J. Manning, *Reading Romantics: Texts and Contexts* (Oxford University Press, 1990), p. 231.
104 See McGann, "The Book of Byron and the Book of a World," *Critical Essays on Lord Byron*, ed. Robert F. Gleckner (New York: G. K. Hall, 1991), pp. 266–82.
105 In 1844, John Murray's son and successor renewed the copyrights to Byron's poetry from Hobhouse, Byron's executor, thus allowing the firm to retain its dominance ("George Paston" [pseud. of Emily Symonds], *At John Murray's: Records of a Literary Circle, 1843–92* [London: John Murray, 1832], p. 40).

106 St. Clair, "The Impact of Byron's Writings: An Evaluative Approach," *Byron: Augustan and Romantic*, ed. Andrew Rutherford (New York: St. Martin's, 1990), pp. 1–25; p. 4.
107 Manning, *Reading Romantics*, pp. 227–30.
108 St. Clair, "Impact," *Byron: Augustan and Romantic*, ed. Rutherford, p. 20.
109 "Preface by a Clergyman," *Don Juan* (London: Hodgson, 1823), p. vi.
110 Hugh J. Luke, "The Publishing of Byron's *Don Juan*," *PMLA* 80 (1965): 199–209.
111 *The Intimate Letters of Hester Piozzi and Penelope Pennington, 1788–1821*, ed. Oswald G. Knapp (London: John Lane, 1914), p. 279.
112 Parry, *The Last Days of Lord Byron* (London: Knight and Lacey, 1825), p. 221.
113 Viscount Chilston, *W. H. Smith* (London: Routledge and Kegan Paul, 1965), pp. 28–29.
114 Walker, *Byron's Readers*, pp. 110–11.
115 Account quoted in Collins, *Thomas Cooper*, p. 19.
116 For Harney, see W. E. Adam, *Memoirs of a Social Atom*, 2 vols. (London: Hutchinson, 1903), I: 227; for Holyoake, see his *Sixty Years of an Agitator's Life*, 2 vols. (London: T. Fisher Unwin, 1892), II: 301.
117 See Bouthaina Shaaban, "The Romantics in the Chartist Press," *Keats-Shelley Journal* 38 (1989): 25–46.
118 Chew, *Byron in England*, pp. 169–93.
119 See Peter Thorslev, *The Byronic Hero: Types and Prototypes* (Minneapolis: University of Minnesota Press, 1962).
120 Taylor, "Preface" to *Philip van Artevelde: A Dramatic Romance*, 2 vols. (Cambridge: James Monroe, 1835), I: xv.
121 Bourdieu, "The Field of Cultural Production, or: The Economic World Reversed," *The Field of Cultural Production*, ed. Randal Johnson (New York: Columbia University Press, 1993), pp. 29–74.

3 CARLYLE, BYRONISM, AND THE PROFESSIONAL INTELLECTUAL

1 Sanders, "The Byron Closed in *Sartor Resartus*," *Studies in Romanticism* 3 (1964): 77–108.
2 Timko, *Carlyle and Tennyson* (Iowa City: University of Iowa Press, 1987), p. 119.
3 Riede, "Transgression, Authority, and the Church of Literature in Carlyle," *Victorian Connections*, ed. Jerome J. McGann (Charlottesville: University of Virginia Press, 1989), pp. 88–120; p. 107.
4 Heyck, *The Transformation of Victorian Intellectual Life* (New York: St. Martin's, 1982), p. 30.

5 See Michael Allen, *Poe and the British Magazine Tradition* (New York: Oxford University Press, 1969), pp. 20–22.

6 See René Wellek, "Carlyle and German Romanticism," *Confrontations: Studies in the Intellectual and Literary Relations Between Germany, England, and the United States During the Nineteenth Century* (Princeton University Press, 1965), pp. 34–81; A. Abbott Ikeler, *Puritan Temper and Transcendental Faith: Carlyle's Literary Vision* (Columbus: Ohio State University Press, 1972); and David J. DeLaura, "The Future of Poetry: A Context for Carlyle and Arnold," *Carlyle and His Contemporaries: Essays in Honor of Charles Richard Sanders,* ed. John Clubbe (Durham: Duke University Press, 1976), pp. 148–80.

7 Scott, "*Childe Harold's Pilgrimage,* Canto III. By Lord Byron," *Quarterly Review* 16 (1816): 172–208; 207.

8 Nietzsche, *Twilight of the Idols,* trans. R. J. Hollingdale (Harmondsworth, Middlesex: Penguin, 1968), p. 74.

9 Carlyle complains that Byron's poetry "is not true" and mocks his "volcanic heroism"; Jeffrey had stated bluntly of a section of canto III of *Childe Harold's Pilgrimage,* "[W]e trust it is not true," and had used the volcano metaphor in the same review ("*Childe Harold's Pilgrimage,* Canto the Third. By Lord Byron," *Edinburgh Review* 27 [1816]: 277–310; 298, 280). Carlyle's discussion of Byron's "superhuman contempt" resembles Walter Scott's description of Byron telling his reader "that neither he, the courteous reader, nor aught the earth had to shew, was worthy the attention of the noble traveller" ("*Childe Harold's Pilgrimage.* Canto IV. By Lord Byron," *Quarterly Review* 19 [1818]: 215–32; 218). Carlyle objects to Byron's "brawling . . . in some paltry tragedy"; John Scott objected to having "our touched sympathies interrupted by the stage-trick of a displayed pocket-handkerchief, or the strut of theatrical magnanimity in martyrdom" ("Living Authors, No. IV: Lord Byron," *London Magazine* 3 [1821]: 50–61; 53). Carlyle's praise of *Don Juan* as his most sincere work may have been influenced by Lockhart's opinion of it as "the only sincere thing" that Byron wrote, as I note in chapter I.

10 For full documentation of the issues discussed in this paragraph, see my "Carlyle, Byron, and Lockhart: A Note," *Carlyle Annual* 12 (1991): 91–95.

11 See David Alec Wilson, *Carlyle to "The French Revolution" (1826–1837)* (London: Kegan Paul, 1924), pp. 65–68.

12 Publisher quoted in Wilson, *Carlyle to "The French Revolution,"* p. 159.

13 G. B. Tennyson, *Sartor Called Resartus: The Genesis, Structure, and Style of Thomas Carlyle's First Major Work* (Princeton University Press, 1965), pp. 133–41.

14 Miriam M. H. Thrall, *Rebellious Fraser's: Nol Yorke's Magazine in the*

Days of Maginn, Thackeray, and Carlyle (New York: Columbia University Press, 1934), pp. 180–81.

15 *Fraser's* actually featured two articles on the fashionable novel; I concentrate on the second because it more directly affected *Sartor*. The *Wellesley Index to Victorian Periodicals, 1824–1900* attributes to Maginn these articles and others important for Carlyle (*The Wellesley Index to Victorian Periodicals*, ed. Walter E. Houghton, 5 vols. [Toronto: University of Toronto, 1966–89], II: 320–26). J. A. Heraud may also have contributed, but I will use Maginn's name; for an account of the relations between Carlyle, Heraud, and Maginn, see Thrall, *Rebellious Fraser's*, pp. 263–75.

16 Alison Adburgham, *Silver Fork Society: Fashionable Life and Literature from 1814 to 1840* (London: Constable, 1983), pp. 131–33.

17 Maginn, "Mr. Edward Lytton Bulwer's Novels; and Remarks on Novel Writing," *Fraser's Magazine* 1 (1830): 509–32; 530.

18 Ibid., p. 514.

19 Ibid., p. 513.

20 Ibid., pp. 514–15.

21 Ibid., p. 532.

22 See Chris R. Vanden Bossche, *Carlyle and the Search for Authority* (Columbus: Ohio State University Press, 1991), pp. 41–44.

23 The following discussion of relations between *Sartor*, Moore's biography, and the reviewers appears with more complete documentation in my "The Sorrows of Carlyle: Byronism and the Philosophic Critic," *Victorian Literature and Culture* 21 (1993): 147–67.

24 Maginn, "Galt's *Life of Byron*," *Fraser's Magazine* 2 (1830): 347–70; 366.

25 Ibid., p. 348.

26 Ibid., pp. 370, 356.

27 Although Carlyle does not mention reading this review specifically, his letters indicate that he was reading *Fraser's* regularly during this time. On October 19, he asked his brother John about the October issue, in which the second part of John's article on St. John Long appeared (*CL*, V: 175, 202); it seems highly probable that Carlyle saw the issue soon afterwards.

28 The earliest evidence for his having read Moore appears in a passing reference to Byron's letters, cited above, in "Schiller, Goethe and Mme. de Staël." These letters occur near the end of Moore's first volume, and were published there for the first time. Carlyle's essay was not published in *Fraser's* until 1832, but on June 6, 1831, he wrote to his brother, "By the way, Fraser, I think, has still a little Paper of mine, 'Goethe, Schiller and Madame de Staël': request him to return it if it does not suit" (*CL*, V: 284). If in June *Fraser's* had had the piece for some time, Carlyle must have written it earlier in 1831, which in turn suggests that he read the first volume of Moore during the winter

or early spring of 1830–31. Further evidence for his having read Moore appears in the letter he wrote to Napier in 1832, after Napier suggested that he write an encyclopedia entry on Byron. Carlyle indicated his unwillingness but added: "If . . . you still persist, then be so good as transmit me your copy of *Moore's Life of Byron* (the second volume of which I have never seen)" (*CL*, VI: 149). He implies that he had at least seen the first volume, which ends with Byron about to leave England after his marriage's failure.

29 Lockhart, Review of Thomas Moore's *"Life of Lord Byron," Quarterly Review* 44 (1831): 168–226; 219.

30 Lockhart in his review of Hunt claimed that "Lord Byron, we have no sort of doubt, indulged his passion for mystifying, at the expense of this gentleman [Hunt], to an improper and unjustifiable extent" (Review of *"Lord Byron and Some of His Contemporaries," Quarterly Review* 37 [1828]: 402–26; 415).

31 Macaulay, *Critical and Historical Essays*, 2 vols. [London: Dent, 1967], II: 614.

32 Carlyle associated Byron explicitly with the Satanic school in a letter to his brother in November 1831: he noted that employment was often difficult to find and "thus Byron writes Satanic Poetry" (*CL*, VI: 46).

33 See Joseph Sigman, " 'Diabolico-angelical Indifference': The Imagery of Polarity in *Sartor Resartus," Southern Review* (Adelaide) 5 (1972): 207–24; 221.

34 G. B. Tennyson, *Sartor Called Resartus*, pp. 114–25.

35 See Chris Vanden Bossche, "Desire and Deferral of Closure in Carlyle's *Sartor Resartus* and *The French Revolution," Journal of Narrative Technique* 16 (1986): 72–78; 75.

36 Jeffrey quoted in Wilson, *Carlyle to "The French Revolution,"* p. 201.

37 See Harrold's discussion in his introduction, *SR*, pp. xl–xlvii.

38 Morley, "Carlyle," *Critical Miscellanies* in *The Works of Lord Morley*, 15 vols. (London: Macmillan, 1921), VI: 66; Roden Noel, "Lord Byron and his Times," *Essays on Poetry and Poets* (London: Kegan Paul, 1886), p. 55.

4 BYRON AT THE MARGINS: EMILY BRONTË AND THE FATE OF MILO

1 Gaskell, *The Life of Charlotte Brontë*, ed. Alan Shelston (Harmondsworth, Middlesex: Penguin, 1975), p. 145.

2 See the work collected in Brian Maidment, *The Poorhouse Fugitives: Self-Taught Poets and Poetry in Victorian Britain* (Manchester: Carcanet, 1987).

3 See my "The Argument between the Rev. Winterbotham and the Rev. Brontë," *Brontë Society Transactions* 20 (1990): 89–94.

4 See Stone, *The Family, Sex and Marriage in England, 1500–1800*, abridged ed. (New York: Harper, 1977), pp. 164–80.
5 Charlotte's story quoted in Winifred Gérin, *Emily Brontë: A Biography* (Oxford: Clarendon, 1971), p. 16.
6 Gaskell, *Life*, ed. Shelston, p. 94.
7 Gérin, *Emily Brontë*, p. 17.
8 Charlotte Brontë, "Biographical Notice of Ellis and Acton Bell," in Emily Brontë, *Wuthering Heights*, eds. Hilda Marsden and Ian Jack (Oxford: Clarendon, 1976), p. 443.
9 Alexander, *The Early Writings of Charlotte Brontë* (Oxford: Blackwell, 1983), p. 12.
10 Gaskell, *Life*, ed. Shelston, p. 117.
11 Branwell Brontë quoted in Winifred Gérin, "Byron's Influence on the Brontës," *Keats-Shelley Memorial Bulletin* 17 (1966): 1–19; 2.
12 *The Brontë Letters*, ed. Muriel Spark (London: Macmillan, 1966), p. 42.
13 Gérin, "Byron's Influence," p. 1.
14 *Brontë Letters*, ed. Spark, p. 47.
15 *Selected Brontë Poems*, ed. Edward Chitham and Tom Winnifrith (Oxford: Basil Blackwell, 1985), pp. 68–86; quotations from the poem are cited by part and line numbers in this edition.
16 *The Poems of Charlotte Brontë: A New Text and Commentary*, ed. Victor A. Neufeldt (New York: Garland, 1985), pp. 120–24; quotations from the poem are cited by line numbers in this edition.
17 See Tom Winnifrith, *The Brontës and Their Background: Romance and Reality* (London and Basingstoke: Macmillan, 1973), p. 100.
18 See Helene Moglen, *Charlotte Brontë: The Self Conceived* (New York: Norton, 1976), pp. 47–57, and John Maynard, *Charlotte Brontë and Sexuality* (Cambridge University Press, 1984), pp. 9–12.
19 *An Edition of the Early Writings of Charlotte Brontë*, ed. Christine Alexander, 2 vols. to present (Oxford: Basil Blackwell, 1987–), vol. II, part 2, pp. 92–93.
20 Charlotte Brontë, *Five Novelettes*, ed. Winifred Gérin (London: Folio Press, 1971), p. 309.
21 Ibid., pp. 351–52.
22 Ibid., p. 353.
23 Many of these were first pointed out in Helen Brown, "The Influence of Byron on Emily Brontë," *Modern Language Review* 34 (1939): 374–81.
24 The "H" refers to Hatfield's numbering in *The Complete Poems of Emily Jane Brontë*, ed. C. W. Hatfield (New York: Columbia University Press, 1941). All references to Emily Brontë's poetry are to line numbers in this edition.
25 Pykett, *Emily Brontë* (Savage, MD: Barnes and Noble, 1989), p. 49.
26 For examples, see the supplementary issue of *The Mirror* 3 (1824): 350–52.

27 *Brontë Letters*, ed. Spark, p. 90.
28 It is difficult to know if her siblings had seen it before, but at some point she stopped showing it, as Charlotte's famous story of stumbling on it by accident suggests ("Biographical Notice of Ellis and Acton Bell," in *Wuthering Heights*, eds. Marsden and Jack, p. 435). Anne's 1845 birthday note also hints that Emily did not show her poetry: "She is writing some poetry, too. I wonder what it is about?" (*Brontë Letters*, ed. Spark, p. 123).
29 For a discussion of problematic transcendence in Emily's poetry, see Margaret Homans, *Women Writers and Poetic Identity* (Princeton University Press, 1980), pp. 104–61.
30 Christine Gallant, "The Archetypal Feminine in Emily Brontë's Poetry," *Women's Studies* 7 (1980): 79–94; 84.
31 Auerbach, "This Changeful Life: Emily Brontë's Anti-Romance," *Shakespeare's Sisters: Feminist Essays on Women Poets*, ed. Sandra M. Gilbert and Susan Gubar (Bloomington: Indiana University Press, 1979), pp. 49–65; p. 58.
32 Pykett, *Emily Brontë*, p. 52.
33 Tayler, *Holy Ghosts: The Male Muses of Emily and Charlotte Brontë* (New York: Columbia University Press, 1990), p. 32.
34 Charlotte Brontë, "Biographical Notice of Ellis and Acton Bell" in *Wuthering Heights*, eds. Marsden and Jack, p. 435.
35 See Tom Winnifrith's introduction to *The Poems of Patrick Branwell Brontë* (New York: New York University Press for the Shakespeare Head Press, 1983), p. xxiii.
36 In her "Biographical Notice" Charlotte claimed that the sisters wrote novels after the poetry's failure (*Wuthering Heights*, eds. Marsden and Jack, pp. 436–37), but her letters reveal that they had started their novels even before their poetry appeared (see *Brontë Letters*, ed. Spark, pp. 129–31).
37 Gaskell, *Life*, ed. Shelston, p. 307.
38 *Brontë Letters*, ed. Spark, p. 65.
39 *The Miscellaneous and Unpublished Writings of Charlotte and Patrick Branwell Brontë*, vols. XVIII–XIX of the Shakespeare Head Brontë, ed. T. J. Wise and J. A. Symington (Oxford: Shakespeare Head, 1938), XIX: 404.
40 Alison quoted in *Victorian Criticism of the Novel*, eds. Edwin M. Eigner and George J. Worth (Cambridge University Press, 1985), p. 60.
41 Andrew Blake, *Reading Victorian Fiction: The Cultural Context and Ideological Content of the Nineteenth-Century Novel* (New York: St. Martin's, 1989), p. 73.
42 Ellis quoted in Vineta Colby, *Yesterday's Woman: Domestic Realism in the English Novel* (Princeton University Press, 1974), p. 38.
43 *The Professor*, eds. Margaret Smith and Herbert Rosengarten (Oxford: Clarendon, 1987), p. 159.
44 Ibid., p. 253.

45 Ibid., p. 180.

46 Rod Mengham, *Wuthering Heights*, Penguin Critical Studies (Harmondsworth, Middlesex: Penguin, 1988), p. 57.

47 See, for example, Terry Eagleton, *Myths of Power: A Marxist Study of the Brontës* (London: Macmillan, 1975), pp. 97–121; Fredric Jameson, *The Political Unconscious: Narrative as a Socially Symbolic Act* (Ithaca: Cornell University Press, 1981), pp. 126–28; Anita Levy, *Other Women: The Writing of Class, Race, and Gender, 1832–1898* (Princeton University Press, 1991), pp. 75–97; and Nancy Armstrong, "Imperialist Nostalgia and *Wuthering Heights*," in *Emily Brontë: Wuthering Heights*, ed. Linda H. Peterson (Boston: St. Martin's, 1992), pp. 428–49.

48 Jameson, *Political Unconscious*, p. 126.

49 Ibid., p. 128.

50 Citations from the novel are to page numbers in *Wuthering Heights*, eds. Hilda Marsden and Ian Jack (Oxford: Clarendon, 1976).

51 For a different but compelling treatment of the binarism of realism and romance, see Nancy Armstrong, "Emily Brontë In and Out of Her Time," *Genre* 15 (1982): 243–64.

52 For a discussion of the stereotypes, see Meg Harris Williams, *A Strange Way of Killing: The Poetic Structure of Wuthering Heights* (Perthshire: Clunie Press, 1987), pp. 205–19.

53 Margiad Evans first discussed *Manfred* and *Wuthering Heights* in detail, and I am indebted to his article for verbal connections ("Byron and Emily Brontë: An Essay," *Life and Letters* 57 [1948]: 193–216); see also Gérin, "Byron's Influence," p. 13.

54 Ewbank, *Their Proper Sphere: A Study of the Brontë Sisters as Early Victorian Female Novelists* (Cambridge, MA: Harvard University Press, 1966), p. 99.

55 Wilson quoted in *The Works of Lord Byron*, [ed. John Wright], 17 vols. (London: John Murray, 1832–33), XI:48.

56 Gérin, *Emily Brontë*, p. 45.

57 *Works of Lord Byron*, [ed. Wright], X:7.

58 Charlotte Brontë, *Novelettes*, ed. Gérin, p. 147.

59 Davies, *Emily Brontë: The Artist as a Free Woman* (Manchester: Carcanet, 1983), pp. 95–113.

60 For a dissenting opinion, see Beth Newman, " 'The Situation of the Looker-On': Gender, Narration, and Gaze in *Wuthering Heights*," *PMLA* 105 (1990): 1029–41.

61 Sandra M. Gilbert and Susan Gubar, *The Madwoman in the Attic: The Woman Writer and the Nineteenth-Century Literary Imagination* (New Haven: Yale University Press, 1979), p. 299.

62 Ibid., p. 299.

5 THE FLIGHT FROM VULGARITY: TENNYSON AND BYRON

1 Taine quoted in *Tennyson: The Critical Heritage*, ed. John D. Jump (London: Routledge and Kegan Paul, 1967), p. 272.
2 "Tennyson's *Maud*," *Essays of George Eliot*, ed. Thomas Pinney (New York: Columbia University Press, 1963), p. 194; [Anon.], "Modern Light Literature–Poetry," *Blackwood's Magazine* 79 (1856): 125–38; 132.
3 Quoted in Hallam Tennyson, *Alfred Lord Tennyson: A Memoir*, 2 vols. (New York: Macmillan, 1897), I: 4.
4 Peckham, *Victorian Revolutionaries: Speculations on Some Heroes of a Culture Crisis* (New York: Braziller, 1970), pp. 8–10.
5 The most detailed treatment of Byron's influence on the 1827 volume occurs in W. D. Paden, *Tennyson in Egypt: A Study of the Imagery in his Early Work* (Lawrence: University of Kansas Press, 1942).
6 Quoted in Leon Edel, *Henry James: The Conquest of London, 1870–83* (Philadelphia and New York: Lippincott, 1962), p. 376.
7 H. Tennyson, *Memoir*, II: 331.
8 Quoted in Hallam Tennyson, *Materials for a Life of Alfred Tennyson*, 4 vols. (privately printed, *c.* 1895), I: 22.
9 For discussion of Coleridgean influence, see John Beer, "Tennyson, Coleridge, and the Cambridge Apostles," *Tennyson: Seven Essays*, ed. Philip Collins (Houndmills, Basingstoke: Macmillan, 1992), pp. 1–35.
10 See Leslie A. Marchand, *The Athenaeum: A Mirror of Victorian Culture* (Chapel Hill: University of North Carolina Press, 1941), esp. pp. 1–24.
11 Maurice, "Sketches of Contemporary Authors, No. XII: Lord Byron," *Athenaeum* 23 (April 8, 1828): 2.
12 Richard Monckton Milnes, "The Wordsworth Society," *Some Writings and Speeches of Lord Houghton, in the Last Year of his Life* (London: Chiswick Press, 1888), pp. 120–21.
13 Speaker quoted in *Letters of Arthur Henry Hallam*, ed. Jack Kolb (Columbus: Ohio State University Press, 1981), p. 341 n.1.
14 *Athenaeum* quoted in Marchand, *The Athenaeum*, p. 260.
15 *Remains in Prose and Verse of Arthur Henry Hallam* (London: John Murray, 1863), p. 24 n.
16 Robert Bernard Martin, *Tennyson: The Unquiet Heart* (Oxford: Clarendon, 1983), p. 162.
17 Neil Fraistat, "Illegitimate Shelley: Radical Piracy and the Textual Edition as Cultural Performance," *PMLA* 109 (1994): 409–23.
18 Unless otherwise noted, citations of Tennyson's poetry are to line numbers in *The Poems of Tennyson*, ed. Christopher Ricks, 3 vols. (Berkeley and Los Angeles: University of California Press, 1987).

19 For discussion of Tennyson's relation to Shelley, see Alan Sinfield, *Alfred Tennyson* (Oxford: Basil Blackwell, 1986), esp. pp. 21–39; Margaret A. Lourie, "Below the Thunders of the Upper Deep: Tennyson as Romantic Revisionist," *Studies in Romanticism* 18 (1979): 2–27; and Herbert F. Tucker, *Tennyson and the Doom of Romanticism* (Cambridge, MA: Harvard University Press, 1988), to which I am indebted throughout this chapter.

20 Tennyson's marginalia in *Works of Lord Byron* (London: John Murray, 1837), p. 123. This edition abbreviated the 1832–33 one and included notes by critics printed in the earlier edition. I thank Susan Gates of the Tennyson Research Centre, Lincoln, England, for making it available.

21 Ibid., p. 60.

22 H. Tennyson, *Materials*, 1: 30.

23 Michael G. Cooke, *The Blind Man Traces the Circle: On the Patterns and Philosophy of Byron's Poetry* (Princeton University Press, 1969), p. 88.

24 I quote the 1832 "Lady of Shalott" from Jerome J. McGann's *New Oxford Book of Romantic Period Verse* (Oxford and New York: Oxford University Press, 1993), pp. 754–59, lines 28–32.

25 George G. Loane pointed out these echoes, not noted by Ricks, in *Echoes in Tennyson and Other Essays* (London: Arthur H. Stockwell, n.d.), p. 4.

26 Albright, *Tennyson: The Muses' Tug-of-War* (Charlottesville: University of Virginia Press, 1986), p. 34.

27 McGann, *Romantic Period Verse*, p. 756, lines 64–72.

28 Ibid., p. 757, lines 125–26.

29 *Tennyson: The Critical Heritage*, ed. Jump, p. 72.

30 McGann, *Romantic Period Verse*, pp. 758–59, lines 174–80.

31 For further discussion of the endings of "The Lady of Shalott," see Kathy Alexis Psomiades's "Beauty's Body: Gender Ideology and British Aestheticism," *Victorian Studies* 36 (1992): 31–52.

32 See my "Contesting Heterodoxy: Mrs. Hemans vs. Lord Byron," paper presented at the North American Society for the Study of Romanticism, August 1993; I am grateful to Herbert Tucker for reinforcing this insight.

33 *The Letters of Alfred, Lord Tennyson*, eds. Cecil Y. Lang and Edgar F. Shannon, Jr., 3 vols. (Cambridge, MA: Harvard University Press, 1981–90), 1: 109.

34 In his first edition of Tennyson, Ricks noted several recollections of Byron; in the second edition, he expanded his annotation based on B. J. Leggett, "Dante, Byron, and Tennyson's Ulysses," *Tennessee Studies in Literature* 15 (1970): 143–159 (see Ricks, ed., *Poems of Tennyson*, 1: 615). More recently, Martin Bidney has argued for the influence of Byron's "The Dream" in "Vision of Wholeness and

Voices from the Deep: Kindred Wanderers in Byron's 'The Dream' and Tennyson's 'Ulysses,'" *Victorian Newsletter* 74 (1988): 41–45.

35 Quoted in *Tennyson: Interviews and Recollections*, ed. Norman Page (Totowa, NJ: Barnes and Noble, 1983), p. 71.

36 *William Allingham: A Diary*, eds. H. Allingham and D. Radford (Harmondsworth, Middlesex: Penguin, 1985), p. 300.

37 For citations, see Oscar José Santucho, ed., *George Gordon, Lord Byron: A Comprehensive Bibliography of Secondary Materials in English, 1807–1924* (Metuchen, NJ: Scarecrow Press, 1977), p. 242.

38 Leggett, "Dante, Byron, and Tennyson's Ulysses," p. 151.

39 Schur, *Victorian Pastoral: Tennyson, Hardy, and the Subversion of Forms* (Columbus: Ohio State University Press, 1989), p. 77.

40 *Hallam Letters*, ed. Kolb, p. 181.

41 Quoted in Maria Trench, *Richard Chenevix Trench, Archbishop: Letters and Memorials*, 2 vols. (London: Kegan Paul, 1888), I: 45.

42 Mill quoted in *Tennyson: The Critical Heritage*, ed. Jump, p. 89.

43 For a discussion of "Tithon" versus "Tithonus," see Linda K. Hughes, *The Manyfacèd Glass: Tennyson's Dramatic Monologues* (Athens, OH: Ohio University Press, 1987), pp. 223–26.

44 Horne quoted in *Tennyson: The Critical Heritage*, ed. Jump, p. 153; Elizabeth Barrett Browning may have written much of this essay.

45 Ibid., p. 160.

46 T. S. Eliot, "*In Memoriam*," rpt. in *Tennyson's Poetry*, ed. Robert W. Hill, Jr. (New York: Norton, 1971), pp. 613–20; p. 617.

47 H. Tennyson, *Memoir*, I: 304–05.

48 Martin, *Unquiet Heart*, p. 342.

49 Allingham, *Diary*, ed. Allingham and Radford, p. 132.

50 Brisman, "*Maud*: The Feminine as the Crux of Influence," *Studies in Romanticism* 31 (1992): 21–43.

51 Ibid., p. 41.

52 *The Poetical Works of Thomas Cooper* (London: Hodder and Stoughton, 1877), p. 52.

53 I am indebted to Mark A. Weinstein, *William Edmondstoune Aytoun and the Spasmodic Controversy* (New Haven: Yale University Press, 1968); see also Jerome Hamilton Buckley, *The Victorian Temper: A Study in Literary Culture* (1951; rpt. New York: Random House, 1964), pp. 41–65.

54 Weinstein, *Spasmodic Controversy*, pp. 63, 65, 128.

55 For discussions of Tennyson and the Spasmodics, see ibid., pp. 174–76, and Antony H. Harrison, *Victorian Poets and Romantic Poems: Intertextuality and Ideology* (Charlottesville: University of Virginia Press, 1990), pp. 72–89.

56 Smith, *A Life-Drama, City Poems, Etc.* (London: Walter Scott, 1907), pp. 37–38.

57 Ibid., p. 23.

58 Tennyson's marginalia in *Poems by Alexander Smith*, 2nd ed. (London: David Bogue, 1853), p. 93; volume in the Tennyson Research Centre, Lincoln, England.

59 "Recent English Poetry," *Selected Prose Works of Arthur Hugh Clough*, ed. Buckner B. Trawick (University of Alabama Press, 1964), pp. 145–46.

60 Gilfillian quoted in Weinstein, *Spasmodic Controversy*, p. 84.

61 Harrison, *Victorian Poets*, p. 73.

62 See Susan Shatto's introduction to *Tennyson's "Maud": A Definitive Edition* (Norman and London: University of Oklahoma Press, 1986), pp. 33–38.

63 Brimley quoted in *Tennyson: The Critical Heritage*, ed. Jump, p. 191.

64 Tennyson later made several alterations to clarify the plot; for discussion, see Edgar F. Shannon, "The Critical Reception of Tennyson's *Maud*," *PMLA* 68 (1953): 397–417.

65 Rader, *Tennyson's "Maud": The Biographical Genesis* (Berkeley and Los Angeles: University of California Press, 1963).

66 Culler, *The Poetry of Tennyson* (New Haven: Yale University Press, 1977), p. 209.

67 Tucker, *Doom*, p. 426.

68 For an alternative view of the effect that this technical control has on *Maud*, see Eric Griffith's *The Printed Voice of Victorian Poetry* (Oxford: Clarendon, 1989), pp. 154–65.

69 Caudwell, *Illusion and Reality: A Study of the Sources of Poetry* (New York: International, 1937), p. 108; despite Caudwell's reputation as a vulgar Marxist, his discussion of Victorian poets deserves to be better known (pp. 99–116).

70 Shannon, "Critical Reception," p. 406.

71 Mann quoted in *Tennyson: The Critical Heritage*, ed. Jump, p. 200.

72 Dixon, "Review of *Maud and Other Poems*," *Athenaeum* 28 (August 4, 1855): 893.

73 *Tennyson Letters*, eds. Lang and Shannon, I: 116.

74 J. Cumming Walters, *Tennyson: Poet, Philosopher, Idealist* (London: Kegan Paul, 1893), p. 125.

75 Saint-Saëns set "A Voice by the Cedar Tree"; Liszt, "Go Not, Happy Day"; and Massenet, "Come into the Garden, Maud" (*Songs from the Published Writings of Alfred Tennyson, Poet Laureate*, ed. W. G. Cusins [London: C. Kegan Paul, 1880], pp. 305–14, 315–22, 323–32).

76 Gordon N. Ray analyzes notes that were taken at one of Tennyson's readings in *Tennyson Reads "Maud"* (Vancouver: University of British Columbia Press, 1968).

77 Allingham, *Diary*, eds. Allingham and Radford, p. 118.

78 H. Tennyson, *Memoir*, I: 398.

79 Ure, *The Philosophy of Manufactures, Or, An Exposition of the Scientific,*

Moral, and Commercial Economy of the Factory System of Great Britain (1835; London: Frank Cass, 1967), p. 13.

80 Smiles quoted in Asa Briggs, *Victorian People: A Reassessment of Persons and Themes, 1851–1867,* rev. ed. (University of Chicago Press, 1970), pp. 127–28.

81 Benjamin, "The Work of Art in the Age of Mechanical Reproduction," *Illuminations,* ed. Hannah Arendt, trans. Harry Zohn (New York: Schocken, 1968), p. 242.

82 My understanding of the role of utopianism in art draws on Fredric Jameson's "Conclusion: The Dialectic of Utopia and Ideology" in *The Political Unconscious: Narrative as a Socially Symbolic Act* (Ithaca: Cornell University Press, 1981), pp. 281–300.

83 Shannon, "Critical Reception," pp. 413–14.

84 "The Lovesong of J. Alfred Prufrock" in *T. S. Eliot: Selected Poems* (New York: HBJ, 1964), p. 12. See W. K. Wimsatt, *Hateful Contraries: Studies in Literature and Criticism* (Louisville: University of Kentucky, 1965), pp. 205–06, and, more generally, Carol T. Christ's *Victorian and Modern Poetics* (University of Chicago Press, 1984).

85 T. S. Eliot, *"In Memoriam,"* rpt. in *Tennyson's Poetry,* ed. Hill, p. 620.

86 H. Tennyson, *Memoir,* i: 69.

6 THE SHADY SIDE OF THE SWORD: BULWER LYTTON, DISRAELI, WILDE, AND BYRON'S HOMOSEXUALITY

1 Sedgwick, *Epistemology of the Closet* (Berkeley: University of California Press, 1990), p. 47.

2 See Jeffrey Weeks, *Sex, Politics, and Society: The Regulation of Sexuality since 1800* (London: Longman, 1981), esp. pp. 96–121; David M. Halperin, *One Hundred Years of Homosexuality* (New York: Routledge, 1990); and Ed Cohen, *Talk on the Wilde Side* (New York: Routledge, 1993).

3 See Wayne Koestenbaum, *Double Talk: The Erotics of Male Literary Collaboration* (New York: Routledge, 1989), and Richard Dellamora, *Masculine Desire: The Sexual Politics of Victorian Aestheticism* (Chapel Hill: University of North Carolina Press, 1990).

4 Foucault, *The History of Sexuality, Vol. 1: An Introduction,* trans. Robert Hurley (New York: Random House, 1978), p. 43.

5 Scott Lash, "Genealogy and the Body: Foucault/Deleuze/Nietzsche," *Theory, Culture & Society* 2 (1984): 1–17; 7.

6 See Bourdieu, *The Field of Cultural Production: Essays on Art and Literature,* ed. Randal Johnson (New York: Columbia University Press, 1993), esp. pp. 29–73.

7 Moi, "Appropriating Bourdieu: Feminist Theory and Pierre Bourdieu's Sociology of Culture," *New Literary History* 22 (1991): 1017–49; 1036.

8 Butler, *Gender Trouble: Feminism and the Subversion of Identity* (London: Routledge, 1990), p. 139.

9 Crompton, *Byron and Greek Love: Homophobia in 19th-Century England* (Berkeley: University of California Press, 1985), p. 11; I am indebted to Crompton's work throughout.

10 Trumbach, "Gender and the Homosexual Role in Modern Western Culture," *Homosexuality, Which Homosexuality?: International Conference on Gay and Lesbian Studies,* ed. Dennis Altman *et al.* (London: GMP Publishers, 1989), pp. 149–69.

11 Cohen, *Talk,* p. 114.

12 Blackstone quoted in Crompton, *Greek Love,* p. 15.

13 Weeks, *Sex, Politics, and Society,* p. 101.

14 For further discussion of these issues, see Jill Campbell, "Politics and Sexuality in Portraits of John, Lord Hervey," *Word & Image* 6 (1990): 281–97.

15 Christensen, *Lord Byron's Strength: Romantic Writing and Commercial Society* (Baltimore and London: Johns Hopkins University Press, 1993), pp. 49–87.

16 *Lady Blessington's Conversations of Lord Byron,* ed. Ernest J. Lovell, Jr. (Princeton University Press, 1969), pp. 6–7; Moore quoted from G. Wilson Knight, *Lord Byron: Christian Virtues* (London: Routledge and Kegan Paul, 1952), p. 81.

17 C. L. Cline, "Unpublished Notes on the Romantic Poets by Isaac D'Israeli," *Studies in English* (University of Texas) 21 (1941): 142.

18 Davies quoted in *His Very Self and Voice: Collected Conversations of Lord Byron,* ed. Ernest J. Lovell, Jr. (New York: Macmillan, 1954), p. 42.

19 For details, see Leslie A. Marchand, *Byron: A Biography,* 3 vols. (New York: Knopf, 1957), esp. vol. II, chs. 15–16.

20 Miller, "Secret Subjects, Open Secrets," *The Novel and the Police* (Berkeley: University of California Press, 1988), pp. 192–220; Sedgwick, *Epistemology,* pp. 67 ff., further develops the "open secret."

21 Adburgham, *Silver-Fork Society: Fashionable Life and Literature from 1814 to 1840* (London: Constable, 1983), p. 118.

22 Woolf, "Hariette Wilson," *Collected Essays,* 4 vols. (New York: Harcourt Brace, 1967), III: 227.

23 *Don Leon* (c. 1833) is anonymous; it is reprinted in Bernard Grebanier, *The Uninhibited Byron: An Account of His Sexual Confusion* (New York: Crown, 1970), pp. 307–49; quotations on p. 349.

24 Bruce R. Smith, *Homosexual Desire in Shakespeare's England: A Cultural Poetics* (University of Chicago Press, 1991), pp. 191–92.

25 Hobhouse quoted in Marchand, *Byron,* p. 586.

26 Opie quoted in *Three Generations of English Women: Memoirs and Correspondence of Susannah Taylor, Sarah Austin, and Lady Duff Gordon,* ed. Janet Ross (London: T. Fisher Unwin, 1893), pp. 58–59.

27 *The Diaries of William Charles Macready*, ed. William Toynbee, 2 vols. (London: Chapman and Hall, 1912), I: 243.

28 Davidoff and Hall, *Family Fortunes: Men and Women of the English Middle Class, 1780–1850* (University of Chicago Press, 1987), p. 229.

29 Adburgham, *Silver-Fork Society*, p. 1. Information in the following paragraphs comes from Adburgham and from E. Beresford Chancellor, *Life in Regency and Early Victorian Times: An Account of the Days of Brummell and D'Orsay, 1800 to 1850* (London: B. T. Batsford, 1927), esp. chs. 2 and 3.

30 Biographers emphasize the admiration that both had for Byron and the formative effects of his dandyism; for Bulwer Lytton, see Michael Sadleir, *Bulwer: A Panorama, Edward and Rosina, 1803–1836* (Boston: Little, Brown, and Company, 1931; the first volume of a never-completed two-volume biography), pp. 26, 29, 52–56, as well as Bulwer Lytton's own comments on Byron in his *England and The English*, ed. Standish Meacham (University of Chicago Press, 1970), pp. 266–81. For Disraeli, see Sarah Bradford, *Disraeli* (New York: Stein and Day, 1982), pp. 88, 178–79.

31 See [Anon.], "Sir Edward Bulwer-Lytton's Remarks on Lady Caroline Lamb Written in his Copy of *Glenarvon*," *Byron Journal* 6 (1978): 113.

32 Fragment printed in the Earl of Lytton, *Life of Edward Bulwer, First Lord Lytton*, 2 vols. (London: Macmillan, 1913), I: 120–21.

33 Doris Langley Moore, *The Late Lord Byron: Posthumous Dramas*, rev. ed. (New York: Harper and Row, 1977), p. 243.

34 *Memoir and Letters of Charles Sumner*, ed. Edward C. Pierce, 2 vols. (Boston: Roberts Brothers, 1877), II: 23.

35 Chorley quoted in Sadleir, *Bulwer*, p. 324.

36 Cartoon reproduced in Michael Sadleir, *Blessington-D'Orsay: A Masquerade* (London: Constable, 1933), p. 264.

37 B. R. Jerman, *The Young Disraeli* (Princeton University Press, 1960), p. 158.

38 Bates quoted in Adburgham, *Silver-Fork Society*, p. 195; Willis, in Wilfred Meynell's *The Man Disraeli* (London: Hutchinson, 1927), p. 38.

39 Quoted in André Maurois, *Disraeli: A Picture of the Victorian Age* (New York: D. Appleton, 1928), p. 47.

40 Bradford, *Disraeli*, p. 51.

41 Gagnier, *Idylls of the Marketplace: Oscar Wilde and the Victorian Public* (Stanford University Press, 1986), p. 76; see pp. 67–90 more generally.

42 Rosina Bulwer Lytton quoted in Virginia Blain, "Rosina Bulwer Lytton and the Rage of the Unheard," *Huntington Library Quarterly* 53 (1990): 211–36; 231.

43 Rosina Bulwer Lytton, *A Blighted Life* (London: London Publishing Office, 1880), p. 76.

44 Bradford, *Disraeli*, p. 218.
45 Sadleir, *Bulwer*, p. 133.
46 Quoted in Bradford, *Disraeli*, p. 24.
47 Ibid., p. 31.
48 Ibid., p. 50.
49 Sedgwick, *Between Men: English Literature and Male Homosocial Desire* (New York: Columbia University Press, 1985).
50 For details, see Adburgham, *Silver-Fork Society*, pp. 69–79.
51 The only full-length book on the subject is Matthew Whiting Rosa, *The Silver-Fork School: Novels of Fashion Preceding "Vanity Fair"* (New York: Columbia University Press, 1936), although Adburgham's *Silver-Fork Society* is an important supplement.
52 Anderson, "The Writings of Catherine Gore," *Journal of Popular Culture* 10 (1976): 404–23; 420.
53 Review quoted in Adburgham, *Silver-Fork Society*, p. 80.
54 All quotations from the novel are from *Pelham, or the Adventures of a Gentleman*, ed. Jerome J. McGann (Lincoln: University of Nebraska Press, 1972).
55 Adburgham, *Silver-Fork Society*, p. 127.
56 Oakley, "The Reform of Honor in Bulwer's *Pelham*," *Nineteenth-Century Literature* 47 (1992): 49–71; 50.
57 Sedgwick, *Between Men*, p. 118.
58 *Examiner* quoted in Sadleir, *Bulwer*, p. 178.
59 Ibid., p. 146.
60 Crompton, *Greek Love*, p. 342. He was surprisingly open about Byron's sexual relationships with women and was harshly criticized for his candor. Lockhart, for example, objected because Moore had become "the instrument of placing before the public . . . full-length pictures of this particular species of profligacy" (review of "Moore's *The Life of Lord Byron*," *Quarterly Review* 44 [1831]: 168–226; 205).
61 John Wilson, Review of "Moore's *Byron*," *Blackwood's Magazine* 27 (1830): 389–420; 417.
62 Beckford quoted with the permission of Yale's Beinecke Library.
63 Quoted from Robert, Lord Lytton, *The Life, Letters, and Literary Remains of Edward Bulwer, Lord Lytton*, 2 vols. (London: Kegan Paul, 1883), II: 318 and from Hughenden MS. 104/1, f. 12, Bodleian Library.
64 On Byronism in Disraeli's other novels, see Peter W. Graham, "Byron and Disraeli," *Victorian Newsletter* 69 (1986): 26–30.
65 Jerman, *Young Disraeli*, p. 289.
66 Bradford, *Disraeli*, p. 93.
67 From *The Court Journal* (1837), quoted in *Disraeli's Novels Reviewed, 1826–1968*, ed. R. W. Stewart (Metuchen, NJ: Scarecrow Press, 1975), p. 163.
68 Garnett quoted in ibid., p. 168.

69 Herbert's first name comes from Scott's *Marmion*, whose hero was a major precursor for Byron's.

70 All quotations from the novel are from *Venetia* (New York: George Routledge, 1853).

71 See John Holloway, *The Victorian Sage: Studies in Argument* (1953; rpt. New York: Norton, 1965), pp. 86–110.

72 *Fraser's* quoted in *Disraeli's Novels Reviewed*, ed. R. W. Stewart, pp. 163, 184.

73 Disraeli's secretary quoted in Jerman, *Young Disraeli*, p. 191.

74 Queensberry quoted in Richard Ellman, *Oscar Wilde* (New York: Random House, 1988), p. 438.

75 See William Whitla, "Browning, The Byron Scandal, and Alfred Austin," *Browning Society Notes* 7.1 (March, 1977): 12–33. Relevant essays in the Arnold-Swinburne quarrel are reprinted in *Byron: The Critical Heritage*, ed. Andrew Rutherford (New York: Barnes and Noble, 1970).

76 See John L. Kijinski, "John Morley's 'English Men of Letters' Series and the Politics of Reading," *Victorian Studies* 34 (1991): 205–25.

77 *The Artist as Critic: Critical Writings of Oscar Wilde*, ed. Richard Ellmann (New York: Random House, 1968), pp. 3–4.

78 Ellman, *Oscar Wilde*, pp. 37–39.

79 *Artist as Critic*, ed. Ellman, pp. 260, 341.

80 Wilde won a bet in 1899 because he recognized that the description of Shelley as a "beautiful, ineffectual angel" came from Arnold's essay on Byron (*The Letters of Oscar Wilde*, ed. Rupert Hart-Davis [London: Rupert Hart-Davis, 1962], pp. 782, 786).

81 Arnold quoted in *Byron: The Critical Heritage*, ed. Rutherford, p. 446.

82 Ibid., p. 459.

83 Ibid., p. 455.

84 *Artist as Critic*, ed. Ellman, p. 262.

85 Knight, *Passages of a Working Life During Half a Century: With a Prelude of Early Reminiscences*, 2 vols. (London: Bradbury and Evans, 1864), I: 112.

86 See Elaine Showalter, *A Literature of Their Own: British Women Novelists from Brontë to Lessing* (Princeton University Press, 1977), pp. 153–81.

87 See Edward Wagenknecht, *Harriet Beecher Stowe: The Known and the Unknown* (New York: Oxford University Press, 1965), Frank Lentricchia, "Harriet Beecher Stowe and the Byron Whirlwind," *Bulletin of the New York Public Library* 70 (1966): 218–28, and Susan Wolstenholme, "Voice of the Voiceless: Harriet Beecher Stowe and the Byron Controversy," *American Literary Realism, 1870–1910* 19.2 (1987): 48–65.

88 Böker, "Lord Byron, Flaubert und Mrs. Braddon," *Byron-Symposium Mannheim 1982*, eds. Werner Huber and Rainer Schöwerling

(Paderborn: Universität-Gesamthochschüle, 1983), pp. 120–41.

89 Braddon, *Aurora Floyd*, 2 vols. (Leipzig: Tauchnitz, 1863), 1: 263, 33.

90 Shaw, *Man and Superman: A Comedy and a Philosophy* (Harmondsworth, Middlesex: Penguin, 1985), p. 13.

91 See Ouida's *Views and Opinions* (London: Methuen, 1895), pp. 255–57, and *Critical Studies* (New York: Cassell and Company, 1900), p. 145; for her early enthusiasm, see Eileen Bigland, *Ouida: The Passionate Victorian* (London: Jarrolds, 1950), p. 22.

92 Ouida, *Folle-Farine*, 2 vols. (1871; Leipzig: Tauchnitz, 1872), 1: 201.

93 *Wilde Letters*, ed. Hart-Davis, p. 831.

94 Ellman, *Oscar Wilde*, pp. 286–94.

95 *Wilde Letters*, ed. Hart-Davis, p. 211. For Wilde and Braddon, see Robert Lee Woolf, *Sensational Victorian: The Life and Fiction of Mary Elizabeth Braddon* (New York and London: Garland, 1979), pp. 263, 329, 336, 389. For Wilde and Ouida, see Horace Wyndham, *Speranza: A Biography of Lady Wilde* (London and New York: T. V. Boardman, 1951), p. 123, and Bigland, *Ouida*, pp. 65, 186, 202.

96 *The Journals of Lady Knightley of Fawsley*, ed. Julia Cartwright (New York: E. P. Dutton, 1916), p. 367.

97 Wyndham, *Speranza*, pp. 112–32.

98 Jane Francesca Elgee, Lady Wilde, *Notes on Men, Women, and Books* (London: Ward and Downey, 1891), p. 250.

99 *Wilde Letters*, ed. Hart-Davis, p. 466.

100 For example, Frederika Macdonald comments on Byron's view of Rousseau ("The Hermitage: An Episode in the Life of Jean Jacques Rousseau," *Woman's World* 1 [1888]: 146–53; 153); Lady Fairlie Cuninghame describes a portrait of him ("A Visit to Hughenden," *Woman's World* 2 [1889]: 484–87; 485); and the Stowe scandal is mentioned in a notice of Stowe's death ([Anon.], "Reviews and Notices," *Woman's World* 3 [1890]: 386–88; 388).

101 For more information on this aspect of Wilde's writing, see Gagnier, *Idylls*, pp. 65–67, and Kerry Powell, "Tom, Dick, and Dorian Gray: Magic-Picture Mania in Late Victorian Fiction," *Philological Quarterly* 62 (1983): 147–70.

102 See *Oscar Wilde: The Critical Heritage*, ed. Karl Beckson (New York: Barnes and Noble, 1970), p. 79.

103 Quoted in Bigland, *Ouida*, p. 217.

104 See Crompton, *Greek Love*, pp. 362–70.

105 Ellman, *Oscar Wilde*, p. 386n.

106 *Wilde Letters*, ed. Hart-Davis, p. 729.

107 Crompton, *Greek Love*, pp. 362–63.

108 All quotations from the novel are from *The Picture of Dorian Gray* (Harmondsworth, Middlesex: Penguin, 1983).

109 See Jeff Nunokawa's "Homosexual Desire and the Effacement of

Self in *The Picture of Dorian Gray*," *American Imago* 49 (1992): 311–21.
110 Cohen, "Writing Gone Wilde: Homoerotic Desire in the Closet of Representation," *PMLA* 102 (1987): 801–13; 809.
111 Noel, "Lord Byron and His Times," *Essays on Poetry and Poets* (London: Kegan Paul, Trench & Co., 1886), p. 65.
112 *The Theatre* quoted in *Wilde: Critical Heritage*, ed. Beckson, p. 82.
113 *St. James's Gazette* quoted in ibid., pp. 71, 72.
114 Sedgwick, *Epistemology*, pp. 163–67.

AFTERWORD

1 *No Priest But Love: Excerpts from the Diaries of Anne Lister, 1824–1826*, ed. Helena Whitbread (New York University Press, 1992), p. 54.
2 Ibid., p. 193.
3 *I Know My Own Heart: The Diaries of Anne Lister, 1791–1840*, ed. Helena Whitbread (New York University Press, 1988), p. 42.
4 William St. Clair, "The Impact of Byron's Writings: An Evaluative Approach," *Byron: Augustan and Romantic*, ed. Andrew Rutherford (New York: St. Martin's, 1990), pp. 1–25; p. 12.
5 Ibid., p. 136.
6 Letter of Helena Whitbread to author, June 1, 1993.
7 *I Know My Own Heart*, ed. Whitbread, p. 203.
8 Ibid., p. 210.
9 See also Elizabeth Mavor's *The Ladies of Llangollen: A Study in Romantic Friendship* (Harmondsworth, Middlesex: Penguin, 1971), p. 176.
10 *I Know My Own Heart*, ed. Whitbread, pp. 49, 131, 344.
11 For a different view, see Terry Castle's discussion of Lister in *The Apparitional Lesbian: Female Homosexuality and Modern Culture* (New York: Columbia University Press, 1993), pp. 92–106.

Index